The Old South

GOLDENTREE BIBLIOGRAPHIES

In American History
under the series editorship of
Arthur S. Link

The Old South

compiled by

Fletcher M. Green

and

J. Isaac Copeland

Director Emeritus of the Southern Historical Collection
and
Professor Emeritus of History
University of North Carolina at Chapel Hill

AHM Publishing Corporation
Arlington Heights, Illinois 60004

F
207
.G7

ISBN 0-88295-580-2, paper
ISBN 0-88295-539-x, cloth

Library of Congress Card Number 79-55730

PRINTED IN THE UNITED STATES OF AMERICA
7129

CONTENTS

CONTENTS

CONTENTS

CONTENTS

Editor's Foreword

Goldentree Bibliographies in American History are designed to provide students, teachers, and librarians with ready and reliable guides to the literature of American history in all its remarkable scope and variety. Volumes in the series cover comprehensively the major periods in American history, while additional volumes are devoted to all important subjects.

Goldentree Bibliographies attempt to steer a middle course between the brief list of references provided in the average textbook and the long bibliography in which significant items are often lost in the sheer number of titles listed. Each bibliography is, therefore, selective, with the sole criterion for choice being the significance—and not the age—of any particular work. The result is bibliographies of all works, including journal articles and doctoral dissertations, that are still useful, without bias in favor of any particular historiographical school.

Each compiler is a scholar long associated, both in research and teaching, with the period or subject of his volume. All compilers have not only striven to accomplish the objective of this series but have also cheerfully adhered to a general style and format. However, each compiler has been free to define his field, make his own selections, and work out internal organization as the unique demands of his period or subject have seemed to dictate.

The single great objective of *Goldentree Bibliographies in American History* will have been achieved if these volumes help researchers and students to find their way to the significant literature of American history.

Arthur S. Link

PREFACE

The organization of this bibliography reflects the nature of the history of the antebellum South as presented by the compilers in their teaching. While the bibliography has been designed principally with advanced undergraduates and beginning graduate students in mind, it is hoped that students whose interests are in other areas of United States history may also find it useful — especially as they prepare for comprehensive examinations. For the scholar whose primary interest is in other fields, it should serve as a convenient, introductory guide.

This is a selective work, with no intent that it be comprehensive. Emphasis is upon the period after 1820, and particular attention has been given to economic, cultural, and social history. Though political history has not been neglected, it occupies a secondary place because this topic is covered in other United States history courses.

For this work the Old South has been defined geographically as including the states of the former Confederate States of America, plus the border states of Maryland, Kentucky, and Missouri. The state of Delaware has been included in a limited fashion. For the first decades of the nineteenth century the citizens of Delaware regarded themselves as southerners, but this feeling waned when slavery became a divisive issue. The references to Delaware relate to the general history of the state and to the cultural and business life of the state through the early national period.

Where the dagger (†) has been used, it is an indication that the volume is currently available as a paperback. In providing bibliographic information for books, the date used is that of latest publication; one should bear this in mind when selecting a title since that particular work may have been published a number of years earlier. This practice was followed also in listing the contemporary travel accounts, diaries, etc., many of which have appeared in different editions and with different editors over a period of years.

Much of the writing about the South done by trained historians has been published in the twentieth century, with the better and more mature works coming after the founding of the Southern Historical Association in 1934. The fact that the South — the recent South as well as the Old

— is a relatively new field of study accounts in part for the large number of monographs and journal articles included in this bibliography. The major work on the South's history is the ten-volume *History of the South*, sponsored jointly by the Littlefield Fund for Southern History of the University of Texas and the Louisiana State University Press. The first to be published was volume five, which appeared in 1947. Eight more volumes have been published since then, and those that pertain to the pre-1860 period have been included in the bibliography. The unpublished volume, number two, which will cover the years 1689-1763, is in the capable hands of Peter H. Wood of Duke University.

The first section of the bibliography includes reference works offering general coverage of United States history, as well as the specialized ones confined to the Old South. In each case the titles are ones with which students should gain familiarity. Section three is composed of a list of travel accounts, diaries, journals, reminiscences, and collected letters. Selections from this list of contemporary works can provide students with some feeling for, and understanding of, the South as it existed prior to 1860. Manuscript collections and unpublished items have not been included. A few doctoral dissertations are listed and these are generally available on microfilm; a very limited number are in printed form, published at the time the degree was received. Perhaps half a dozen master's theses are included, and these constitute the only exception to the statement regarding unpublished items.

Finally, certain debts must be acknowledged. In the late 1960s Anthony Miller was a graduate assistant who spent much time during one academic year searching the journal literature for articles relating to the antebellum South, transcribing the bibliographical information to cards, and sorting cards into a broad classification. Thanks are due him.

I am indebted to every member of the Humanities Reference staff of Wilson Library of the University of North Carolina at Chapel Hill. On more than one occasion these able people tracked a fragmentary reference to its source or established a reference that had been cited inaccurately in some bibliography or footnote.

The actual editing, with its endless checking of authors and titles and verification of pages and volume numbers, was done while Wilson Library was undergoing major renovation and expansion, and a warehouse was filled with books and journals in storage. Completion of the construction work was followed immediately by a program of reclassification, with the Dewey classification being replaced by that of the Library of Congress. Under these circumstances the job was frequently frustrating, and but for William Walker, the library's stack supervisor, and Mrs. Anna Akerman, tracer of lost and misplaced volumes, the frustration would have been overwhelming. A very special debt is owed these two people.

PREFACE

Fletcher Green did not live to see this bibliography completed. Had his advice and great store of knowledge about the South been available, the finished product would have been improved.

J. I. C.

Abbreviations

Ag Hist	Agricultural History
Ala Hist Q	Alabama Historical Quarterly
Ala Rev	Alabama Review
Am Ec Rev	American Economic Review
Am-Ger Rev	American-German Review
Am Heritage	American Heritage
Am Hist Rev	American Historical Review
Am J Ec Soc	American Journal of Economics and Sociology
Am J Soc	American Journal of Sociology
Am Lit	American Literature
Am Neptune	American Neptune
Am Pol Sci Rev	American Political Science Review
Am Q	American Quarterly
Am Sch	American Scholar
Am Speech	American Speech
Ann Am Acad Pol Soc Sci	Annals of the American Academy of Political and Social Science
Ann Assn Am Geog	Annals of the Association of American Geographers
Ann Rept Am Hist Assn	Annual Report of the American Historical Association
Antioch Rev	Antioch Review
Antiques	Antiques
Ark Hist Q	Arkansas Historical Quarterly
Bapt Hist Heritage	Baptist History and Heritage
Black Schol	Black Scholar
Bul Bus Hist Soc	Bulletin of the Business Historical Society
Historian	Historian
Hist Mag Prot Epis Church	Historical Magazine of the Protestant Episcopal Church
Hist Meth Newsletter	Historical Methods Newsletter
Hist Ed Q	History of Education Quarterly
Hist Today	History Today
Ind Mag Hist	Indiana Magazine of History
J Am Hist	Journal of American History
J Am Stud	Journal of American Studies
J Black Stud	Journal of Black Studies
J Ec Hist	Journal of Economic History
J Interdis Hist	Journal of Interdisciplinary History

ABBREVIATIONS

J Lib Hist	Journal of Library History
J Miss Hist	Journal of Mississippi History
J Neg Ed	Journal of Negro Education
J Neg Hist	Journal of Negro History
J Pol Ec	Journal of Political Economy
J Pol	Journal of Politics
J Presb Hist	Journal of Presbyterian History
J Soc Hist	Journal of Social History
J S Hist	Journal of Southern History
J Hist Ideas	Journal of the History of Ideas
J Hist Med Al Sc	Journal of the History of Medicine and Allied Sciences
J Presb Hist Soc	Journal of the Presbyterian Historical Society
J Soc Arch Hist	Journal of the Society of Architectural Historians
J West	Journal of the West
J Urban Hist	Journal of Urban History
Kan Hist Q	Kansas Historical Quarterly
Lab Hist	Labor History
Lib Q	Library Quarterly
La Hist Q	Louisiana Historical Quarterly
La Hist	Louisiana History
La Stud	Louisiana Studies
McNeese Rev	McNeese Review
Md Hist Mag	Maryland Historical Magazine
Meth Hist	Methodist History
Mich Hist	Michigan History
Mid-Am	Mid-America
Miss Q	Mississippi Quarterly
Miss Val Hist Rev	Mississippi Valley Historical Review
Mo Hist Rev	Missouri Historical Review
Neg Hist Bul	Negro History Bulletin
N Eng Q	New England Quarterly
N-Y Hist Soc Q	New-York Historical Society Quarterly
N C Hist Rev	North Carolina Historical Review
Ohio Hist Q	Ohio Historical Quarterly
Oral Hist Rev	Oral History Review
Pac Hist Rev	Pacific Historical Review
Part Rev	Partisan Review
Peabody J Ed	Peabody Journal of Education
Pa Hist	Pennsylvania History
Pa Mag Hist Biog	Pennsylvania Magazine of History and Biography
Pers Am Hist	Perspectives in American History
Phylon	Phylon
Pol Sci Q	Political Science Quarterly
Proc S C Hist Assn	Proceedings of the South Carolina Historical Association
Proc Wis Hist Soc	Proceedings of the Wisconsin Historical Society
Quaker Hist	Quaker History
Red Riv Val Hist Rev	Red River Valley Historical Review
Reg Ky Hist Soc	Register of the Kentucky Historical Society
Rur Soc	Rural Sociology

ABBREVIATIONS

Russian Rev	Russian Review
Sci and Soc	Science and Society
Sew Rev	Sewanee Review
Soc Sci Res Coun Bul	Social Science Research Council Bulletin
S Atl Q	South Atlantic Quarterly
S C Hist Gen Mag	South Carolina Historical and Genealogical Magazine
S C Hist Mag	South Carolina Historical Magazine
S Assn Q	Southern Association Quarterly
S Ec J	Southern Economic Journal
S Folklore Q	Southern Folklore Quarterly
S Hum Rev	Southern Humanities Review
S Lit J	Southern Literary Journal
S Q	Southern Quarterly
S Rev	Southern Review
S Speech J	Southern Speech Journal
Sou Stud	Southern Studies
SW Rev	Southwest Review
SW Hist Q	Southwestern Historical Quarterly
Tech Cult	Technology and Culture
Tenn Hist Mag	Tennessee Historical Quarterly
Tequesta	Tequesta
Texana	Texana
Text Hist Rev	Textile History Review
Trans Ala Hist Soc	Transactions of the Alabama Historical Society
Trans Huguenot Soc S C	Transactions of the Huguenot Society of South Carolina
Van Law Rev	Vanderbilt Law Review
Va Cav	Virginia Cavalcade
Va Mag Hist Biog	Virginia Magazaine of History and Biography
Va Q Rev	Virginia Quarterly Review
Washington Univ Stud	Washington University Studies
Wel Rev	Welfare in Review
W Tenn Hist Soc Pap	West Tennessee Historical Society Papers
W Va Hist	West Virginia History
W Ec J	Western Economic Journal
W Hist Q	Western Historical Quarterly
Wm Mar Q	William and Mary Quarterly
Winterthur Port	Winterthur Portfolio
Wis Mag Hist	Wisconsin Magazine of History
Yale Law J	Yale Law Journal
Yal Rev	Yale Review

I. Reference Works and Bibliographical Guides

1. Selected Reference Works, Including Atlases

1 ADAMS, James T., ed. *Dictionary of American History.* Rev. ed. 8 vols., incl. index. New York, 1976

2 CARRUTH, Gorton, et al. *Encyclopedia of American Facts and Dates.* 5th ed. New York, 1970.

3 CLARK, Thomas D., ed. *Travels in the Old South.* 3 vols. Norman, Okla. 1956–1959.

4 *Dictionary of American Biography.* Eds. Allen Johnson and Dumas Malone. 11 vols., incl. index, plus supplements 3, 4, and 5. New York, 1976–1978.

5 GRAY, Wood, et al. *Historian's Handbook: A Key to the Study and Writing of History.* 2nd ed. Boston, 1964.†

6 JAMES, Edward T., Janet Wilson JAMES, and Paul S. BOYER, eds. *Notable American Women, 1607–1950.* 3 vols. Cambridge, Mass., 1971.

7 KULL, Irving S., and Nell M. KULL, eds. *A Short Chronology of American History.* New Brunswick, N.J., 1952.

8 MORRIS, Richard B., and Jeffrey B. MORRIS, eds. *Encyclopedia of American History.* 5th ed. New York, 1976.

9 MORRISON, Olin D., comp. *The American South: Historical Atlas.* 3 vols. in 4. Athens, Ohio, 1965.

10 PAULLIN, Charles O. *Atlas of the Historical Geography of the United States.* Ed. John K. Wright. Westport, Conn., 1975.

11 POULTON, Helen J. *The Historian's Handbook: A Descriptive Guide to Reference Works.* Norman, Okla., 1972.†

12 STEPHENSON, Wendell H. *The South Lives in History.* New York, 1969.

13 STEPHENSON, Wendell H. *Southern History in the Making: Pioneer Historians of the South.* Baton Rouge, 1964.

14 U.S. CONGRESS. *Biographical Directory of the American Congress, 1774–1971.* Washington, D.C., 1971.

2. Statistical and Documentary Compilations

15 DeBOW, J. D. B. *The Industrial Resources, Statistics, etc., of the United States, and More Particularly of the Southern and Western States.* 3 vols. New York, 1966.

16 DODD, Donald B., and Wynelle S. DODD, comps. *Historical Statistics of the South, 1790–1970.* University, Ala., 1973.

17 ELLIOT, Jonathan, ed. *The Debates in the Several State Conventions on the Adoption of the Federal Constitution.* 5 vols. New York, 1968.

18 THORPE, Francis N., comp. *The Federal and State Constitutions, Colonial Charters, and Other Organic Laws of the States. . . .* 7 vols. Grosse Point, Mich., 1968.

19 *Tribune Almanac and Political Register, 1838–1914.* New York, 1838–1914. Title varies. First published as *Whig Almanac and Political Register.*

20 U.S. BUREAU OF THE CENSUS. *Historical Statistics of the United States: Colonial Times to 1970.* 2 vols. Washington, D.C., 1975.

3. General Bibliographies

21 *America: History and Life: A Guide to the Periodical Literature.* Vol. 1–, July, 1964–. Santa Barbara, Cal., 1964–.

22 American Historical Association. *Guide to Historical Literature.* New York, 1961.

23 *Appalachian Bibliography.* 3 vols. Morgantown, West Va., 1975. This work incorporates the entries in Robert F. Munn, *The Southern Appalachians; A Bibliography and Guide to Studies.* Morgantown, West Va., 1961, with four supplements, and *Appalachian Outlook,* October 1964 through July 1975.

24 BEERS, Henry P., comp. *Bibliographies in American History.* New York, 1961.

25 BEMIS, Samuel F., and Grace G. GRIFFIN, eds. *Guide to the Diplomatic History of the United States, 1775–1921.* Magnolia, Mass., 1976.

26 FREIDEL, Frank B., and Richard K. SHOWMAN, eds. *Harvard Guide to American History.* Rev. ed. 2 vols. Cambridge, Mass., 1974.

27 KAPLAN, Louis, et al., comps. *Bibliography of American Autobiographies.* Madison, Wis., 1961.

28 KUEHL, Warren F., comp. *Dissertations in History: An Index to Dissertations Completed in History Departments of the United States and Canadian Universities, 1873–1960.* Lexington, Ky., 1965.

29 KUEHL, Warren F., comp. *Dissertations in History . . . 1961–June 1970.* Lexington, Ky., 1972.

30 LINK, Arthur S., and Rembert W. PATRICK, eds. *Writing Southern History: Essays in Historiography in Honor of Fletcher M. Green.* Baton Rouge, 1967.†

31 McMANIS, Douglas R. *Historical Geography of the United States: A Bibliography.* Ypsilanti, Mich., 1965.†

32 MATTHEWS, William, comp. *American Diaries: An Annotated Bibliography of American Diaries Written Prior to the Year 1861.* Boston, 1959.

33 MILLER, Elizabeth W., and Mary FISHER, comps. *The Negro in America: A Bibliography.* 2nd ed., rev. and enl. Cambridge, Mass., 1970.

34 "Recent Articles Concerning the Seaboard, Middle Atlantic, and Southern Sections." Each issue of the *Journal of American History*, beginning with June 1937 of the *Mississippi Valley Historical Review*, has included the South in its list of "Recent Articles." The bibliography appeared originally as the concluding section of "Historical News and Comments." It is currently an independent section of each issue; the classification is topical and geographical.

35 RUBIN, Louis D., Jr., ed. *Bibliographical Guide to the Study of Southern Literature*. Baton Rouge, 1969.

36 "Southern History in Periodicals, 19–: A Selected Bibliography." In the *Journal of Southern History*, appearing annually since 1964.

37 U.S. LIBRARY OF CONGRESS. General Reference and Bibliography Division. *Guide to the Study of the United States of America: Representative Books Reflecting the Development of American Life and Thought*. Washington, D.C., 1960. *Supplement*, 1956–1965, Washington, D.C., 1976.

38 *Writings on American History, 1902–1960*. Princeton, New York, New Haven, Conn., and Washington, D.C., 1904–1961. Various editors. Not published for the years 1904–1905, 1941–1947. There is a cumulative index.

39 *Writings on American History, 1962–1973: A Subject Bibliography of Articles*. 4 vols. Washington, 1976. Continued by *Writings on American History*, 1973/74–. Ed. James J. Dougherty et al. Washington, D.C., 1974–.

4. *Edited Papers*

40 CALHOUN, John C. *Papers*. Ed. Robert L. Meriwether; W. Edwin Hemphill; Clyde N. Wilson. v. 1–. Columbia, S.C., 1959–.

41 CLAY, Henry. *Papers*. Eds. James F. Hopkins and Mary W. M. Hargreaves. v. 1–. Lexington, Ky., 1959–.

42 DAVIS, Jefferson. *Papers*. Ed. Haskell M. Monroe, Jr.; James T. McIntosh. v. 1–. Baton Rouge, 1971–.

43 JACKSON, Andrew. *Correspondence*. Ed. John Spencer Bassett. 7 vols. Washington, D.C., 1926–1935.

44 JACKSON, Andrew. *Papers*. With Sam B. Smith as editor, work was started on the *Papers of Andrew Jackson* in 1971.

45 JEFFERSON, Thomas. *Papers*. Eds. Julian P. Boyd and Ruth W. Lester. v. 1–. Princeton, 1950–.

46 JOHNSON, Andrew. *Papers*. Eds. LeRoy P. Graf, Ralph W. Haskins, and Patricia P. Clark. v.1–. Knoxville, Tenn., 1967–.

47 MADISON, James. *Papers*. Eds. William T. Hutchinson and William M. E. Rachal; Robert A. Rutland, et al. v. 1–. Chicago, 1962–.

48 MARSHALL, John. *Papers*. Eds. Herbert A. Johnson and Charles T. Cullen. v. 1–. Chapel Hill, 1974–.

49 MASON, George. *Papers*. Ed. Robert A. Rutland. 3 vols. Chapel Hill, 1970.

50 MONROE, James. *Papers, 1758–1839*. 11 reels microfilm. Washington, D.C., 1960.

51 POLK, James K. *Correspondence*. Eds. Herbert Weaver and Wayne Cutler. v. 1–. Nashville, Tenn., 1969–.

52 WASHINGTON, George. *Papers*. These papers are in process of being edited. Donald Jackson is the editor.

53 WASHINGTON, George, *Writings*. Ed. John C. Fitzpatrick. 39 vols. Washington, D.C., 1931–1944.

II. General Works

1. Textbooks and General Histories of the Antebellum South

54 ABERNETHY, Thomas P. *The South in the New Nation, 1789–1819*. Baton Rouge, 1961.

55 BILLINGTON, Monroe L. *The American South: A Brief History*. New York, 1971†.

56 COTTERILL, Robert S. *The Old South*. 2nd ed. rev. Glendale, Cal., 1949.

57 CRAVEN, Avery O. *The Growth of Southern Nationalism, 1848–1861*. Baton Rouge, 1953.

58 EATON, Clement. *The Growth of Southern Civilization, 1790–1860*. New York, 1961†.

59 EATON, Clement. *History of the Old South*. 3rd ed. New York, 1975.

60 HESSELTINE, William B., and David L. SMILEY. *The South in American History*. 2nd ed. Englewood Cliffs, N.J., 1960.

61 SIMKINS, Francis B., and Charles P. ROLAND. *History of the South*. 4th ed. New York, 1972.

62 STEPHENSON, Wendell H. *Basic History of the Old South*. New York, 1959†.

63 SYDNOR, Charles S. *Development of Southern Sectionalism, 1819–1848*. Baton Rouge, 1964.†

64 WERTENBAKER, Thomas J. *The Old South: The Founding of American Civilization*. New York, 1942.

2. State Histories

65 AMBLER, Charles H., and Festus P. SUMMERS. *West Virginia, the Mountain State*. Englewood Cliffs, N.J., 1958.

66 CLARK, Thomas D. *History of Kentucky*. Rev. ed. Lexington, Ky., 1960.

67 COLEMAN, Kenneth, ed. *History of Georgia*. Athens, Ga., 1977.

68 CONNOR, Seymour V. *Texas*. New York, 1971.

69 COULTER, E. Merton. *Georgia, a Short History*. Rev. ed. Chapel Hill, 1960.

70 DAVIS, Edwin A. *Louisiana: A Narrative History*. 2nd ed. Baton Rouge, 1965.

71 FISHWICK, Marshall W. *Virginia: A New Look at the Old Dominion*. New York, 1959.

72 FOLMSBEE, Stanley J., et al. *Tennessee: A Short History*. Knoxville, Tenn., 1969.

73 HOGAN, William R. *The Texas Republic*. Norman, Okla., 1946.

74 LANDER, Ernest M., Jr., and Robert K. ACKERMAN, eds. *Perspectives in South Carolina History: The First 300 Years*. Columbia, S.C., 1973.

75 LEFLER, Hugh T., and Albert Ray NEWSOME. *North Carolina, the History of a Southern State*. 3rd ed. Chapel Hill, 1973.

76 LEFLER, Hugh T., ed. *North Carolina History Told by Contemporaries*. 4th ed. Chapel Hill, 1965.

77 McCANDLESS, Perry. *History of Missouri: 1820–1860*. Columbia, Mo., 1972.

78 McLEMORE, Richard A., ed. *History of Mississippi*. 2 vols. Hattiesburg, Miss., 1973.

79 MONROE, John A. *Federalist Delaware, 1775–1817*. New Brunswick, N.J., 1954.

80 MOORE, Albert B. *History of Alabama*. University, Ala., 1934.

81 REED, H. Clay, ed. *Delaware: A History of the First State*. 3 vols. New York, 1947.

82 RICE, Otis K. *The Allegheny Frontier: West Virginia Beginnings, 1730–1830*. Lexington, Ky., 1970.

83 RICHARDSON, Rupert N. *Texas, the Lone Star State*. 2nd ed. Englewood Cliffs, N.J., 1958.

84 TEBEAU, Charlton W. *History of Florida*. Coral Gables, Fla., 1971.

85 THOMAS, David Y., ed. *Arkansas and Its People, a History, 1541–1930*. 4 vols. New York, 1930.

86 WALLACE, David Duncan. *South Carolina, a Short History, 1520–1948*. Chapel Hill, 1951.

87 WALSH, Richard, and William L. FOX, eds. *Maryland: A History, 1632–1974*. Baltimore, Md., 1974.

3. State Histories—Bibliographies

88 ALDERSON, William T., and Robert H. WHITE, eds. *Guide to the Study and Reading of Tennessee History*. Nashville, Tenn., 1959.†

89 COLEMAN, J. Winston, Jr., comp. *Bibliography of Kentucky History.* Lexington, Ky., 1949.

90 COX, Richard J., comp. "A Bibliography of Articles and Books on Maryland History, 1974." *Md Hist Mag,* 70 (1975), 211–223. Published annually since this date.

91 EASTERBY, J. Harold, ed. *Guide to the Study and Reading of South Carolina History, with . . . a Selected List of Books and Reprints of Books on South Carolina History Published since 1950, by Noel Polk.* Spartanburg, S.C., 1975.

92 "Florida History in Periodicals." *Fla Hist Q,* 52 (1973), 67–71. Published annually since this date. Compiler's name not given.

93 HARRIS, Michael H., comp. *Florida History: A Bibliography.* Metuchen, N.J., 1972.

94 JONES, Lewis P., comp. *Books and Articles on South Carolina History: A List for Laymen.* Columbia, S.C., 1970.†

95 LEFLER, Hugh T., ed. *Guide to the Study and Reading of North Carolina History.* 3rd ed. Chapel Hill, 1969.†

96 REED, H. Clay, and Marion B. REED, comps. *Bibliography of Delaware through 1960.* Newark, Del., 1966.†

97 ROWLAND, Arthur Ray, and James E. DORSEY, comps. *Bibliography of the Writings on Georgia History, 1900–1970.* Rev. ed. Spartanburg, S.C., 1978.

98 SMITH, Hale G., Herbert J. DOHERTY, Jr., and Charlton W. TEBEAU. "Florida Bibliography and Historiography." *Fla Hist Q,* 37 (1958), 156–177.

99 SMITH, Sam B., ed. and comp. *Tennessee History, a Bibliography.* Knoxville, Tenn., 1974.

100 SWEM, Earl G., comp. *Bibliography of Virginia.* 5 vols. Richmond, Va., 1916–1955.

101 TURNBULL, Robert J., comp. *Bibliography of South Carolina, 1563–1950.* 5 vols, plus index. Charlottesville, Va., 1956–1960.

102 VIRGINIA. STATE LIBRARY, RICHMOND. *Virginia Local History: A Bibliography.* Richmond, Va., 1971.

103 WILKINSON, Norman B., comp. "Bibliography of Delaware History, 1968–1970." *Del Hist,* 14 (1971), 217–222. Published annually since this date. Compilation is currently prepared by Elizabeth E. Moyne.

III. Travel Accounts, Diaries, Journals, Reminiscences, and Collected Letters

104 ABDY, Edward S. *Journal of a Residence and Tour in the United States of North America, 1833–1834.* 3 vols. St. Clair Shores, Mich., 1976.

105 ADAMS, Nehemiah. *South-Side View of Slavery*. Westport, Conn., 1969.

106 ARFWEDSON, Carl D. *The United States and Canada in 1832, 1833, and 1834*. 2 vols. New York, 1969.

107 ARNDT, Karl J. R., ed. "A Bavarian's Journey to New Orleans and Nacogdoches in 1853–1854." *La Hist Q*, 23 (1940), 485–500.

108 AUDUBON, John J. *Journal . . . Made During the Trip to New Orleans in 1820–1821*. Ed. Howard Corning. Boston, 1929.

109 BARNARD, Henry. "The South Atlantic States in 1833, as Seen by a New Englander. . . ." Ed. Barnard C. Steiner. *Md Hist Mag*, 13 (1918), 267–294, 295–386.

110 BARROW, Bennet H. *Plantation Life in the Florida Parishes of Louisiana, 1836–1846, as Reflected in the Diary of Bennet H. Barrow*. Ed. Edwin A. Davis, New York, 1943.

111 BENTON, Thomas H. *Thirty Years' View*. 2 vols. St. Clair Shores, Mich., 1976.

112 BREMER, Frederika. *The Homes of the New World, Impressions of America*. 2 vols. New York, 1968.

113 BUCKINGHAM, James Silk. *The Slave States of America*. 2 vols. New York, 1968.

114 BYRD, William. *Another Secret Diary of William Byrd of Westover, for the Years 1739–1741*. Eds. Maude H. Woodfin and Marion Tinling. Richmond, Va., 1942.

115 BYRD, William. *Histories of the Dividing Line Betwixt Virginia and North Carolina*. Ed. W. K. Boyd. New York, 1968.†

116 BYRD, William. *The Secret Dairy of William Byrd of Westover, 1709–1712*. Ed. Louis B. Wright and Marion Tinling. New York, 1972.

117 CAUTHEN, Charles E., ed. *Family Letters of the Three Wade Hamptons, 1782–1901*. Columbia, S. C., 1953.

118 CHASTELLUX, Francois-Jean, Marquis de. *Travels in North America in the Years 1780, 1781, 1782*. Ed. Howard W. Rice, Jr. 2 vols. Chapel Hill, 1963.

119 CLARK, Thomas D., ed. *South Carolina: The Grand Tour, 1780–1865*. Columbia, S. C., 1973.

120 EASTERBY, J. Harold, ed. *The South Carolina Rice Plantation as Revealed in the Papers of Robert F. W. Allston*. Fairfield, N. J., [n. d.].

121 FEATHERSTONHAUGH, George W. *Excursion through the Slave States, from Washington on the Potomac to the Frontier of Mexico. . . .* 2 vols. Westport, Conn., 1968.

122 FITHIAN, Philip V. *Journal and Letters of Philip Vickers Fithian, 1773–1774: A Plantation Tutor of the Old Dominion*. Ed. Hunter D. Farish. Charlottesville, Va., 1968.†

123 FREUND, Susanne H., and Alice B. KEITH, trs. and eds. "Prince Bernhard's Travels in the Carolinas, December, 1925." *N C Hist Rev*, 26 (1949), 446–459.

124 GRUND, Francis J. *The Americans in Their Moral, Social, and Political Relations*. 2 vols. in 1. New York, 1968.

125 HALL, Captain Basil. *Travels in North America in the Years 1827–28*. 3 vols. in 1. New York, 1974.

126 HARROWER, John. *The Journal of John Harrower, an Indentured Servant in the Colony of Virginia, 1773–1776*. Ed. Edward M. Riley. Charlottesville, Va., 1963.

127 INGRAHAM, Joseph H. *South-West, by a Yankee*. 2 vols. Westport, Conn., 1968.

128 INGRAHAM, Jospeh H. *The Sunny South: Or the Southerner at Home*. Westport, Conn, 1968.

129 JOHNSON, William. *William Johnson's Natchez: The Ante-Bellum Diary of a Free Negro*. Ed. William R. Hogan and Edwin A. Davis. 1 vol. in 2. Port Washington, N. Y., 1968.

130 KEMBLE, Frances Anne. *Journal of a Residence on a Georgian Plantation in 1838–1839*. Ed. John A. Scott. New York, 1975.†

131 LYELL, Sir Charles. *A Second Visit to the United States of North America*. 2 vols. St. Clair Shores, Mich., [n. d.].

132 MARTINEAU, Harriet. *Society in America*. 3 vols. New York, 1966.

133 MYERS, Robert M., ed. *Children of Pride*. 1 vol. in 3. New Haven, Conn., 1975.†

134 NORTHUP, Solomon. *Twelve Years a Slave*. Ed. Sue Eakin and Joseph Logsdon. Baton Rouge, 1968.

135 OLMSTED, Frederick L. *The Cotton Kingdom: A Traveller's Observations on Cotton and Slavery in the American Slave States*. Ed. Arthur M. Schlesinger, Sr. New York, 1953. This work is based on the author's three volumes subsequently listed.

136 OLMSTED, Frederick L. *Journey in the Back Country*. Intro. Clement Eaton. New York, 1970.†

137 OLMSTED, Frederick L. *Journey in the Seaboard Slave States*. Westport, Conn., 1968.

138 OLMSTED, Frederick L. *Journey through Texas, or a Saddle Trip on the Southwestern Frontier*. Austin, Tex., 1978.†

139 OLMSTED, Frederick L. *The Slave States before the Civil War*. Ed. Harvey Wish. New York, 1959. Based on selections from the author's three journeys.†

140 PARSONS, Charles G. *Inside View of Slavery, or a Tour among the Planters*. St. Clair Shores, Mich., 1970.

141 PAULDING, James K. *Letters from the South, Written during an Excursion in the Summer of 1816*. 2 vols. in 1. New York, 1973.

142 POWER, Tyronne. *Impressions of America, during the Years 1833, 1834, and 1835*. 2 vols. in 1. New York, 1971.

143 ROBINSON, Solon. *Solon Robinson, Pioneer and Agriculturist: Selected Writings*. Ed. Herbert A. Kellar. 2 vols. New York, 1968.

144 ROYALL, Anne N. *Letters from Alabama, 1812–1822, on Various Subjects*. Ed. Lucille Griffith. University, Ala., 1969.

145 ROYALL, Anne N. *Mrs. Royall's America, 1828 to 1831*. 7 vols. in 6. New York, 1972.

146 RUFFIN, Edmund. *The Diary of Edmund Ruffin*. Ed. William K. Scarborough. v. 1–. Baton Rouge, 1972–.

147 [SCHAW, Janet]. *Journal of a Lady of Quality . . . 1774 to 1776*. Eds. Evangeline W. Andrews and Charles M. Andrews. Spartanburg, S. C., 1971.

148 SCHULTZ, Charles R., ed. "New Orleans in December 1860." *La Hist*, 9 (1968), 53–61.

149 SCHWAAB, Eugene L., comp. *Travels in the Old South, Selected from Periodicals of the Times.* Ed. with . . . Jacqueline Bull. 2 vols. Lexington, Ky., 1973.

150 SELDEN, John A. *The Westover Journal of John A. Selden, Esqr., 1858–1862.* Ed. John Spencer Bassett. Northampton, Mass., 1921.

151 SMEDES, Susan Dabney. *Memorials of a Southern Planter.* Ed. Fletcher M. Green. New York, 1965.

152 SPARKS, Jared. "Journal of a Southern Tour in 1826," in *The Life and Writings of Jared Sparks.* . . . Ed. Herbert Baxter Adams. 2 vols. Boston, 1893.

153 TOCQUEVILLE, Alexis de. *Democracy in America.* Ed. Phillips Bradley. 2 vols. New York, 1945.†

154 WHIPPLE, Henry B. *Bishop Whipple's Southern Diary, 1843–1844.* Ed. Lester B. Shippee. New York, 1968.

155 WOOD, Virginia Steele. "James Keen's Journal of a Passage from Philadelphia to Blackbeard Island, Georgia, for Live Timber, 1817–1818." *Am Neptune*, 35 (1975), 227–247.

156 WOODMASON, Charles. *The Carolina Backcountry on the Eve of the Revolution.* Ed. Richard J. Hooker. Chapel Hill, 1969.†

IV. From Settlement to Founding of the New Nation

1. Geography of the Region

157 BARROWS, Harlan H. *Lectures on the Historical Geography of the United States.* . . . Ed. William A. Koelsch. Chicago, 1962. (University of Chicago, Department of Geography, Research Paper, #77)

158 BROWN, Ralph H. *Historical Geography of the United States.* New York, 1948.

159 CUMMING, William P. "Geographical Misconceptions of the Southeast in the Cartography of the Seventeenth and Eighteenth Centuries." *J S Hist*, 4 (1938), 476–492.

160 PARKINS, Almon E. "The Antebellum South: A Geographer's Interpretation." *Ann Assn Am Geog*, 21 (1931), 1–33.

161 PARKINS, Almon E. *The South: Its Economic-Geographic Development.* Westport, Conn., 1970.

162 VANCE, Rupert. *Human Geography of the South.* 2nd ed. New York, 1968.

163 VANCE, Rupert. "The Profile of Southern Culture." *Culture in the South.* Ed. W. T. Couch. Westport, Conn., 1970.

2. Indians, the First Inhabitants

164 ALDEN, John. *John Stuart and the Southern Colonial Frontier*. Ann Arbor, Mich., 1944.

165 ATKIN, Edmond. *The Appalachian Indian Frontier: The Edmond Atkin Report and Plan of 1755*. Ed. Wilbur R. Jacobs. Lincoln, Neb., 1967.†

166 CORKRAN, David H. *The Carolina Indian Frontier*. Columbia, S.C., 1970.†

167 CORKRAN, David H. *The Cherokee Frontier: Conflict and Survival, 1740–63*. Norman, Okla, 1962.

168 COTTERILL, Robert S. *The Old South*. See **56**.

169 COTTERILL, Robert S. *The Southern Indians: The Story of the Civilized Tribes before Removal*. Norman, Okla., 1954.

170 HUDSON, Charles M. *The Southeastern Indians*. Knoxville, Tenn., 1976.

171 MALONE, Henry T. *Cherokees of the Old South*. Athens, Ga., 1956.

172 MILLING, Chapman J. *Red Carolinians*. 2nd ed. Columbia, S. C., 1969.

173 POUND, Merritt B. "Colonel Benjamin Hawkins—North Carolinian—Benefactor of the Southern Indians." *N C Hist Rev*, 19 (1942), 1–21, 168–186.

174 ROTHROCK, Mary U. "Carolina Traders among the Overhill Cherokees, 1690–1760." *E Tenn Hist Soc Pub*, 1 (1929), 3–18.

175 SWANTON, John R. *Indians of the Southeastern United States*. Washington, D. C., 1946.

3. European Settlers

176 American Council of Learned Societies. "Report of Committee on Linguistic and National Stocks in the United States." *Ann Rept Am Hist Assn*, 1931, I, 103–408.

177 CHILDS, St. Julien Ravenel. "French Origins of Carolina." *Trans Huguenot Soc S C*, 50 (1945), 24–44.

178 COULTER, E. Merton. "The Acadians in Georgia." *Ga Hist Q*, 47 (1963), 68–75.

179 COULTER, E. Merton. "Was Georgia Settled by Debtors?" *Ga Hist Q*, 53 (1969), 442–454.

180 CUNZ, Dieter. *The Maryland Germans, a History*. Princeton, 1948.

181 DAVIS, Nora M. "The French Settlement at New Bordeaux." *Trans Huguenot Soc S C*, 56 (1951), 28–57.

182 FAUST, Albert B. "Swiss Emigration to the American Colonies in the Eighteenth Century." *Am Hist Rev*, 22 (1916), 21–44.

183 FRIES, Adelaide L. "The Moravian Contribution to Colonial North Carolina." *N C Hist Rev*, 7 (1930), 1–14.

184 FRIES, Adelaide L. *The Road to Salem.* Chapel Hill, 1944.

185 GRAHAM, Ian C. *Colonists from Scotland: Emigration to North America, 1707–1783.* Ithaca, N. Y., 1956.

186 HAMER, Marguerite B. "The Fate of the Exiled Acadians in South Carolina." *J S Hist,* 4 (1938), 199–208.

187 HANSEN, Marcus L. *The Atlantic Migration, 1607–1860.* Magnolia, Mass., [n. d.].

188 HIRSCH, Arthur H. *Huguenots of Colonial South Carolina.* Hamden, Conn., 1973.

189 HUDNUT, Ruth, and Hayes BAKER-CROTHERS. "Acadian Transients in South Carolina." *Am Hist Rev,* 43 (1938), 500–513.

190 LANNING, John Tate. *The Spanish Missions of Georgia.* St. Clair Shores, Mich., 1971.

191 LEYBURN, James G. *The Scotch-Irish: A Social History.* Chapel Hill, 1962.

192 McDERMOTT, John F., ed. *The French in the Mississippi Valley.* Urbana, Ill., 1965.

193 McDERMOTT, John F., ed. *Frenchmen and French Ways in the Mississippi Valley.* Urbana, Ill., 1969.

194 McDERMOTT, John F., ed. *The Spanish in the Mississippi Valley, 1762–1804.* Urbana, Ill., 1974.

195 MILLING, Chapman J. *Exile without an End.* Columbia, S. C., 1943.

196 PRIOR, Granville T. "Huguenot Descendants in Ante-Bellum South Carolina." *Trans Huguenot Soc S C,* 52 (1947), 24–37.

197 PURYEAR, Elmer L. "The Huguenots of the Upper South." *Trans Huguenot Soc S C,* 66 (1961), 5–12.

198 URLSPERGER, Samuel, ed. *Detailed Reports on the Salzburger Emigrants Who Settled in America.* . . . Ed. and tr. George F. Jones et al. v. 1–. Athens, Ga., 1968–.

199 VOIGHT, Gilbert P. "Cultural Contributions of German Settlers to South Carolina." *S C Hist Mag,* 53 (1952), 183–189.

200 VOIGHT, Gilbert P. "The Germans and the German-Swiss in South Carolina, 1732–1765." *Proc S C Hist Assn,* 5 (1935), 17–25.

4. The Colonial South, the Revolution, and the South in the New Nation

201 ABERNETHY, Thomas P. *The South in the New Nation, 1789–1819.* See **54**.

202 ABERNETHY, Thomas P. *Three Virginia Frontiers.* Magnolia, Mass., 1962.

203 ALDEN, John R. *The First South.* Baton Rouge, 1971.†

204 ALDEN, John R. *The South in the Revolution, 1763–1789.* Baton Rouge, 1976.†

205 BAILYN, Bernard. *Ideological Origins of the American Revolution.* Cambridge, Mass., 1967.†

206 BARNWELL, Robert W., Jr. "The Migration of Loyalists from South Carolina." *Proc S C Hist Assn*, 7 (1937), 34–42.

207 BOLTON, S. C. "South Carolina and the Reverend Doctor Francis LeJau: Southern Society and the Conscience of an Anglican Missionary." *Hist Mag Prot Epis Church*, 40 (1971), 63–80.

208 BRIDENBAUGH, Carl. *Myths and Realities: Societies of the Colonial South.* New York, 1966.†

209 BROWN, Richard M. *The South Carolina Regulators.* Cambridge, Mass., 1963.

210 BYRD, William. *Another Secret Diary of William Byrd of Westover.* See **114**.

211 BYRD, William. *Histories of the Dividing Line Betwixt Virginia and North Carolina.* See **115**.

212 BYRD, William. *The Secret Diary of William Byrd of Westover.* See **116**.

213 CRANE, Verner W. *The Southern Frontier, 1676–1732.* Westport, Conn., 1977.

214 CRAVEN, Wesley F. *The Southern Colonies in the Seventeenth Century, 1607–1689.* Baton Rouge, 1949.†

215 DAVIS, Richard Beale. *Intellectual Life in the Colonial South, 1583–1763.* 3 vols. Knoxville, Tenn., 1978.

216 DeMOND, Robert O. *Loyalists in North Carolina during the Revolution.* Durham N. C., 1940.

217 EVANS, Emory G. "Planter Indebtedness and the Coming of the Revolution to Virginia." *Wm Mar Q*, 3rd ser., 19 (1962), 511–533.

218 FITHIAN, Philip V. *Journal and Letters of Philip Vickers Fithian, 1773–1774: A Plantation Tutor of the Old Dominion.* See **122**.

219 FRANKLIN, John Hope. "The North, the South, and the American Revolution." *J Am Hist*, 62 (1975), 5–23.

220 GREENE, Jack P. *The Quest for Power: The Lower House of Assembly in the Southern Royal Colonies, 1689–1776.* Chapel Hill, 1964.

221 HARRELL, Isaac S. "North Carolina Loyalists." *N C Hist Rev*, 3 (1926), 575–590.

222 HARROWER, John. *The Journal of John Harrower, an Indentured Servant in the Colony of Virginia, 1773–1776.* See **126**.

223 KETCHAM, Earle H. "The Sources of the North Carolina Constitution of 1776." *N C Hist Rev*, 6 (1929), 215–236.

224 KING, Spencer B., Jr. "Georgia and the American Revolution: Three Shades of Opinion." *Ga Rev*, 23 (1969), 44–50.

225 KLINGBERG, Frank J. *An Appraisal of the Negro in Colonial South Carolina.* Philadelphia, 1975.

226 LAND, Aubrey C. "Economic Behavior in a Planting Society: The Eighteenth-Century Chesapeake." *J S Hist*, 33 (1967), 469–485.

227 LANNING, John Tate. *The Spanish Missions of Georgia.* See **190**.

228 LEVETT, Ella P. "Loyalism in Charleston, 1761–1784." *Proc S C Hist Assn*, 6 (1936), 3–17.

229 McCULLOCH, Samuel C. "Dr. Bray's Trip to Maryland: a Study in Militant Anglican Humanitarianism." *Wm Mar Q*, 3rd ser., 2 (1945), 15–32.

230 MARAMBAUD, Pierre. "William Byrd of Westover: Cavalier, Diarist, and Chronicler." *Va Mag Hist Biog*, 78 (1970), 144–183.

231 MEADE, Robert D. *Patrick Henry*. 2 vols. Philadelphia, Pa., 1957, 1959.

232 MEADOWS, Milo M., Jr. "The Virginia Constitution of 1776." *Filson Club Hist Q*, 43 (1969), 5–22.

233 MILLER, Helen H. *George Mason, Gentleman Revolutionary*. Chapel Hill, 1975.

234 OLSON, Gary D. "Loyalists and the American Revolution: Thomas Brown and the South Carolina Backcountry, 1775–1776." *SC Hist Mag*, 68 (1967), 201–219; 69 (1968), 44–56.

235 ROGERS, George C., Jr. *Charleston in the Age of the Pinckneys*. Norman, Okla., 1969.

236 RUTLAND, Robert A. *The Birth of the Bill of Rights*. New York, 1962.

237 SIEBERT, Wilbur H. "The Loyalists in West Florida and the Natchez District." *Miss Val Hist Rev*, 2 (1916), 465–483.

238 SIRMANS, M. Eugene. *Colonial South Carolina: A Political History, 1663–1763*. Chapel Hill, 1966.

239 SMITH, Abbot E. *Colonists in Bondage, White Servitude and Convict Labor in America, 1607–1776*. Chapel Hill, 1947.

240 SPRUILL, Julia C. *Women's Life and Work in the Southern Colonies*. New York, 1972.†

241 TRENHOLME, Louise I. *Ratification of the Federal Constitution in North Carolina*. New York, 1967.

242 WALLACE, David Duncan. *Henry Laurens*. New York, 1967.

243 WOODMASON, Charles. *The Carolina Backcountry on the Eve of the Revolution*. See **156**.

244 WRIGHT, Louis B. *The First Gentlemen of Virginia: Intellectual Qualities of the Early Colonial Ruling Class*. San Marino, Cal., 1940.

V. Slavery

1. Documentary Sources

A. Documents, Narratives by Slaves and by Travelers, and Contemporary Writings

245 ADAMS, Nehemiah. *South-Side View of Slavery*. See **105**.

246 BEAR, James A., Jr. *Jefferson at Monticello*. Charlottesville, Va., 1967.

247 CAIRNES, John Elliott. *The Slave Power*. Westport, Conn., 1975.

248 CATTERALL, Helen T., ed. *Judicial Cases Concerning American Slavery and the Negro*. 5 vols. New York, 1968.

249 DONNAN, Elizabeth, ed. *Documents Illustrative of the Slave Trade to America*. 4 vols. New York, 1965.

250 DOUGLASS, Frederick. *My Bondage and My Freedom*. Intro. Philip Foner. New York, 1969.

251 ELLIOTT, Ebenezer Newton, ed. *Cotton is King, and Pro-Slavery Arguments: Comprising the Writings of Hammond, Harper, Christy, Stringfellow, Hodge, Bledsoe, and Cartwright*. New York, 1969.

252 FITZHUGH, George. *Cannibals All: Or, Slaves without Masters*. Ed. C. Vann Woodward. Cambridge, Mass., 1960.†

253 FITZHUGH, George. *Sociology of the South*. New York, 1965.

254 HENSON, Josiah. *Autobiography of the Reverend Josiah Henson*. Reading, Mass., 1969.†

255 HUNDLEY, Daniel R. *Social Relations in Our Southern States*. New York, 1973.

256 HURD, John C. *The Law of Freedom and Bondage in the United States*. 2 vols. Westport, Conn., 1968.

257 LAND, Lunsford. *The Narrative of Lunsford Lane*. Boston, 1848.

258 MILLER, Randall M. *"Dear Master," Letters of a Slave Family*. Ithaca, N. Y., 1978.

259 NICHOLS, Charles H. *Many Thousands Gone: The Ex-Slaves' Accounts of Their Bondage and Freedom*. Bloomington, Ind., 1969.†

260 NICHOLLS, Michael L., ed. "News from Monrovia, 1834–1846: The Letters of Peyton Skipworth to John Hartwell Cocke." *Va Mag Hist Biog*, 85 (1977), 65–85.

261 NORTHUP, Solomon. *Twelve Years a Slave*. See **134**.

262 PARSONS, Charles G. *Inside View of Slavery*. See **140**.

263 PHILLIPS, Ulrich B., ed. *Plantation and Frontier Documents, 1649–1863*. 2 vols. New York, 1969.

264 RAWICK, George P., ed. *The American Slave: A Composite Autobiography*. 19 vols. Westport, Conn., 1972. *Supplementary Series*. 12 vols. Westport, Conn., 1977.

265 STAROBIN, Robert S., ed. *Blacks in Bondage: Letters of American Slaves*. New York, 1974.†

266 VIRGINIA. CONSTITUTIONAL CONVENTION, 1829–1830. *Proceedings and Debates of the Virginia State Convention of 1828–1830*. Richmond, Va., 1830.

267 WOODSON, Carter G., ed. *The Mind of the Negro as Reflected in Letters Written during the Crisis, 1800–1860*. Westport, Conn., 1969.

268 YETMAN, Norman R., ed. *Life under the "Peculiar Institution": Selections from the Slave Narrative Collection*. Huntingdon, N.Y., 1976.

B. Commentaries on Documents and Narratives

269 BLASSINGAME, John W. "Using the Testimony of Ex-Slaves: Approaches and Problems." *J S Hist* 41 (1975), 473–492.

270 NICHOLS, Charles H. "Slave Narratives and the Plantation Legend." *Phylon*, 10 (1949), 201–210.

271 SOAPES, Thomas F. "The Federal Writers' Project Slave Interviews: Useful Data or Misleading Sources." *Oral Hist Rev* (1977), 33–38.

272 WOODWARD, C. Vann. "History from Slave Sources." *Am Hist Rev*, 79 (1974), 470–481. Review of *The American Slave*, edited by George P. Rawick.

2. General

273 APTHEKER, Herbert, and V. Della CHIESA. "The Study of American Negro Slavery." *Sci and Soc*, 21 (1957), 257–263.

274 BELLAMY, Donnie D. "Slavery in Microcosm: Onslow County, North Carolina." *J Neg Hist*, 62 (1977), 339–350.

275 BLASSINGAME, John W. *The Slave Community: Plantation Life in the Ante-Bellum South.* New York, 1973.†

276 COHEN, William. "Thomas Jefferson and the Problem of Slavery." *J Am Hist*, 56 (1969), 503–526.

277 COLEMAN, J. Winston, Jr. *Slavery Times in Kentucky.* New York, 1970.

278 COOPER, William J., Jr. *The South and the Politics of Slavery, 1828–1856.* Baton Rouge, 1978.

279 DAVID, Paul A., et al. *Reckoning with Slavery: A Critical Study in the Quantitative History of American Negro Slavery.* New York, 1976.

280 DAVIS, David Brion. *The Problem of Slavery in the Age of Revolution, 1770–1823.* Ithaca, N.Y., 1976.†

281 DAVIS, David Brion. *The Problem of Slavery in Western Culture.* Ithaca, N.Y., 1969.†

282 DAVIS, David Brion. *The Slave Power Conspiracy and the Paranoid Style.* Baton Rouge, 1969.

283 DAVIS, David Brion. "Slavery and the Post-World War II His- torians."*Daedalus*, 103 (Spring, 1974), 1–16.

284 DAVIS, David Brion. *Was Thomas Jefferson an Authentic Enemy of Slavery?* Oxford, Eng., 1970.

285 DEGLER, Carl N. "Slavery and the Genesis of American Race Prejudice." *Comp Stud Soc Hist*, 2 (1959), 49–66.

286 EATON, Clement. *The Mind of the Old South*. Rev. ed. Baton Rouge, 1967.†

287 ELKINS, Stanley M. *Slavery: A Problem in American Institutional and Intellectual Life*. 3rd ed. Chicago, 1976.†

288 FLANDERS, Ralph B. *Plantation Slavery in Georgia*. Cos Cob, Conn., 1967.

289 FRANKLIN, John Hope. *From Slavery to Freedom: History of American Negroes*. 4th ed. New York, 1974.†

290 FRANKLIN, John Hope. "Slaves Virtually Free in Ante-Bellum North Carolina." *J Neg Hist*, 28 (1943), 284–310.

291 FRAZIER, E. Franklin. "The Negro Slave Family." *J Neg Hist*, 15 (1930), 198–259.

292 FREDRICKSON, George M. *The Black Image in the White Mind: The Debate on Afro-American Character and Destiny, 1817–1914*. New York, 1977.†

293 FREDRICKSON, George M. "A Man but Not a Brother: Abraham Lincoln and Racial Equality." *J S Hist*, 41 (1975), 39–58.

294 FREEHLING, William W. "The Founding Fathers and Slavery," *Am Hist Rev*, 77 (1972), 80–93.

295 GENOVESE, Eugene D. "Materialism and Idealism in the History of Negro Slavery in the Americas." *J Soc Hist*, 1 (1968), 371–394.

296 GENOVESE, Eugene D. "Rebelliousness and Docility in the Negro Slave: A Critique of the Elkins Thesis." *Civ War Hist*, 13 (1967), 293–314.

297 GENOVESE, Eugene D. *Roll, Jordan, Roll: The World the Slaves Made*. New York, 1976.†

298 GENOVESE, Eugene D. *The World the Slaveholders Made*. New York, 1969.

299 GOLDIN, Claudia D. *Urban Slavery in the American South, 1820–1860: A Quantitative History*. Chicago, 1976.

300 GUTMAN, Herbert G. *The Black Family in Slavery and Freedom, 1750–1925*. New York, 1976.

301 HANDLIN, Oscar, and Mary HANDLIN. "Origins of the Southern Labor System." *Wm Mar Q*, 3rd ser., 7 (1950), 199–222.

302 HERNDON, G. Melven. "Slavery in Antebellum Virginia: William Galt, Jr., 1839–1851, a Case Study." *Sou Stud*, 16 (1977), 309–320.

303 JOHNSTON, James H. *Race Relations in Virginia and Miscegenation in the South, 1776–1860*. Amherst, Mass., 1970.

304 JONES, Bobby F. "A Cultural Middle Passage: Slave Marriage and Family in the Ante-Bellum South." Doctoral dissertation, University of North Carolina, 1965.

305 JORDAN, Winthrop D. *White over Black: American Attitudes toward the Negro, 1550–1812*. New York, 1977.†

306 KING, Richard H. "Marxism and the Slave South." *Am Q*, (1977), 117–131. A review essay.

307 LANE, Ann J., ed. *The Debate over Slavery: Stanley Elkins and His Critics*. Urbana, Ill, 1971.†

308 McCOLLEY, Robert. *Slavery and Jeffersonian Virginia*. 2nd ed. Urbana, Ill., 1974.†

309 McPHERSON, James M. "Slavery and Race." *Pers Am Hist*, 3 (1969), 460–473.

310 MENN, Joseph K. "The Large Slaveholders of the Deep South, 1860." Doctoral dissertation, University of Texas, 1964.

311 MILLER, Elinor, and Eugene D. GENOVESE, eds. *Plantation, Town, and County—Essays on the Local History of American Slave Society.* Urbana, Ill., 1974.†

312 MILLER, John Chester. *The Wolf by the Ears, Thomas Jefferson and Slavery.* Riverside, N. J., 1977.

313 MILLER, William L. "Slavery and the Population of the South." *S Ec J*, 28 (1961), 46–54.

314 MOONEY, Chase C. *Slavery in Tennessee.* Westport, Conn., 1971.

315 MOORE, John Hebron. "Simon Gray, Riverman: A Slave Who Was Almost Free." *Miss Val Hist Rev*, 49 (1962), 472–484.

316 MORRIS, Richard B. "The Measure of Bondage in the Slave States." *Miss Val Hist Rev*, 41 (1954), 219–240.

317 NEWTON, James E. "Slave Artisans and Craftsmen: The Roots of Afro-American Art." *Black Schol*, 9 (November, 1977), 35–42.

318 NYE, Russel B. "The Slave Power Conspiracy, 1830–1860." *Sci and Soc*, 10 (1946), 262–274.

319 OWENS, Harry P., ed. *Perspectives and Irony in American Slavery.* Jackson, Miss., 1976.

320 OWENS, Leslie H. *This Species of Property: Slave Life and Culture in the Old South.* New York, 1977.†

321 PHIFER, Edward W. "Slavery in Microcosm: Burke County, North Carolina." *J S Hist*, 28 (1962), 137–165.

322 PHILLIPS, Ulrich B. *American Negro Slavery.* Foreword, Eugene Genovese. Baton Rouge, 1966.†

323 PHILLIPS, Ulrich B. "The Central Theme of Southern History." *Am His Rev*, 34 (1928), 30–43.

324 PHILLIPS, Ulrich B. *Life and Labor in the Old South.* Boston, 1963. Intro. C. Vann Woodward.†

325 RAMSDELL, Charles W. "The Natural Limits of Slavery Expansion." *Miss Val Hist Rev*, 16 (1929), 151–171.

326 RICE, C. Duncan. *The Rise and Fall of Black Slavery.* Baton Rouge, 1976.†

327 SCARPINO, Phillip V. "Slavery in Calloway County, Missouri: 1845–1855." *Mo Hist Rev*, 71 (1976), 22–43; (1977), 266–283.

328 SCHWENINGER, Loren. "A Slave Family in the Ante Bellum South." *J Neg Hist*, 60 (1975), 29–44.

329 SELLERS, Charles G., Jr. "The Travail of Slavery." *The Southerner as American.* Ed. Charles G. Sellers, Jr. New York, 1966.†

330 SELLERS, James B. *Slavery in Alabama.* University, Ala., 1950.

331 SHALOPE, Robert E. "Race, Class, Slavery, and the Antebellum Southern Mind." *J S Hist*, 37 (1971), 557–574.

332 SMALLWOOD, James. "Blacks in Antebellum Texas: A Reappraisal." *Red Riv Val Hist Rev*, 2 (1975), 443–466.

333 SMITH, Julia F. *Slavery and Plantation Growth in Florida, 1821–1860.* Gainesville, Fla., 1973.

334 STAMPP, Kenneth M. "The Historian and Southern Negro Slavery." *Am Hist Rev*, 57 (1952), 613–624.

335 STAMPP, Kenneth M. "Interpreting the Slaveholders' World: A Review." *Ag Hist*, 44 (1970), 407–412.

336 STAMPP, Kenneth M. *The Peculiar Institution: Slavery in the Ante-Bellum South.* New York, 1964.†

337 STAMPP, Kenneth M. "Rebels and Sambos: The Search for the Negro's Personality in Slavery." *J S Hist*, 37 (1971), 367–392.

338 STRICKLAND, Arvarh E. "Aspects of Slavery in Missouri, 1821." *Mo Hist Rev*, 65 (1971), 505–526.

339 SUTCH, Richard C. "The Treatment Received by American Slaves: A Critical Review of the Evidence Presented in *Time on the Cross." Exp Ec Hist*, 12 (1975), 335–438.

340 SYDNOR, Charles S. *Slavery in Mississippi.* Magnolia, Mass., [n. d.].

341 TAYLOR, Joe Gray. *Negro Slavery in Louisiana.* Westport, Conn., 1977.

342 TAYLOR, Orville W. *Negro Slavery in Arkansas.* Durham, N. C., 1958.

343 TURNER, Wallace B. "Kentucky Slavery in the Last Ante Bellum Decade." *Reg Ky Hist Soc*, 58 (1960), 291–307.

344 WADE, Richard C. *Slavery in the Cities: The South, 1820–1860.* New York, 1976.†

345 WALL, Bennett H. "An Epitaph for Slavery." *La Hist*, 16 (1975), 229–256.

346 WEINSTEIN, Allen, and Frank Otto GATELL, eds. *American Negro Slavery, a Modern Reader.* 3rd ed. New York, 1979.†

347 WILLIAMS, Edwin L., Jr. "Negro Slavery in Florida." *Fla Hist Q*, 28 (1949), 93–110; (1950), 182–204.

348 WILTSHIRE, Susan Ford. "Jefferson, Calhoun, and the Slavery Debate." The Classics and the Two Minds of the South." *S Hum Rev*, (1977), 33–40. A special unnumbered issue of the *Southern Humanities Review*, entitled "The Classical Tradition in the South."

349 WYATT-BROWN, Bertram. "Stanley Elkins' *Slavery*: The Antislavery Interpretation Reexamined." *AM Q*, 25 (1973), 154–176.

3. The Slave Trade

350 ANSTEY, Robert. *The Atlantic Slave Trade and British Abolition, 1760–1810.* Atlantic Highlands, N. J., 1975.

351 BANCROFT, Frederic. *Slave-Trading in the Old South.* New York, 1970.†

352 BERNSTEIN, Barton J. "Southern Politics and Attempts to Reopen the African Slave Trade." *J Neg Hist*, 51 (1966), 16–35.

353 BRADY, Patrick S. "The Slave Trade and Sectionalism in South Carolina, 1787–1808." *J S Hist*, 38 (1972), 601–620.

354 CALDERHEAD, William. "How Extensive Was the Border State Slave Trade? A New Look." *Civ War Hist*, 18 (1972), 42–55.

355 CALDERHEAD, William. "The Role of the Professional Slave Trader in a Slave Economy: Austin Woolfolk, a Case Study." *Civ War Hist*, 23 (1977), 195–211.

356 CARSTENSEN, F. V., and S. E. GOODMAN. "Trouble on the Auction Block: Interregional Slave Sales and the Reliability of a Linear Equation." *J Interdis Hist*, 8 (1977), 315–318.

357 CLARK, Thomas D. "The Slave Trade between Kentucky and the Cotton Kingdom." *Miss Val Hist Rev*, 21 (1934), 331–342.

358 COLEMAN, J. Winston, Jr. "Lexington's Slave Dealers and Their Southern Trade." *Filson Club Hist Q*, 12 (1938), 1–23.

359 COLLINS, Winfield H. *The Domestic Slave Trade of the Southern United States.* Port Washington, N. Y., 1969.

360 CURTIN, Philip D. *The Atlantic Slave Trade: A Census.* Madison, Wis., 1969.†

361 DAVIS, Robert R., Jr., ed. "Buchanian Espionage: A Report on Illegal Slave Trading in the South in 1859." *J S Hist*, 37 (1971), 271–278.

362 DONNAN, Elizabeth, ed. *Documents Illustrative of the Slave Trade to America.* See **249.**

363 DuBOIS, W. E. B. "The Enforcement of the Slave-Trade Laws." *Ann Rept Am Hist Assn*, (1891), 163–194.

364 DuBOIS, W. E. B. *The Suppression of the African Slave Trade to the United States of America.* Foreword, John Hope Franklin. Baton Rouge, 1970.†

365 EVANS, Robert J. "Some Economic Aspects of the Domestic Slave Trade, 1830–1860." *S Ec J*, 27 (1961), 329–337.

366 FORNELL, Earl W. "Agitation in Texas for Reopening the Slave Trade." *SW Hist Q*, 60 (1956), 245–259.

367 HENDRIX, James P., Jr. "The Efforts to Reopen the African Slave Trade in Louisiana." *La Hist*, 10 (1969), 97–123.

368 HOWELL, Isabel. "John Armfield, Slave-Trader." *Tenn Hist Q*, 2 (1943), 2–39.

369 JILLSON, Calvin, and Thornton ANDERSON. "Realignments in the Convention of 1787: The Slave Trade Compromise." *J Pol*, 39 (1977), 712–729.

370 KIPLE, Kenneth F. "The Case against a Nineteenth-Century Cuba-Florida Slave Trade." *Fla Hist Q*, 49 (1971), 346–355.

371 KOTLIKOFF, Laurence J., and Sebastian PINERA. "The Old South's Stake in the Inter-Regional Movement of Slaves, 1850–1860." *J Ec Hist*, 37 (1977), 434–450.

372 LANDRY, Harral E. "Slavery and the Slave Trade in Atlantic Diplomacy, 1850–1861." *J S Hist*, 27 (1961), 184–207.

373 LLOYD, Christopher. *The Navy and the Slave Trade: The Suppression of the African Slave Trade in the Nineteenth Century.* London, 1949.

374 LOWE, Richard G., and Randolph B. CAMPBELL. "The Slave-Breeding Hypothesis: A Demographic Comment on the 'Buying' and 'Selling' States." *J S Hist*, 42 (1976), 401–412.

375 MILLER, William L. "A Note on the Importance of the Interstate Slave Trade of the Ante Bellum South." *J Pol Ec*, 73 (1965), 181–187.

376 ROTTENBERG, Simon. "The Business of Slave Trading." *S Atl Q*, 66 (1967), 409–423.

377 STAFFORD, Frances J. "Illegal Importations: Enforcement of the Slave Trade Laws along the Florida Coast, 1810–1828."*Fla Hist Q*, 46 (1967), 124–133.

378 STEPHENSON, Wendell H. *Isaac Franklin, Slave Trader and Planter of the Old South*. Magnolia, Mass., 1968.

379 TAKAKI, Ronald T. "The Movement to Reopen the African Slave Trade in South Carolina." *S C Hist Mag*, 66 (1965), 38–54.

380 TAKAKI, Ronald T. *A Pro-Slavery Crusade: The Agitation to Reopen the African Slave Trade*. New York, 1971.

381 THOMAS, Robert P., and Richard N. BEAN. "The Fishers of Men: The Profits of the Slave Trade." *J Ec Hist*, 34 (1974), 885–915.

382 WARD, W. E. F. *The Royal Navy and the Slavers: The Suppression of the Atlantic Slave Trade*. New York, 1969.†

383 WAX, Darold D. "Robert Ellis, Philadelphia Merchant and Slave Trader." *Pa Mag Hist Biog*, 88 (1964), 52–69.

384 WELLS, Tom H. "Charles Augustus Lafayette Lamar: Gentleman Slave Trader." *Ga Hist Q*, 47 (1963), 158–168.

385 WELLS, Tom H. *The Slave Ship Wanderer*. Athens, Ga., 1967.

386 WHITRIDGE, Arnold. "The American Slave-Trade." *Hist Today*, 8 (1958), 462–472.

387 WHITTEN, David O. "Slave Buying in 1853 Virginia as Revealed by Letters of a Louisiana Negro Sugar Planter [Andrew Durnford]." *La Hist*, 11 (1970), 231–244.

388 WILLIAMS, Jack K. "The Southern Movement to Reopen the African Slave Trade, 1854–1860: A Factor in Secession." *Proc S C Hist Assn*, 30 (1960), 23–31.

389 WISH, Harvey. "The Revival of the African Slave Trade in the United States, 1856–1860." *Miss Val Hist Rev*, 27 (1941), 569–588.

4. Health of Slaves

390 JORDAN, Weymouth T. "Plantation Medicine in the Old South." *Ala Rev*, 3 (1950), 83–107.

391 KIPLE, Kenneth F., and Virginia H. KIPLE. "Black Tongue and Black Men: Pellagra and Slavery in the Antebellum South." *J S Hist*, 43 (1977), 411–428.

392 LEE, Ann S., and Everett S. LEE. "The Health of Slaves and the Health of Freedmen: A Savannah Study." *Phylon*, 38 (1977), 170–180.

393 POSTELL, William D. *The Health of Slaves on Southern Plantations*. Magnolia, Mass., 1970.

394 SAVITT, Todd L. *Medicine and Slavery: The Health and Care of Slaves in Antebellum Virginia*. Urbana, Ill., 1978.

395 SAVITT, Todd L. "Slave Life Insurance in Virginia and North Carolina." *J S Hist*, 43 (1977), 583–600.

396 SIKES, Lewright. "Medical Care for Slaves: A Preview of the Welfare State." *Ga Hist Q*, 52 (1968), 405–413.

397 WALL, Bennett H. "Medical Care of Ebenezer Pettigrew's Slaves." *Miss Val Hist Rev*, 37 (1950), 451–470.

398 WHITTEN, David O. "Medical Care of Slaves: Louisiana Sugar Region and South Carolina Rice District." *Sou Stud*, 16 (1977), 153–180.

5. Economics of Slavery

399 ANDERSON, Ralph V., and Robert E. GALLMAN. "Slaves as Fixed Capital: Slave Labor and Southern Economic Development." *J Am Hist*, 64 (1977), 24–26.

400 AUFHAUSER, R. Keith. "Slavery and Scientific Management." *J Ec Hist*, 33 (1973), 811–824.

401 BELL, Rudolph M. "Slavery as an Investment: Dollars and Humans." *Hist Meth Newsletter*, 10 (1976), 1–9.

402 CANARELLA, Giorgio, and John A. TOMASKE. "The Optimal Utilization of Slaves." *J Ec Hist*, 35 (1975), 621–629.

403 CONRAD, Alfred H., and John R. MEYER. *The Economics of Slavery, and Other Studies in Econometric History*. Chicago, 1964.

404 CONRAD, Alfred H., and John R. MEYER. "The Economics of Slavery in the Ante-Bellum South." *J Pol Ec*, 66 (1958), 95–130.

405 CONRAD, Alfred H., and John R. MEYER. "Slavery as an Obstacle to Economic Growth in the United States: A Panel Discussion." *J Ec Hist*, 27 (1967), 518–560.

406 DAVID, Paul A., et al. *Reckoning with Slavery: A Critical Study in Quantitative History of American Negro Slavery*. New York, 1976. A critique of *Time on the Cross*.†

407 ENGERMAN, Stanley L. "The Antebellum South: What Probably Was and What Should Have Been." *Ag Hist*, 44 (1970), 127–142.

408 ENGERMAN, Stanley L., and Eugene D. GENOVESE, eds. *Race and Slavery in the Western Hemisphere: Quantitative Studies*. Princeton, 1975.†

409 FINDLAY, Ronald. "Slavery, Incentive, and Manumission: A Theoretical Model." *J Pol Ec*, 83 (1975), 923–933.

410 FOGEL, Robert W., and Stanley L. ENGERMAN. "Explaining the Relative Efficiency of Slave Agriculture in the Antebellum South." *Am Ec Rev*, 67 (1977), 275–296.

411 FOGEL, Robert W. "Three Phases of Cliometric Research on Slavery and its Aftermath." *Am Ec Rev*, 65 (May 1975), 37–46. This is a special issue, paged separately.

412 FOGEL, Robert W., and Stanley L. ENGERMAN. *Time on the Cross: The Economics of American Negro Slavery*. 2 vols. Boston, 1974.†

413 FONER, Philip S. *Business and Slavery: The New York Merchant and the Irrepressible Conflict*. New York, 1968.

414 FOUST, James D., and Dale E. SWAN. "Productivity and Profitability of Antebellum Slave Labor: A Micro-Approach." *Ag Hist*, 44 (1970), 39–62.

415 GENOVESE, Eugene D. "The Low Productivity of Southern Slave Labor: Causes and Effects." *Civ War Hist*, 9 (1963), 365–382.

416 GENOVESE, Eugene D. "The Medical and Insurance Costs of Slaveholding in the Cotton Belt." *J Neg Hist*, 45 (1960), 141–155.

417 GENOVESE, Eugene D. *The Political Economy of Slavery: Studies in the Economy and Society of the Old South*. New York, 1967.†

418 GENOVESE, Eugene D. "The Significance of the Slave Plantation for Southern Economic Development." *J S Hist*, 28 (1962), 422–437.

419 GOVAN, Thomas P. "Was Plantation Slavery Profitable?" *J S Hist*, 8 (1942), 513–535.

420 GRAY, Lewis C. "Economic Efficiency and Competitive Advantages of Slavery under the Plantation System." *Ag Hist*, 4 (1930), 31–47.

421 GUTMAN, Herbert G. *Slavery and the Numbers Game: A Critique of Time on the Cross*. Urbana, Ill., 1975.†

422 JONES, Archer, and Paul H. HOEPNER. "The South's Economic Investment in Slavery." *Am J Ec Soc*, 26 (1967), 297–299.

423 McPHERSON, James M. "The Political Economy of Slavery: Studies in the Economy and Society of the Slave South. A Review Article." *J Soc Hist*, 1 (1968), 280–285.

424 MILLER, William L. "J. E. Cairnes on the Economics of American Negro Slavery." *S Ec J*, 30 (1964), 333–341.

425 NIEMI, Albert W., Jr. "Inequality in the Distribution of Slave Wealth: The Cotton South and Other Southern Agricultural Regions." *J Ec Hist*, 37 (1977), 747–754.

426 PARKER, William N. "Slavery and Southern Economic Development: An Hypothesis and Some Evidence." *Ag Hist*, 44 (1970), 115–126.

427 PHILLIPS, Ulrich B. *The Slave Economy of the Old South: Selected Essays in Economic and Social History*. Ed. Eugene D. Genovese. Baton Rouge, 1968.†

428 RUSSEL, Robert R. "The Economic History of Negro Slavery in the United States." *Ag Hist*, 11 (1937), 308–321.

429 RUSSEL, Robert R. "The Effects of Slavery upon Nonslaveholders in the Ante Bellum South." *Ag Hist*, 15 (1941), 112–126.

430 RUSSEL, Robert R. "The General Effects of Slavery upon Southern Economic Progress." *J S Hist*, 4 (1938), 34–54.

431 SARAYDAR, Edward. "A Note on the Profitability of Ante-Bellum Slavery." *S Ec J*, 30 (1964), 325–332.

432 SAVITT, Todd L. "Slave Life Insurance in Virginia and North Carolina." See **395**.

433 SMITH, Robert W. "Was Slavery Unprofitable in the Ante-Bellum South?" *Ag Hist*, 20 (1946), 62–64.

434 *The Structure of the Cotton Economy of the Antebellum South*. Ed. William N. Parker. Washington, D. C., 1970.

435 SUTCH, Richard C. "The Breeding of Slaves for Sale and the Westward Expansion of Slavery, 1850–1860." *Race and Slavery in the Western Hemisphere: Quantitative Studies*. Eds. Stanley L. Engerman and Eugene D. Genovese. Princeton, 1975.

436 SUTCH, Richard C. "The Profitability of Ante-Bellum Slavery—Revisited." *S Ec J*, 31 (1965), 365–376.

437 VEDDER, Richard K., and David C. STOCKDALE. "The Profitability of Slavery: A Different Approach." *Ag Hist*, 49 (1975), 392–404.

438 VEDDER, Richard K., and David C. STOCKDALE. "The Slave Exploitation (Expropriation) Rate." *Exp Ec Hist*, 12 (1975), 453–457.

439 WAYLAND, Francis F. "Slavebreeding in America: The Stevenson-O'Connell Imbroglios of 1838." *Va Mag Hist Biog*, 50 (1942), 47–54.

440 WHITTEN, David O. "Sugar Slavery: A Profitability Model for Slave Investments in the Antebellum Louisiana Sugar Industry." *La Stud*, 12 (1973), 423–442.

441 WILLIAMS, Eric E. *Capitalism and Slavery*. New York, 1966.†

442 WOODMAN, Harold D. "The Profitability of Slavery: A Historical Perennial." *J S Hist*, 29 (1963), 303–325.

443 WOOLFOLK, George R. "Planter Capitalism and Slavery: The Labor Thesis." *J Neg Hist*, 41 (1956), 103–116.

444 WRIGHT, Gavin. "New and Old Views on the Economics of Slavery." *J Ec Hist*, 33 (1973), 452–466. A review article.

6. Slave Unrest

445 ADDINGTON, Wendell G. "Slave Insurrection in Texas." *J Neg Hist*, 35 (1950), 408–434.

446 APTHEKER, Herbert. *American Negro Slave Revolts*. New York, 1969.†

447 BAUER, Raymond A., and Alice H. BAUER. "Day to Day Resistance to Slavery." *J Neg Hist*, 27 (1942), 388–419.

448 CARROLL, Joseph C. *Slave Insurrections in the United States, 1800–1865*. Westport, Conn., 1968.

449 DEW, Charles B. "Black Ironworkers and the Slave Insurrection Panic of 1856.' *J S Hist*, 41 (1975), 321–338.

450 DUFF, John B., and Peter M. MITCHELL, eds. *The Nat Turner Rebellion: The Historical Event and the Modern Controversy*. New York, 1971.†

451 ELLIOTT, Robert N. "The Nat Turner Insurrection as Reported in the North Carolina Press." *N C Hist Rev*, 38 (1961), 1–18.

452 FREDRICKSON, George M., and Christopher LASCH. "Resistance to Slavery." *Civ War Hist*, 13 (1967), 315–330.

453 GREENE, Lorenzo J. "Mutiny on the Slave Ships." *Phylon*, 5 (1944), 346–354.

454 KILSON, Marion D. "Towards Freedom: An Analysis of Slave Revolts in the United States." *Phylon*, 25 (1964) , 175–187.

455 MILES, Edwin A. "The Mississippi Slave Insurrection Scare of 1835." *J Neg Hist*, 42 (1957), 48–60.

456 MULLIN, Gerold W. *Flight and Rebellion: Slave Resistance in Eighteenth-Century Virginia.* New York, 1974.†

457 OATES, Stephen B. *The Fires of Jubilee: Nat Turner's Fierce Rebellion.* New York, 1976.†

458 PEASE, Jane H., and William H. PEASE. *They Who Would Be Free: Blacks' Search for Freedom, 1830–1861.* New York, 1974.

459 TRAGLE, Henry I. *The Southampton Slave Revolt of 1831: A Compilation of Source Material.* Amherst, Mass., 1971.†

460 WADE, Richard. "The Vesey Plot: A Reconsideration." *J S Hist*, 30 (1964), 143–161.

461 WISH, Harvey. "American Slave Insurrections before 1861." *J Neg Hist*, 22 (1937), 299–320.

7. The Slave and the Law

462 BEATTY-BROWN, Florence R. "Legal Status of Arkansas Negroes before Emancipation." *Ark Hist Q*, 28 (1969), 6–13.

463 CATTERALL, Helen T., ed. *Judicial Cases Concerning American Slavery and the Negro.* See **248**.

464 CLARK, Ernest J., Jr. "Aspects of the North Carolina Slave Code, 1715–1860." *N C Hist Rev*, 39 (1962), 148–164.

465 COVER, Robert M. *Justice Accused: Antislavery and the Judicial Process.* New Haven, Conn., 1975.

466 DEW, Charles B. "Disciplining Slave Ironworkers in the Antebellum South: Coercion, Conciliation, and Accommodation." *Am Hist Rev*, 79 (1974), 393–418.

467 EDWARDS, John C. "Slave Justice in Four Middle Georgia Counties." *Ga Hist Q*, 57 (1973), 265–273.

468 FLANIGAN, Daniel J. "Criminal Procedure in Slave Trials in the Antebellum South." *J S Hist*, 40 (1974), 537–564.

469 HENRY, Howell M. *The Police Control of the Slave in South Carolina.* Westport Conn., 1968.

470 HOWARD, Warren S. *American Slavers and the Federal Law, 1837–1862.* Westport, Conn., 1976.

471 HURD, John C. *The Law of Freedom and Bondage in the United States.* See **256**.

471a JANUARY, Alan F. "The South Carolina Association: An Agency for Race Control in Antebellum Charleston." *S C Hist Mag*, 78 (1977), 191–201.

472 KLEBANER, Benjamin J. "American Manumission Laws and the Responsibility for Supporting Slaves." *Va Mag Hist Biog*, 63 (1955), 443–453.

473 MANGUM, Charles S. *The Legal Status of the Negro.* New York, 1970.

474 YANUCK, Julius. "Thomas Ruffin and North Carolina Slave Law." *J S Hist*, 21 (1955), 456–475.

475 YOUNGER, Richard D. "Southern Grand Juries and Slavery." *J Neg Hist*, 40 (1955), 166–178.

8. Fugitives

476 BRIDNER, Elwood L., Jr. "The Fugitive Slaves of Maryland." *Md Hist Mag*, 66 (1971), 33–50.

477 BUCKMASTER, Henrietta. *Let My People Go: The Story of the Underground Railroad and the Growth of the Abolition Movement.* Boston, 1959.†

478 CAMPBELL, Stanley W. *The Slave Catchers: Enforcement of the Fugitive Law, 1850–1860.* New York, 1972.†

479 GARA, Larry. " The Fugitive Slave Law: A Double Paradox." *Civ War Hist*, 10 (1964), 229–240.

480 WILSON, Benjamin C. "Kentucky Kidnappers, Fugitives, and Abolitionists in Antebellum Cass County, Michigan." *Mich Hist*, 60 (1976), 339–59.

9. Industrial Slavery

481 DEW, Charles B. "Black Ironworkers and the Slave Insurrection Panic of 1856." See **449**.

482 DEW, Charles B. "David Ross and the Oxford Iron Works: A Study of Industrial Slavery in the Early Nineteenth-Century South." *Wm Mar Q*, 3rd ser., 31 (1974), 189–224.

483 EATON, Clement. "Slave-Hiring in the Upper South: A Step toward Freedom." *Miss Val Hist Rev*, 46 (1960), 663–678.

484 LANDER, Ernest M., Jr. "Slave Labor in South Carolina Cotton Mills." *J Neg Hist*, 38 (1953), 161–173.

485 LEWIS, Ronald L. "Slave Families at Early Chesapeake Ironworks." *Va Mag Hist Biog*, 86 (1978), 169–179.

486 MOORE, John Hebron. "Simon Gray, Riverman: A Slave Who was Almost Free." See **315**.

487 PREYER, Norris W. "The Historian, the Slave, and the Ante-Bellum Textile Industry." *J Neg Hist*, 46 (1961), 67–82.

488 STAROBIN, Robert S. "Disciplining Industrial Slaves in the Old South." *J Neg Hist*, 53 (1968), 111–128.

489 STAROBIN, Robert S. "The Economics of Industrial Slavery in the Old South." *Bus Hist Rev*, 44 (1970), 131–174.

490 STAROBIN, Robert S. *Industrial Slavery in the Old South.* New York, 1971.†

490a STEALEY, John E., III. "Slavery and the Western Virginia Salt Industry." *J Neg Hist*, 59 (1974), 105–131.

10. The Defense of Slavery

491 BOOKER, H. Marshall. "Thomas Roderick Dew: Forgotten Virginian." *Va Cav*, 19 (Autumn, 1969), 20–29.

492 CARSELL, Wilfred. "The Slaveholders' Indictment of Northern Wage Slavery." *J S Hist*, 6 (1940), 504–520.

493 DONALD, David. "The Pro-Slavery Argument Reconsidered." *J S Hist*, 37 (1971), 3–18.

494 DURDEN, Robert F. "J. D. B. DeBow: Convolutions of a Slavery Expansionist." *J S Hist*, 17 (1951), 441–461.

495 EATON, Clement. "Mob Violence in the Old South." *Miss Val Hist Rev*, 29 (1942), 351–370.

496 FITZHUGH, George. *Cannibals All: Or, Slaves without Masters.* Ed. C. Vann Woodward. See **252**.

497 FITZHUGH, George. *Sociology for the South.* See **253**.

498 GARDNER, Robert. "A Tenth Hour Apology for Slavery." *J S Hist*, 26 (1960), 352–367.

499 GUILLORY, James D. "The Pro-Slavery Arguments of Dr. Samuel A. Cartwright." *La Hist*, 9 (1968), 209–227.

500 HARRISON, Lowell. "Thomas Roderick Dew: Philosopher of the Old South." *Va Mag Hist Biog*, 57 (1949), 390–404.

501 HESSELTINE, William B. "Some New Aspects of the Pro-Slavery Argument." *J Neg Hist*, 21 (1936), 1–14.

502 JENKINS, William S. *Pro-Slavery Thought in the Old South.* Chapel Hill, 1935.

503 McKITRICK, Eric L., ed. *Slavery Defended: The Views of the Old South.* Englewood Cliffs, N. J., 1963.†

504 MANSFIELD, Stephen S. "Thomas Roderick Dew: Defender of the Southern Faith." Doctoral dissertation, University of Virginia, 1968.

505 MORROW, Ralph E. "The Proslavery Argument Revisited." *Miss Val Hist Rev*, 48 (1961), 79–94.

506 PERKINS, Howard C. "The Defense of Slavery in the Northern Press on the Eve of the Civil War." *J S Hist*, 9 (1943), 501–531.

507 ROGERS, Tommy W. "Dr. F. A. Ross and the Presbyterian Defense of Slavery." *J Presb Hist*, 45 (1967), 112–124.

508 SMITH, Harmon L. "William Capers and William A. Smith, Neglected Advocates of the Pro-Slavery Moral Argument." *Meth Hist*, 3 (October, 1964), 23–32.

509 STAMPP, Kenneth M. "An Analysis of T. R. Dew's *Review of the Debate in the Virginia Legislature.*" *J Neg Hist*, 27 (1942), 380–387.

509a TISE, Larry E. "Pro-Slavery Ideology: A Social and Intellectual History of the Defense of Slavery in America, 1790–1840." Doctoral dissertation, University of North Carolina, 1975.

510 WILSON, Harold. "Basil Manly, Apologist for Slavocracy." *Ala Rev*, 15 (1962), 38–53.

511 WISH, Harvey. *George Fitzhugh, Propagandist of the Old South.* Baton Rouge, 1943.

11. Comparative Studies of the Slave System

512 ALEXANDER, Herbert B. "Brazilian and United States Slavery Compared." *J Neg Hist*, 7 (1922), 349–364.

513 BERGER, Max. "American Slavery as Seen by British Visitors, 1836–1860." *J Neg Hist*, 30 (1945), 181–202.

514 CONRAD, Robert. *The Destruction of Brazilian Slavery, 1850–1888.* Berkeley, Cal., 1972.†

515 COTTROL, Robert L. "Comparative Slave Studies: Urban Slavery as a Model. Travelers Accounts as a Source—Bibliographic Essay." *J Black Stud*, 8 (1977), 3–12.

516 DEGLER, Carl N. *Neither Black nor White: Slavery and Race Relations in Brazil and the United States.* New York, 1971.†

517 DEGLER, Carl N. "Slavery in Brazil and the United States: An Essay in Comparative History." *Am Hist Rev*, 75 (1970), 1004–1028.

518 DUNN, Richard S. "A Tale of Two Plantations: Slave Life at Mesopotamia in Jamaica and Mount Airy in Virginia, 1799 to 1828." *Wm Mar Q*, 3rd ser., 34 (1977), 32–65.

519 ELKINS, Stanley, and Eric McKITRICK. "Institutions and the Law of Slavery: The Dynamics of Unopposed Capitalism." *Am Q*, 9 (1957), 3–21.

520 ELKINS, Stanley, and Eric McKITRICK. "Institutions and the Law of Slavery: Slavery in Capitalist and Non-Capitalist Cultures." *Am Q*, 9 (1957), 159–179.

521 FONER, Laura, and Eugene D. GENOVESE, eds. *Slavery in the New World: A Reader in Comparative History.* Englewood Cliffs, N. J., 1969.†

522 GENOVESE, Eugene D. "A Georgia Slaveholder Looks at Africa." *Ga Hist Q*, 51 (1967), 186–193.

523 HINE, William C. "American Slavery and Russian Serfdom: A Preliminary Comparison." *Phylon*, 36 (1975), 378–384.

524 KLEIN, Herbert S. "Anglicanism, Catholicism, and the Negro Slave." *Comp Stud Soc Hist*, 8 (1966), 295–327, and commentary 328–330.

525 KLEIN, Herbert S. *Slavery in the Americas: A Comparative Study of Cuba and Virginia.* New York, 1972.

526 LURAGHI, Raimondo. "Wage Labor in the 'Rice Belt' of Northern Italy and Slave Labor in the American South—A First Approach." *Sou Stud*, 16 (1977).

527 SIO, Arnold A. "Interpretations of Slavery: The Slave Status in the Americas." *Comp Stud Soc Hist*, 7 (1965), 289–308.

528 TANNENBAUM, Frank. *Slave and Citizen: The Negro in the Americas*. New York, 1963.

529 WILLIAMS, Mary W. "The Treatment of Slaves in the Brazilian Empire: A Comparison with the United States." *J Neg Hist*, 15 (1930), 315–336.

VI. The Free Black

530 BARR, Ruth B., and Modeste HARGIS. "The Voluntary Exile of Free Negroes of Pensacola." *Fla Hist Q*, 17 (1938), 3–14.

531 BEDINI, Silvio A. *The Life of Benjamin Banneker*. New York, 1971.

532 BELL, Howard H. "Free Negroes of the North, 1830–1835: A Study in National Cooperation." *J Neg Ed*, 26 (1957), 447–455.

533 BELL, Howard H. "The National Negro Convention, 1848." *Ohio Hist Q*, 67 (1958), 357–368.

534 BELLAMY, Donnie D. "Free Blacks in Antebellum Missouri, 1820–1860." *Mo Hist Rev*, 67 (1973), 198–226.

535 BERKELEY, Edmund, Jr. "Prophet without Honor: Christopher McPherson, Free Person of Color." *Va Mag Hist Biog*, 77 (1969), 180–190.

536 BERLIN, Ira. *Slaves without Masters: The Free Negro in the Antebellum South*. New York, 1976.†

537 BOUCHER, Morris R. "The Free Negro in Alabama Prior to 1860." Doctoral dissertation, State Unversity of Iowa, 1950.

538 BREWER, James H. "Negro Property Owners in Seventeenth-Century Virginia." *Wm Mar Q*, 3rd ser., 12 (1955), 575–580.

539 BROWN, Letitia W. *Free Negroes in the District of Columbia, 1790–1846*. New York, 1972.

540 BROWNING, James B. "The Free Negro in Ante-Bellum North Carolina." *N C Hist Rev*, 15 (1938), 23–33.

541 CHRISTENSEN, Lawrence O. "Cyprian Clamorgan, *The Colored Aristocracy of St. Louis* (1858)." *Bul Mo Hist Soc*, 31 (1974), 3–31.

542 COHEN, David W., and Jack P. GREEN, eds. *Neither Slave nor Free: The Freedman of African Descent in the Slave Societies of the New World*. Baltimore, Md., 1972.

543 DAVIS, Edwin A., and William R. HOGAN. *The Barber of Natchez*. Baton Rouge, 1973.†

544 DAVIS, Edwin A. "William Johnson: Free Negro Citizen of Ante-Bellum Mississippi." *J Miss Hist*, 15 (1953), 57–72.

545 DELLA, M. Ray, Jr. "The Problems of Negro Labor in the 1850's." *Md Hist Mag*, 66 (1971), 14–32.

546 DesCHAMPS, Margaret Burr. "John Chavis as a Preacher to Whites." *N C Hist Rev*, 32 (1955), 165–172.

547 DOHERTY, Herbert J., Jr., ed. "A Free Negro Purchases His Daughter." *Fla Hist Q*, 29 (1950), 38–43.

548 DOUGLASS, Frederick. *My Bondage and My Freedom*. See **250**.

·549 EATON, Clement. *The Mind of the Old South*. See **286**.

550 ENGLAND, J. Merton. "The Free Negro in Ante-Bellum Tennessee." Doctoral dissertation, Vanderbilt University, 1941.

551 ENGLAND, J. Merton. "The Free Negro in Ante-Bellum Tennessee." *J S Hist*, 9 (1943), 37–58.

552 EVERETT, Donald E. "Emigres and Militiamen: Free Persons of Color in New Orleans, 1803–1815." *J Neg Hist*, 38 (1953), 377–402.

553 EVERETT, Donald E. "Free Persons of Color in Colonial Louisiana." *La Hist*, 7 (1966), 21–50.

554 EVERETT, Donald E. "The Free Persons of Color in New Orleans, 1803–1865." Doctoral dissertation, Tulane University, 1952.

555 FISCHER, Roger A. "Racial Segregation in Ante-Bellum New Orleans." *Am Hist Rev*, 74 (1969), 926–937.

556 FITCHETT, E. Horace. "The Origin and Growth of the Free Negro Population of Charleston, South Carolina." *J Neg Hist*, 26 (1941), 421–437.

557 FITCHETT, E. Horace. "The Status of the Free Negro in Charleston, South Carolina." *J Neg Hist*, 32 (1947), 430–451.

558 FITCHETT, E. Horace. "The Traditions of the Free Negro in Charleston, South Carolina." *J Neg Hist*, 25 (1940), 139–152.

559 FLANDERS, Ralph B. "The Free Negro in Ante-Bellum Georgia." *N C Hist Rev*, 9 (1932), 250–272.

560 FONER, Laura. "The Free People of Color in Louisiana and St. Domingue: A Comparative Portrait of Two Three-Caste Slave Societies." *J Soc Hist*, 3 (1970), 406–430.

561 FRANKLIN, John Hope. "The Enslavement of Free Negroes in North Carolina." *J Neg Hist*, 29 (1944), 401–428.

562 FRANKLIN, John Hope. *The Free Negro in North Carolina*. New York, 1971.†

563 FRANKLIN, John Hope. "The Free Negro in the Economic Life of Ante-Bellum North Carolina." *N C Hist Rev*, 19 (1942), 239–259, 359–375.

564 FRANKLIN, John Hope. "James Boon, Free Negro Artisan." *J Neg Hist*, 30 (1945), 150–180.

565 FRAZIER, E. Franklin. *The Free Negro Family: A Study of Family Origins before the Civil War*. New York, 1968.

566 GARVIN, Russell. "The Free Negro in Florida before the Civil War." *Fla Hist Q*, 46 (1967), 1–17.

567 HALLIBURTON, R., Jr. "Free Black Owners of Slaves: A Reappraisal of the [Carter G.] Woodson Thesis." *S C Hist Mag*, 76 (1975), 129–142.

568 HANCOCK, Harold B. "Not Quite Men: The Free Negro in Delaware in the 1830's." *Civ War Hist*, 17 (1971), 320–331.

569 HITE, Roger W. "Voice of a Fugitive: Henry Bibb and Ante-Bellum Black Separatism." *J Black Stud*, 4 (1974), 269–284.

570 JACKSON, Luther P. *Free Negro Labor and Property Holding in Virginia 1830–1860*. New York, 1969.

571 JACKSON, Luther P. "Free Negroes of Petersburg, Virginia." *J Neg Hist*, 12 (1927), 365–388.

572 JACKSON, Luther P. "The Virginia Free Negro Farmer and Property Owner, 1830–1860." *J Neg Hist*, 24 (1939), 390–439.

573 JACKSON, Luther P. "Virginia Negro Soldiers and Seamen in the American Revolution." *J Neg Hist*, 27 (1942), 247–287.

574 JOHNSON, William. *William Johnson's Natchez: The Ante-Bellum Diary of a Free Negro*. See **129**.

575 JOHNSTON, James H. *Race Relations in Virginia and Miscegenation in the South*. See **303**.

576 KNIGHT, Edgar W. "Notes on John Chavis." *N C Hist Rev*, 7 (1930), 326–345.

577 LITWACK, Leon F. *North of Slavery: The Negro in the Free States, 1790–1860*. Chicago, 1965.†

578 MALVIN, John. *North into Freedom: The Autobiography of John Malvin, Free Negro, 1795–1880*. Ed. Allan Peskin. Cleveland, Ohio, 1966.

579 MATHIAS, Frank F. "John Randolph's Freedmen: The Thwarting of a Will." *J S Hist*, 39 (1973), 263–272.

580 MILLS, Gary B. "A Portrait of Achievement: Augustin Metoyer." *Red Riv Val Hist Rev*, 2 (1975), 333–348.

581 MORGAN, Edmund S. "Slavery and Freedom: The American Paradox." *J Am Hist*, 59 (1972), 5–29.

582 MUIR, Andrew F. "The Free Negro in Fort Bend County, Texas."*J Neg Hist*, 33 (1948), 77–85.

583 MUIR, Andrew F. "The Free Negro in Harris County, Texas." *SW Hist Q*, 46 (1943), 214–238.

584 MUIR, Andrew F. "The Free Negro in Jefferson and Orange Counties, Texas. *J Neg Hist*, 35 (1950), 183–206.

585 MYERS, John L. "American Antislavery Society Agents and the Free Negro, 1833–1838." *J Neg Hist*, 52 (1967), 200–219.

586 PORTER, Kenneth W. "Florida Slaves and Free Negroes in the Seminole War, 1835–1842." *J Neg Hist*, 28 (1943), 390–421.

587 PROVINE, Dorothy. "The Economic Position of Free Blacks in the District of Columbia, 1800–1860." *J Neg Hist*, 58 (1973), 61–72.

588 REINDERS, Robert C. "The Decline of the New Orleans Free Negro in the Decade before the Civil War." *J Miss Hist*, 24 (1962), 88–98.

589 REINDERS, Robert C. "The Free Negro in the New Orleans Economy, 1850–1860." *La Hist*, 6 (1965), 273–285.

590 ROBINSON, Henry S. "Some Aspects of the Free Negro Population of Washington, D. C., 1800–1862." *Md Hist Mag*, 64 (1969), 43–64.

591 ROGERS, W. McDowell. "Free Negro Legislation in Georgia before 1865." *Ga Hist Q*, 16 (1932), 27–37.

592 RUSSELL, John H. "Colored Freemen as Slave Owners in Virginia." *J Neg Hist*, 1 (1916), 233–242.

593 RUSSELL, John H. *The Free Negro in Virginia, 1619–1865.* New York, 1969.

594 SAVAGE, W. Sherman. "The Influence of John Chavis and Lunsford Lane on the History of North Carolina." *J Neg Hist,* 25 (1940), 14–24.

595 SCHOEN, Harold. "The Free Negro in the Republic of Texas." *SW Hist Q,* 39 (1936), 292–308; 40 (1936), 26–34, 85–113, 169–199, (1937), 267–289; 41 (1937), 83–108.

596 SCHWENINGER, Loren. "John H. Rapier, Sr.: A Slave and Freedman in the Ante-Bellum South." *Civ War Hist,* 20 (1974), 23–34.

597 SEIP, Terry L. "Slaves and Free Negroes in Alexandria, 1850–1860." *La Hist,* 10 (1969), 125–145.

598 SELLERS, James B. "Free Negroes of Tuscaloosa County before the Thirteenth Amendment." *Ala Rev,* 23 (1970), 110–127.

599 SENESE, Donald J. "The Free Negro and the South Carolina Courts, 1790–1860." *S C Hist Mag,* 68 (1967), 140–153.

600 SHUGG, Roger W. "Negro Voting in the Ante-Bellum South." *J Neg Hist,* 21 (1936), 357–364.

601 SOUTHALL, Eugene P. "Negroes in Florida Prior to the Civil War." *J Neg Hist,* 19 (1934), 77–86.

602 STAHL, Annie Lee West. "The Free Negro in Ante-Bellum Louisiana." *La Hist Q,* 25 (1942), 301–396.

603 STAVISKY, Leonard P. "The Negro Artisan in the South Atlantic States, 1800–1860: A Study of Status and Economic Opportunity with Special Reference to Charleston." Doctoral dissertation, Columbia University, 1958.

604 STERKX, H. E. *The Free Negro in Ante-Bellum Louisiana, 1724–1860.* Rutherford, N. J., 1972.

605 SWEAT, Edward F. "The Free Negro in Ante-Bellum Georgia." Doctoral dissertation, Indiana University, 1957.

606 SWEAT, Edward F. "Social Status of the Free Negro in Antebellum Georgia." *Neg Hist Bul,* 21 (1958), 129–131.

607 SYDNOR, Charles S. "The Free Negro in Mississippi before the Civil War." *Am Hist Rev,* 32 (1927), 769–788.

608 VOEGELI, V. Jacque. *Free but not Equal: The Midwest and the Negro during the Civil War.* Chicago, 1970.†

609 WHITTEN, David O. "A Black Entrepreneur in Antebellum Louisiana." *Bus Hist Rev,* 45 (1971), 201–219.

610 WIKRAMANAYAKE, Marina. *A World in Shadow: The Free Black in Antebellum Carolina.* Columbia, S. C., 1973.

611 WINSTON, James E. "The Free Negro in New Orleans, 1803–1860." *La Hist Q,* 21 (1938), 1075–1085.

612 WOODSON, Carter G. *Free Negro Heads of Families in the United States in 1830.* Washington, D. C., 1925.

613 WOODSON, Carter G., ed. *Free Negro Owners of Slaves in the United States in 1830. . . .* Westport, Conn., 1968.

614 WRIGHT, James M. *The Free Negro in Maryland, 1634–1860.* New York, 1971.

VII. The Crusade against Slavery: Colonization, Manumission, Abolition

1. General

615 BARNES, Gilbert H. *The Antislavery Impulse, 1830–1844.* Intro W. G. McLoughlin. New York, 1964.†

616 BEAN, William G. "The Ruffner Pamphlet of 1847: An Antislavery Aspect of Virginia Sectionalism." *Va Mag Hist Biog,* 61 (1953), 260–282.

617 BOROMÉ, Joseph A., ed. "Henry Clay and James G. Birney: An Exchange of Views." *Filson Club Hist Q,* 35 (1961), 122–124.

618 BOYD, William M. "Southerners in the Anti-Slavery Movement, 1800–1830." *Phylon,* 9 (1948), 153–163.

619 CARDOSO, Jack J. "Southern Reaction to Helper's *The Impending Crisis.*" *Civ War Hist,* 16 (1970), 5–17.

620 CATE, Margaret D. "Mistakes in Fanny Kemble's Georgia Journal." *Ga Hist Q,* 44 (1960), 1–17.

621 COVER, Robert M. *Justice Accused: Antislavery and the Judicial Process.* New Haven, Conn., 1975.

622 DEGLER, Carl N. *The Other South: Southern Dissenters in the Nineteenth Century.* New York, 1975.†

623 DesCHAMPS, Margaret B. "Antislavery Presbyterians in the Carolina Piedmont." *Proc S C Hist Assn,* 24 (1954), 6–13.

624 EMINHIZER, Earl E. "Alexander Campbell's Thoughts on Slavery and Abolition." *W Va Hist,* 33 (1972), 109–123.

625 FILLER, Louis. *The Crusade against Slavery, 1830–1860.* New York, 1960.†

626 FINNIE, Gordon E. "The Antislavery Movement in the Upper South before 1840." *J S Hist,* 35 (1969), 319–342.

627 FISHER, Miles Mark. "Friends of Humanity: A Quaker Anti-Slavery Influence." *Church Hist,* 4 (1935), 187–202.

628 FLADELAND, Betty. *Men and Brothers: Anglo-American Antislavery Cooperation.* Urbana, Ill., 1972.

629 GARA, Larry. "Friends and the Underground Railroad." *Quaker Hist,* 51 (1962), 3–19.

630 GARA, Larry. *The Liberty Line: The Legend of the Underground Railroad.* Lexington, Ky., 1967.†

631 GARA, Larry. "Propaganda Uses of the Underground Railroad." *Mid-Am*, 34 (1952), 155–171.

632 GOODLOE, Daniel R. *An Inquiry into the Causes Which Have Retarded. . . the Southern States*. Washington, D. C., 1846.

633 HANCOCK, Harold B., ed. "William Yates's Letter of 1837: 'Slavery, and Colored People in Delaware'." *Del Hist*, 14 (1971), 205–216.

634 HICKIN, Patricia P. "Antislavery in Virginia, 1831–1861." Doctoral dissertation, University of Virginia, 1968.

635 HICKIN, Patricia. "Gentle Agitator: Samuel M. Janney and the Antislavery Movement in Virginia, 1842–1851." *J S Hist,* 37 (1971), 159–190.

636 HICKIN, Patricia P. "John C. Underwood and the Antislavery Movement in Virginia, 1847–1860." *Va Mag Hist Biog*, 73 (1965), 156–168.

637 JORDAN, Winthrop D. "An Antislavery Proslavery Document?" *J Neg Hist*, 47 (1962), 54–56.

638 KATES, Don B., Jr. "Abolition, Deportation, Integration: Attitudes toward Slavery in the Early Republic." *J Neg Hist*, 53 (1968), 33–47.

639 MARTIN, Asa E. "Pioneer Anti-Slavery Press." *Miss Val Hist Rev*, 2 (1916), 509–528.

640 NYE, Russel B. "Civil Liberties and the Antislavery Controversy." *Sci and Soc*, 9 (1945), 125–146.

641 PEASE, William H., and Jane H. PEASE, eds. *The Antislavery Argument*. Indianapolis, Ind., 1965.

642 RATNER, Lorman A. "Northern Opposition to the Anti-Slavery Movement, 1831–1840." Doctoral dissertation, Cornell University, 1961.

643 RICE, C. Duncan. "The Anti-Slavery Mission of George Thompson to the United States, 1834–1835." *J Am Stud*, 2 (1968), 13–31.

644 ROBERT, Joseph C. *The Road from Monticello: A Study of the Virginia Slavery Debate of 1832*. New York, 1970.

645 RUSH, D. Orwin. "Lucretia Mott and the Philadelphia Antislavery Fairs." *Bul Friends Hist Assn*, 35 (1946), 69–75.

646 SHANKS, Caroline L. "The Biblical Anti-Slavery Argument of the Decade, 1830–1840." *J Neg Hist*, 16 (1931), 132–157.

647 STAMPP, Kenneth M. "The Fate of the Southern Anti-Slavery Movement." *J Neg Hist*, 28 (1943), 10–22.

648 STAMPP, Kenneth M. "The Southern Refutation of the Pro-Slavery Argument." *N C Hist Rev*, 21 (1944), 35–45.

649 STEELY, Will F. "Antislavery in Kentucky, 1850–1860." Doctoral dissertation, University of Rochester, 1956.

650 STEINER, Bruce E., ed. "A Planter's Troubled Conscience." *J S Hist*, 28 (1962), 343–347.

2. *Colonization*

651 BELL, Howard H. "Negro Nationalism: A Factor in Emigration Projects, 1858–1861." *J Neg Hist*, 47 (1962), 42–53.

652 BLACKETT, Richard. "Martin R. Delany and Robert Campbell: Black Americans in Search of an African Colony." *J Neg Hist*, 62 (1977), 1–25.

653 CAMPBELL, Penelope. *Maryland in Africa: The Maryland State Colonization Society, 1831–1857.* Urbana, Ill., 1971.

654 CAMPBELL, Penelope. "Some Notes on Frederick County's Participation in the Maryland Colonization Scheme." *Md Hist Mag*, 66 (1971), 51–59.

655 COLEMAN, J. Winston, Jr. "Henry Clay, Kentucky, and Liberia." *Reg Ky Hist Soc*, 45 (1945), 309–322.

656 COLEMAN, J. Winston, Jr. "The Kentucky Colonization Society." *Reg Ky Hist Soc*, 39 (1941), 1–9.

657 DYER, Brainerd. "The Persistence of the Idea of Negro Colonization." *Pac Hist Rev*, 12 (1943), 53–65.

658 EARP, Charles A. "The Role of Education in the Maryland Colonization Movement." *J Neg Hist*, 26 (1941), 365–388.

659 HOYT, William D., Jr. "John McDonogh and Maryland Colonization in Liberia, 1834–35." *J Neg Hist*, 24 (1939), 440–453.

660 KEITH, Jean E. "Joseph Rogers Underwood, Friend of African Colonization." *Filson Club Hist Q*, 22 (1948), 117–132.

661 KENDALL, Lane C. "John McDonogh, Slave Owner." *La Hist Q*, 15 (1932), 646–654; 16 (1933), 125–134.

662 LANDON, Fred. "Henry Bibb, a Colonizer." *J Neg Hist*, 5 (1920), 437–447.

663 LOGAN, Rayford W. "Some New Interpretations of the Colonization Movement." *Phylon*, 4 (1943), 328–334.

663a MITCHELL, Memory F. "Off to Africa—With Judicial Blessing." *N C Hist Rev*, 53 (1976), 265–287.

664 OPPER, Peter K. "The Mind of the White Participant in the African Colonization Movement, 1816–1840." Doctoral dissertation, University of North Carolina, 1972.

665 OPPER, Peter K. " 'Old Jane Seems to be a Coming Too': A History of the Migration, Emigration, and Colonization of the North Carolina Negro, 1816–1836." Master's thesis, University of North Carolina, 1969.

666 SHERWOOD, Henry N. "Early Negro Deportation Projects."*Miss Val Hist Rev*, 2 (1916), 484–508.

667 SHERWOOD, Henry N. "The Formation of the American Colonization Society." *J Neg Hist*, 2 (1917), 209–228.

668 STANGE, Douglas C. "Lutheran Involvement in the American Colonization Society." *Mid-Am*, 49 (1967), 140–151.

669 STAUDENRAUS, Philip J. *The African Colonization Movement, 1816–1865.* New York, 1961.

670 WEEKS, Louis, III. "John Holt Rice and the American Colonization Society." *J Presb Hist*, 46 (1968), 26–41.

3. Manumission

671 BLACKFORD, L. Minor. *Mine Eyes Have Seen the Glory: The Story of a Virginia Lady . . . Who Taught Her Sons to Hate Slavery and Love the Union.* Cambridge, Mass., 1954.

672 CHILDS, William T. *John McDonogh, His Life and Work.* Baltimore, Md., 1939.

673 DAVIS, J. Treadwell. "Nashoba: Frances Wright's Experiment in Self-Emancipation." *S Q,* 11 (1972), 63–90.

674 EATON, Clement, ed. "Minutes and Resolutions of an Emancipation Meeting in Kentucky in 1849." *J S Hist,* 14 (1948), 541–545.

675 EMERSON, O. B. "Francis Wright and the Nashoba Experiment." *Tenn Hist Q,* 6 (1947), 291–314.

676 KETCHAM, Ralph L. "The Dictates of Conscience: Edward Coles and Slavery." *Va Q Rev,* 36 (1960), 46–62.

677 LANGHORNE, Elizabeth. "Edward Coles, Thomas Jefferson, and the Rights of Man." *Va Cav,* 23 (Summer, 1973), 30–37.

678 MATISON, Sumner E. "Manumission by Purchase." *J Neg Hist,* 33 (1948), 146–167.

679 MATTHEWS, Paul Aaron. "Francis Wright and the Nashoba Experiment: A Transitional Period in Antislavery Attitudes." *E Tenn Hist Soc Pub,* 46 (1974), 37–52.

680 NORTH CAROLINA MANUMISSION SOCIETY. *Minutes of the North Carolina Manumission Society, 1816–1834.* Ed. H. M. Wagstaff. Chapel Hill, 1934. (James Sprunt Historical Studies, v. 22, nos. 1–2)

681 PAYNE-GAPOSCHKIN, Cecilia Helena. "The Nashoba Plan for Removing the Evil of Slavery: Letters of Frances and Camilla Wright, 1820–1829." *Harvard Lib Bul,* 23 (1975), 221–251, 429–461.

682 PEASE, William H., and Jane H. PEASE. "A New View of Nashoba." *Tenn Hist Q,* 19 (1960), 99–109.

683 RICE, Otis K. "Eli Thayer and the Friendly Invasion of Virginia." *J S Hist,* 37 (1971), 575–596.

684 SOWLE, Patrick. "The North Carolina Manumission Society, 1816–1834." *N C Hist Rev,* 42 (1965), 47–69.

685 TILLY, Bette B. "The Spirit of Improvement: Reformism and Slavery in West Tennessee." *W Tenn Hist Soc Pap,* 28 (1974), 25–42.

686 TROXLER, George. "Eli Caruthers: A Silent Dissenter in the Old South." *J Presb Hist,* 45 (1967), 95–111.

4. Abolition

687 ABZUG, Robert H. "The Influence of Garrisonian Abolitionists' Fears of Slave Violence on the Antislavery Argument, 1829–1840." *J Neg Hist,* 55 (1970), 15–28.

688 ATHERTON, Lewis E. "Daniel Howell Hise, Abolitionist and Reformer." *Miss Val Hist Rev,* 26 (1939), 343–358.

689 BAILEY, Hugh C. *Hinton Rowan Helper: Abolitionist—Racist.* University, Ala., 1965.

690 BAILEY Hugh C. "Hinton Rowan Helper and *The Impending Crisis.*" *La Hist Q,* 40 (1957), 133–145.

691 BARTLETT, Irving H. "Wendell Phillips and the Eloquence of Abuse." *Am Q,* 1 (1959), 509–520.

692 BIERBAUM, Milton E. "Frederick Starr, a Missouri Border Abolitionist: The Making of a Martyr." *Mo Hist Rev*, 58 (1964), 309–325.

693 BIRNEY, James G. *Letters of James Gillespie Birney, 1831–1857*. Ed. D. L. Dumond. 2 vols. Magnolia, Mass., 1966.

694 BRAWLEY, Benjamin. "Lorenzo Dow." *J Neg Hist*, 1 (1916), 265–275.

695 BREWER, William M. "Henry Highland Garnet." *J Neg Hist*, 13 (1928), 36–52.

696 BREWER, William M. "John B. Russwurm." *J Neg Hist*, 13 (1928), 413–422.

697 BUCKMASTER, Henrietta. *Let My People Go*. See **477**.

698 CALVERT, Monte A. "The Abolition Society of Delaware, 1801–1807." *Del Hist*, 10 (1963), 295–320.

699 CARDOSO, Joaquín José. "Hinton Rowan Helper: A Nineteenth-Century Pilgrimage." Doctoral dissertation, University of Wisconsin, 1967.

700 CARDOSO, Jack J. "Hinton Rowan Helper as a Racist in the Abolitionist Camp." *J Neg Hist*, 55 (1970), 323–330.

701 CARDOSO, Jack J. "Lincoln, Abolitionism, and Patronage: The Case of Hinton Rowan Helper." *J Neg Hist*, 53 (1968), 144–160.

702 CHEEK, William F. "John Mercer Langston: Black Protest Leader and Abolitionist." *Civ War Hist*, 16 (1970), 101–120.

703 DAVIS, David Brion. "The Emergence of Immediatism in British and American Antislavery Thought." *Miss Val Hist Rev*, 49 (1962), 209–230.

704 DILLON, Merton L. "The Abolitionists: A Decade of Historiography, 1959–1969." *J S Hist*, 35 (1969), 500–522.

705 DILLON, Merton L. "The Abolitionists as a Dissenting Minority." *Dissent: Explorations in the History of American Radicalism*. Ed. Alfred F. Young. DeKalb, Ill., 1968.†

706 DILLON, Merton L. *The Abolitionists: The Growth of a Dissenting Minority*. DeKalb, Ill., 1974.†

707 DILLON, Merton L. *Benjamin Lundy and the Struggle for Negro Freedom*. Urbana, Ill., 1966.

708 DILLON, Merton L. "Benjamin Lundy in Texas." *SW Hist Q*, 63 (1959), 46–62.

709 DILLON, Merton L. *Elijah P. Lovejoy, Abolitionist Editor*. Urbana, Ill., 1961.

710 DILLON, Merton L. "The Failure of the American Abolitionists." *J S Hist*, 25 (1959), 159–177.

711 DUBERMAN, Martin B. "The Abolitionists and Psychology." *J Neg Hist*, 47 (1962), 183–191.

712 DUBERMAN, Martin, ed. *The Antislavery Vanguard: New Essays on the Abolitionists*. Princeton, 1965.†

713 DUMOND, Dwight L. *Antislavery: The Crusade for Freedom in America*. New York, 1966.†

714 DUMOND, Dwight L. *Antislavery Origins of the Civil War in the United States*. Ann Arbor, Mich., 1959.†

715 DURDEN, Robert F. "The Ambiguous Antislavery Crusade of James S. Pike." *S C Hist Mag*, 56 (1955), 187–195.

716 EATON, Clement. "A Dangerous Pamphlet in the Old South." *J S Hist*, 2 (1936), 323–334.

717 FLADELAND, Betty L. *James Gillespie Birney: Slaveholder to Abolitionist*. Westport, Conn., 1969.

718 FLADELAND, Betty. "Who Were the Abolitionists?" *J Neg Hist*, 49 (1964), 99–115.

719 GARA, Larry. "The Professional Fugitive in the Abolition Movement." *Wis Mag Hist*, 48 (1965), 196–204.

720 GARRISON, William L. *The Letters of William Lloyd Garrison*. Ed. Walter M. Merrill, and Louis Rachames for vol. 4. 4 vols. Cambridge, Mass., 1973.

721 HARRISON, Lowell H. "The Anti-Slavery Career of Cassius M. Clay." *Reg Ky Hist Soc*, 59 (1961), 295–317.

722 HAWKINS, William G. *Lunsford Lane: Or, Another Helper from North Carolina*. New York, 1969.

723 HELPER, Hinton R. *The Impending Crisis of the South: How to Meet It*. Ed. G. M. Fredrickson. Cambridge, Mass., 1968.

724 HENIG, Gerald S. "The Jacksonian Attitude toward Abolitionism in the 1830's." *Tenn Hist Q*, 28 (1969), 42–56.

725 JOHNSON, Clifton H. "Abolitionist Missionary Activities in North Carolina." *N C Hist Rev*, 40 (1963), 295–320.

726 JOHNSON, Clifton H. "The American Missionary Association, 1846–1861: A Study of Christian Abolitionism." Doctoral dissertation, University of North Carolina, 1959.

727 JONES, F. Dudley. "The Grimké Sisters." *Proc S C Hist Assn* 3 (1933), 12–21.

728 KEARNS, Francis E. "Margaret Fuller and the Abolition Movement." *J Hist Ideas*, 25 (1964), 120–127.

729 KRADITOR, Aileen S. *Means and Ends in American Abolitionism: Garrison and His Critics on Strategy and Tactics, 1834–1850*. New York, 1969.

730 LANE, Lunsford. *The Narrative of Lunsford Lane*. See **257**.

731 LERNER, Gerda. "The Grimké Sisters and the Struggle against Race Prejudice." *J Neg Hist*, 48 (1963), 277–291.

732 LERNER, Gerda. *The Grimké Sisters from South Carolina: Rebels against Slavery*. New York, 1971.†

733 LITWACK, Leon. "The Abolitionist Dilemma: The Anti-Slavery Movement and the Northern Negro." *N Eng Q*, 34 (1961), 50–73.

734 LOFTON, Williston H. "Abolition and Labor." *J Neg Hist*, 33 (1948), 249–283.

735 LOVELAND, Anne C. "Evangelicalism and 'Immediate Emancipation' in American Antislavery Thought." *J S Hist*, 32 (1966), 172–188.

736 LUMPKIN, Katharine. *The Emancipation of Angelina Grimké*. Chapel Hill, 1974.

737 MATHEWS, Donald G. "The Abolitionists on Slavery: The Critique behind the Social Movement." *J S Hist*, 33 (1967), 163–182.

738 MAYNARD, Douglas H. "The World's Anti-Slavery Convention of 1840." *Miss Val Hist Rev*, 47 (1960), 452–471.

739 MERIDETH, Robert. "A Conservative Abolitionist at Alton: Edward Beecher's *Narrative*." *J Presb Hist Soc*, 42 (1964), 39–53, 92–103.

740 MERKEL, Benjamin G. [sic] "The Underground Railroad and the Missouri Borders, 1840–1860." *Mo Hist Rev*, 37 (1943), 271–285.

741 MERRILL, W. M. *Against Wind and Tide: A Biography of William Lloyd Garrison.* Cambridge, Mass., 1963.

742 MYERS, John L. "Organization of 'the Seventy' to Arouse the North against Slavery." *Mid-Am*, 48 (1966), 29–46.

743 OATES, Stephen B. *To Purge This Land with Blood, a Biography of John Brown.* New York, 1972.†

744 PEASE, William H., and Jane H. PEASE. "Antislavery Ambivalence: Immediatism, Expendiency, Race." *Am Q*, 17 (1965), 682–695.

745 PEASE, William H., and Jane H. PEASE. "Walker's *Appeal* Comes to Charleston: A Note and Documents." *J Neg Hist*, 59 (1974), 287–292.

746 PERRY, Lewis. "Versions of Anarchism in the Antislavery Movement." *Am Q*, 20 (1968), 768–782.

747 POLK, William. "The Hated Helper." *S Atl Q*, 30 (1931), 177–189.

748 QUARLES, Benjamin. "Sources of Abolitionist Income." *Miss Val Hist Rev*, 32 (1945), 63–76.

749 ROPPOLO, Jospeh P. "Harriet Beecher Stowe and New Orleans: A Study in Hate." *N Eng Q*, 30 (1957), 346–362.

750 RUCHAMES, Louis. *The Abolitionist: A Collection of Their Writings.* New York, 1963.

751 SAVAGE, W. Sherman. "Abolitionist Literature in the Mails, 1835–1836." *J Neg Hist*, 13 (1929), 150–184.

752 SEWELL, Richard H. *John P. Hale and the Politics of Abolition.* Cambridge, Mass., 1965.

753 SIMMS, Henry H. "A Critical Analysis of Abolition Literature, 1830–1840." *J S Hist*, 6 (1960), 368–382.

754 SMILEY, David L. "Cassius M. Clay and John G. Fee: A Study in Southern Anti-Slavery Thought." *J Neg Hist*, 42 (1957), 201–213.

755 SMILEY, David L. *Lion of Whitehall: The Life of Cassius M. Clay.* Magnolia, Mass., 1969.

756 SMITH, Robert P. "William Cooper Nell: Crusading Black Abolitionist." *J Neg Hist*, 55 (1970), 182–199.

757 SOUTHALL, Eugene P. "Arthur Tappan and the Anti-Slavery Movement." *J Neg Hist*, 15 (1930), 162–197.

758 STEELY, Will F. "William Shreve Bailey, Kentucky Abolitionist." *Filson Club Hist Q*, 31 (1957), 274–281.

759 STEWART, James B. "The Aims and Impact of Garrisonian Abolitionism, 1840–1860." *Civ War Hist*, 15 (1969), 197–209.

760 STEWART, James B. *Holy Warriors: The Abolitionists and American Slavery.* New York, 1976.

761 THOMAS, Benjamin P. *Theodore Weld, Crusader for Freedom.* New York, 1973.

762 THOMAS, John L. *The Liberator, William Lloyd Garrison, a Biography.* Boston, 1963.

763 THOMAS, John L., ed. *Slavery Attacked: The Abolitionist Crusade.* Englewood Cliffs, N. J., 1964.†

764 TOLBERT, Noble J. "Daniel Worth: Tar Heel Abolitionist." *N C Hist Rev*, 39 (1962), 284–304.

765 TOPLIN, Robert B. "Peter Still Versus the Peculiar Institution." *Civ War Hist*, 13 (1967), 340–349.

766 WALKER, David. *David Walker's Appeal . . . to the Coloured Citizens of the World . . . .* Ed. with introduction, Charles M. Wiltse. New York, 1965.

767 WALKER, Peter. *Moral Choices, Memory, Desire, and Imagination in Nineteenth-Century American Abolition.* Baton Rouge, 1978.

768 WELD, Theodore D. *Letters of Theodore Dwight Weld, Angelina Grimké Weld, and Sarah Grimké, 1822–1844.* Eds. G. H. Barnes and D. L. Dumond. 2 vols. Magnolia, Mass., 1965.

769 WOLF, Hazel C. "An Abolition Martyrdom in Maryland." *Md Hist Mag*, 47 (1952), 224–233.

770 WYATT-BROWN, Bertram. *Lewis Tappan and the Evangelical War against Slavery.* New York, 1971.†

771 WYATT-BROWN, Bertram. "William Lloyd Garrison and Antislavery Unity: A Reappraisal." *Civ War Hist*, 13 (1967), 5–24.

VIII. The Structure of Southern Society

1. General

722 APPLEWHITE, Joseph D. "Some Aspects of Society in Rural South Carolina in 1850." *N C Hist Rev*, 29 (1952), 39–63.

773 BOYD, Minnie C. *Alabama in the Fifties: A Social Study.* New York, 1966.

774 CARPENTER, Charles, ed. "Henry Dana Ward: Early Diary Keeper of the Kanawha Valley." *W Va Hist*, 37 (1975), 34–48.

775 DAVENPORT, F. Garvin. *Ante-Bellum Kentucky, a Social History, 1800–1860.* Oxford, Ohio, 1943.

776 DAVENPORT, F. Garvin. "Cultural Versus Frontier in Tennessee, 1825–1850." *J S Hist*, 5 (1959), 18–33.

777 DesCHAMPS, Margaret Burr. "The Free Agricultural Population in Sumter District, South Carolina, 1850–1860." *N C Hist Rev*, 32 (1955), 81–91.

778 DODD, Dorothy. "Florida in 1845." *Fla Hist Q*, 23 (1945), 3–27.

779 DODD, William E. "The Social Philosophy of the Old South." *Am J Soc*, 23 (1918), 735–746.

780 DOW, Roger. "Seichas: A Comparison of Pre-Reform Russia and the Ante-Bellum South." *Russian Rev*, 7 (1947), 1–15.

781 EATON, Clement. "Class Differences in the Old South." *Va Q Rev*, 33 (1957), 357–370.

782 EATON, Clement. *The Growth of Southern Civilization*. See **58**.

783 HUNDLEY, Daniel R. *Social Relations in Our Southern States*. See **255**.

784 JOHNSON, Guion Griffis. *Ante-Bellum North Carolina, a Social History*. Chapel Hill, 1937.

785 JOHNSON, Guion Griffis. "Social Characteristics of Ante-Bellum North Carolina." *N C Hist Rev*, 6 (1929), 140–157.

786 JOHNSON, Guion Griffis. *A Social History of the Sea Islands*. Chapel Hill, 1930.

787 JORDAN, Weymouth T. *Ante-Bellum Alabama, Town and Country*. Tallahassee, Fla., 1957.

788 LINDEN, Fabian. "Economic Democracy in the Slave South: An Appraisal of some Recent Views." *J Neg Hist*, 31 (1946), 140–189.

789 McDONALD, Forrest, and Grady McWHINEY. "The Antebellum Southern Herdsman: A Reinterpretation." *J S Hist*, 41 (1975), 147–166.

790 MITCHELL, Broadus. *Frederick Law Olmsted, a Critic of the Old South*. New York, 1968.

791 OLMSTED, Frederick L. *Journey in the Back Country*. See **136**.

792 OLMSTED, Ferderick L. *Journey in the Seaboard Slave States*. See **137**.

793 OLMSTED, Frederick L. *Journey through Texas*. See **138**.

794 OWSLEY, Frank L., and Harriet C. OWSLEY. "The Economic Basis of Society in the Late Ante-Bellum South."*J S Hist*, 6 (1940), 24–45.

795 OWSLEY, Frank L., and Harriet C. OWSLEY. "The Economic Structure of Rural Tennessee, 1850–1860." *J S Hist*, 8 (1942), 161–182.

796 PATTON, JAMES W. "Facets of the South in the 1850's." *J S Hist*, 23 (1957), 3–24.

797 PHILLIPS, Ulrich B. *Life and Labor in the Old South*. Intro. C. Vann Woodward. See **324**.

798 POSEY, Walter B. "The Public Manners of Ante-Bellum Southerners." *J Miss Hist*, 19 (1957), 219–233.

799 ROGERS, Benjamin G. "Florida Seen through the Eyes of Nineteenth Century Travellers." *Fla Hist Q*, 34 (1955), 177–189.

800 ROPER, Laura W. *F. L. O.: A Biography of Frederick Law Olmsted*. Baltimore, Md., 1973.

801 SCHLESINGER, Arthur M. "Was Olmsted an Unbiased Critic of the South?" *J Neg Hist*, 37 (1952), 173–187.

802 SMITH, H. Shelton. "The Church and the Social Order in the Old South as Interpreted by James H. Thornwell." *Church Hist*, 7 (1938), 115–124.

803 TAYLOR, Rosser H. *Ante-Bellum South Carolina*. New York, 1970.

804 TAYLOR, Rosser H. "The Mud-Sill Theory in South Carolina." *Proc S C Hist Assn*, 9 (1939), 35–43.

805 TURNER, Frederick J. "The South, 1820–1830." *Am Hist Rev*, 11 (1906), 559–573.

805a WEAVER, Blanche H. C. "D. R. Hundley: Subjective Sociologist." *Ga Rev*, 10 (1956), 222–234.

806 WHIPPLE, Henry B. *Bishop Whipple's Southern Diary, 1843–1844.* See **154**.

807 WHITE, Laura A. "The South in the 1850's as Seen by British Consuls." *J S Hist*, 1 (1935), 29–48.

808 YODER, Paton. "Private Hospitality in the South, 1775–1850." *Miss Val Hist Rev*, 47 (1960), 419–433.

2. *The Westward Movement and Frontier Life*

809 ABERNETHY, Thomas P. *From Frontier to Plantation in Tennessee.* University, Ala., 1967.

810 ATHERTON, Lewis E. "Life, Labor, and Society in Boone County, Missouri, 1834–1852, as Revealed in the Correspondence of an Immigrant Slave Owning Family from North Carolina." *Mo Hist Rev*, 38 (1944), 277–304, 408–429.

811 ATHERTON, Lewis E. "Missouri's Society and Economy in 1821." *Mo Hist Rev*, 65 (1971), 450–477.

812 BALDWIN, Joseph G. *The Flush Times of Alabama and Mississippi.* Magnolia, Mass., 1959.

813 BARNHART, John D. "Frontiersmen and Planters in the Formation of Kentucky." *J S Hist*, 7 (1941), 19–36.

814 BARNHART, John D. "Sources of Migration into the Old Northwest." *Miss Val Hist Rev*, 22 (1935), 49–62.

815 BARNHART, John D. "The Southern Element in the Leadership of the Old Northwest." *J S Hist*, 1 (1935), 186–197.

816 BARNHART, John D. "The Southern Influence in the Formation of Ohio." *J S Hist*, 3 (1937), 28–42.

817 BIEHLE, Reba S. "Edward Oxford, Pioneer Farmer of Middle Georgia." *Ga Hist Q*, 52 (1968), 187–198.

818 CHAMBERS, Nella J. "Early Days in East Alabama." *Ala Rev*, 13 (1960), 177–185.

819 CLARK, Thomas D. *The Rampaging Frontier.* Westport, Conn., 1976.

820 CRAVEN, Avery. "The 'Turner Theories' and the South." *J S Hist*, 5 (1939), 291–314.

821 DICK, Everett. *The Dixie Frontier, a Social History.* New York, 1974.

822 EATON, Clement. "Social Structure and Social Mobility in the Old Southwest." *The Americanization of the Gulf Coast, 1803–1850.* Ed. L. F. Ellsworth, Jr. Pensacola, Fla., 1972. (Gulf Coast History and Humanities Conference, no. 4, University of West Florida)†

823 FRIEND, Llerena B. "The Texan of 1860." *SW Hist Q*, 62 (1958), 1–17.

824 GREEN, Fletcher M., ed. *The Lides Go South . . . and West: The Record of a Planter Migration in 1835.* Columbia, S. C., 1952.†

825 HAMILTON, William B. "The Southwestern Frontier, 1795–1817: An Essay in Social History." *J S Hist*, 10 (1944), 389–403.

826 HARR, John L. "The Ante-Bellum Southwest, 1815–61." Doctoral dissertation, University of Chicago, 1941.

827 HIGHSAW, Mrs. Mary W. "A History of Zion Community in Maury County, 1806–1860." *Tenn Hist Q*, 5 (1946), 3–34, 111–140, 222–233.

828 JORDAN, Terry G. "The Imprint of the Upper and Lower South in Mid-Nineteenth Century Texas." *Ann Assn Am Geog*, 57 (1967), 667–690.

829 LEWIS, Robert. "Frontier and Civilization in the Thought of Frederick Law Olmsted." *Am Q*, 29 (1977), 385–403.

830 MOORE, Arthur K. *The Frontier Mind: A Cultural Analysis of the Kentucky Frontiersman.* Lexington, Ky., 1957.†

831 OWSLEY, Frank L. "The Pattern of Migration and Settlement on the Southern Frontier." *J S Hist*, 11 (1945), 147–176.

832 OWSLEY, Harriet C. "Westward to Tennessee." *Tenn Hist Q*, 24 (1965), 31–38.

833 PHILLIPS, Ulrich B. "The Origin and Growth of the Southern Black Belts." *Am Hist Rev*, 11 (1906), 798–816.

834 ROGERS, Tommy W. "The Great Population Exodus from South Carolina: 1850–1860." *S C Hist Mag*, 68 (1967), 14–21.

835 ROGERS, Tommy W. "Migration from Tennessee during the Nineteenth Century, I: Origin and Destination of Tennessee Migrants, 1850–1860." *Tenn Hist Q*, 27 (1969), 118–122. For companion study, see **837**.

836 ROGERS, Tommy W. "Migration Patterns of Alabama's Population, 1850 to 1860." *Ala Hist Q*, 28 (1966), 45–50.

837 SCOTT, Thomas A. "Migration from Tennessee during the Nineteenth Century, II: The Impact of Tennessee's Migrating Songs." *Tenn Hist Q*, 27 (1968), 123–141.

838 SILVER, James W. "Edward Pendleton Gaines and Frontier Problems, 1801–1849." *J S Hist*, 1 (1935), 320–344.

839 SMEDES, Susan Dabney. *Memorials of a Southern Planter.* See **151**.

840 STEEL, Edward M., Jr. "A Pioneer Farmer in the Choctaw Purchase." *J Miss Hist*, 16 (1954), 229–241.

841 WALZ, Robert B. "Migration into Arkansas, 1834–1880." Doctoral dissertation, University of Texas, 1958.

842 WELLS, Tom H. "Moving a Plantation to Louisiana." *La Stud*, 6 (1967), 280–289.

3. *Planters*

843 BARROW, Bennet H. *Plantation Life in the Florida Parishes of Louisiana.* See **110**.

844 BLACKFORD, John. *Ferry Hill Plantation Journal, January 4, 1838–January 15, 1839.* Ed. Fletcher M. Green. Chapel Hill, 1961.†

845 BREWSTER, Lawrence F. "Planters from the Low-Country and Their Summer Travels." *Proc S C Hist Assn*, 13 (1943), 35–41.

846 CAMPBELL, Randolph B. "Planters and Plain Folk: Harrison County, Texas, as a Test Case, 1850–1860." *J S Hist*, 40 (1974), 369–398.

847 CHESTNUT, Mary Boykin. *Diary from Dixie*. Ed. Ben Ames Williams. Boston, 1961.†

848 DAVIDSON, Chalmers G. *The Last Foray; The South Carolina Planters of 1860: A Sociological Study*. Columbia, S.C., 1971.

849 DAVIS, Edwin A. "Bennet A. Barrow, Ante-Bellum Planter of the Felicianas." *J S Hist*, 5 (1939), 431–446.

850 DORMON, James H. "Aspects of Acadiana Plantation Life in the Mid-Nineteenth Century: A Microcosmic View." *La Hist*, 16 (1975), 361–370.

851 EATON, Clement. *The Civilization of the Old South*. Ed. Albert D. Kirwan. Lexington, Ky., 1968.

852 EATON, Clement. *The Waning of the Old South Civilization*. New York, 1969.†

853 FISHWICK, Marshall. "F. F. V.'s." *Am Q*, 11 (1959), 147–156.

854 GAINES, Francis P. *The Southern Plantation: A Study in the Development and Accuracy of a Tradition*. Magnolia, Mass., 1962.

855 HOFSTADTER, Richard. "U. B. Phillips and the Plantation Legend." *J Neg Hist*, 29 (1944), 109–124.

856 HOLBROOK, Abigail C. "A Glimpse of Life on Antebellum Slave Plantations in Texas." *SW Hist Q*, 76 (1973), 361–383.

857 JOHNSON, Guion Griffis. *A Social History of the Sea Islands*. See **786**.

858 JONES, Katherine, ed. *The Plantation South*. Indianapolis, Ind., 1957.

859 JONES, Lewis P. "William Elliott, South Carolina Nonconformist." *J S Hist*, 17 (1951), 361–381.

860 MYERS, Robert M., ed. *The Children of Pride*. See **133**.

861 PEASE, Jane H. "A Note on Patterns of Conspicuous Consumption among Seaboard Planters, 1820–1860." *J S Hist*, 35 (1969), 381–393.

862 POSTELL, Paul E. "John Hampden Randolph, a Louisiana Planter." *La Hist Q*, 25 (1942), 149–223.

863 SINGAL, Daniel J. "U. B. Phillips: The Old South as the New." *J Am Hist*, 63 (1977), 871–891.

864 SITTERSON, J. Carlyle. "The McCollams: A Planter Family of the Old and New South." *J S Hist*, 6 (1940), 347–367.

865 TAYLOR, Rosser H. "The Gentry of Ante-Bellum South Carolina." *N C Hist Rev*, 17 (1940), 114–131.

866 TOLEDANO, Roulhac B. "Louisiana's Golden Age: Valcour Aime in St. James Parish." *La Hist*, 10 (1969), 211–224.

867 TROUTMAN, Richard L. "The Physical Setting of the Bluegrass Planter." *Reg Ky Hist Soc*, 66 (1968), 367–377.

868 WOOSTER, Ralph A. "Wealthy Texans, 1860." *SW Hist Q*, 71 (1967), 163–180.

4. Overseers

869 BASSETT, John Spencer, ed. *The Southern Plantation Overseer as Revealed in His Letters*. Westport, Conn., 1968.

870 SCARBOROUGH, William K. *The Overseer: Plantation Management in the Old South*. Baton Rouge, 1966.

871 SCARBOROUGH, William K. "The Southern Plantation Overseer: A Re-Evaluation." *Ag Hist*, 38 (1964), 13–20.

5. Yeomen Farmers

872 ABBOTT, Richard H. "The Agricultural Press Views the Yeoman, 1819–1860." *Ag Hist*, 42 (1968), 35–48.

873 BIEHLE, Reba S. "Edward Oxford, Pioneer Farmer of Middle Georgia." See **817**.

874 CLARK, Blanche H. *The Tennessee Yeoman, 1840–1860*. New York, 1971.

875 EATON, Clement. *The Mind of the Old South*. See **286**.

876 EATON, Clement. *The Waning of the Old South Civilization*. See **852**.

877 FIELDS, Emmett B. "The Agricultural Population of Virginia, 1850–1860." Doctoral dissertation, Vanderbilt University, 1953.

878 GENOVESE, Eugene D. "Yeomen Farmers in a Slaveholder's Democracy." *Ag Hist*, 49 (1975), 331–342.

879 LAMBERT, Robert S. "The Oconaluftee Valley, 1800–1860: A Study of the Sources for Mountain History."*N C Hist Rev*, 35 (1958), 415–426.

880 LONGSTREET, Augustus Baldwin. *Georgia Scenes*. Upper Saddle River, N. J., 1969.

881 OWSLEY, Frank L. *Plain Folk of the Old South*. New York, 1965.†

882 SCHLEBECKER, John T. "Farmers in the Lower Shenandoah Valley, 1850." *Va Mag Hist Biog*, 79 (1971), 426–476.

883 SHUGG, Roger W. *Origins of the Class Struggle in Louisiana: A Social History of White Farmers and Laborers during Slavery and After, 1840–1875*. Baton Rouge, 1968.†

884 SUAREZ, Raleigh A. "Louisiana's Struggling Majority: The Ante-Bellum Farmer." *McNeese Rev*, 14 (1963), 14–31.

885 SUAREZ, Raleigh A. "Rural Life in Louisiana, 1850–1860." Doctoral dissertation, Louisiana State University, 1954.

885a WEAVER, Herbert. *Mississippi Farmers, 1850–1860*. Magnolia, Mass., 1968.

6. *Poor Whites*

886 BUCK, Paul. "The Poor Whites of the Ante-Bellum South." *Am Hist Rev*, 31 (1925), 41–54.

887 CRAVEN, Avery O. "Poor Whites and Negroes in the Ante-Bellum South." *J Neg Hist*, 15 (1930), 14–25.

888 DEN HOLLANDER, A. N. J. "The Tradition of 'Poor Whites'." *Culture in the South*. Ed. W. T. Couch. Westport, Conn., 1970.

889 HUNDLEY, Daniel R. *Social Relations in Our Southern States*. See **255**.

890 LAPP, Rudolph M. "The Ante-Bellum Poor Whites of the South Atlantic States." Doctoral dissertation, University of California, Berkeley, 1956.

891 McILWAINE, Shields. *The Southern Poor-White from Lubberland to Tobacco Road*. New York, 1970.

892 WYATT-BROWN, Bertram. "Religion and Formation of Folk Culture: Poor Whites of the Old South." *The Americanization of the Gulf Coast, 1803–1850*. Ed. L. F. Ellsworth, Jr. Pensacola, Fla., 1972. (Gulf Coast History and Humanities Conference, no. 4, University of West Florida)

7. *Women*

893 BOATWRIGHT, Eleanor M. "The Political and Civil Status of Women in Georgia, 1783–1860." *Ga Hist Q*, 25 (1941), 301–324.

894 BONNER, James C., ed. "Plantation Experiences of a New York Woman." *N C Hist Rev*, 33 (1956), 384–412, 529–546.

895 CRAVEN, Avery O. *Rachel of Old Louisiana*. Baton Rouge, 1975.

896 GASS, W. Conrad. "A Felicitous Life: Lucy Martin Battle, 1805–1874." *N C Hist Rev*, 52 (1975), 367–393.

897 GEARHART, Virginia. "The Southern Woman, 1840–1860." Doctoral dissertation, University of Wisconsin, 1927.

898 GIFFEN, Jerena E. "Missouri Women in the 1820's ." *Mo Hist Rev*, 65 (1971), 478–504.

899 GRAY, Virginia G. "Activities of Southern Women: 1840–1860." *S Atl Q*, 27 (1928), 264–279.

900 SCOTT, Anne F. *The Southern Lady: From Pedestal to Politics, 1830–1930*. Chicago, 1970.

901 SCOTT, Anne F. "Women's Perspective on the Patriarchy in the 1850's." *J Am Hist*, 61 (1974), 52–64.

8. Foreigners, Yankees, and Other Minority Groups

902 ABBOTT, Richard H. "Yankee Farmers in Northern Virginia, 1840–1860." *Va Mag Hist Biog*, 76 (1968), 56–63.

903 BAKER, Virgil L. "Albert Pike: Citizen Speechmaker of Arkansas." *Ark Hist Q*, 10 (1951), 138–156.

904 BIESELE, Rudolph L. "The History of the German Settlements in Texas, 1831–1861." Doctoral dissertation, University of Texas, 1928.

905 CHALKER, Fussell. "Irish Catholics in the Building of the Ocmulgee and Flint Railroad." *Ga Hist Q*, 54 (1970), 507–516.

906 CHENAULT, William W., and Robert C. REINDERS. "The Northern-Born Community of New Orleans in the 1850's." *J Am Hist*, 51 (1964), 232–247.

907 CLARK, Robert T., Jr. "The German Liberals in New Orleans (1840–1860)." *La Hist Q*, 20 (1937), 137–151.

908 COULTER, E. Merton. "William Bacon Stevens: Physician, Historian, Teacher, Preacher." *Ga Rev*, 2 (1948), 221–235.

909 DAVIS, Edwin A., ed. "A Northern Sojourner's Remembrances of the Mississippi." *J Miss Hist*, 12 (1950), 127–152.

910 DINNERSTEIN, Leonard, and Mary Dale PALSSON, eds. *Jews in the South*. Baton Rouge, 1973.

911 EMERSON, O. B. "The Bonapartist Exiles in Alabama." *Ala Rev*, 11 (1958), 135–143.

912 FAULK, Odie B. "The Icarian Colony in Texas, 1848." *Texana*, 5 (1967), 132–140.

913 GREEN, Fletcher M. *The Role of the Yankee in the Old South*. Athens, Ga., 1972.

914 HICKIN, Patricia. "Yankees Come to Fairfax County, 1840–1850." *Va Cav*, 26 (1977), 100–109.

915 HILLDRUP, Robert L. "Cold War against the Yankees in the Ante-Bellum Literature of Southern Women." *N C Hist Rev*, 31 (1954), 370–384.

916 JORDAN, Terry G. *German Seed in Texas Soil: Immigrant Farmers in Nineteenth-Century Texas*. Austin, Texas, 1975.†

917 KANTOR, Harvey A. "The Barth Family, a Case Study of Pioneer Immigrant Merchants." *Mo Hist Rev*, 62 (1969), 410–430.

918 NIEHAUS, Earl F. *The Irish in New Orleans, 1800–1860*. New York, 1976.

919 PATTON, James W. "Glimpses of North Carolina in the Writings of Northern and Foreign Travelers, 1783–1860." *N C Hist Rev*, 45 (1968), 298–323.

920 PAYNE, Darwin. "Early Norwegians in Northeast Texas." *SW Hist Q*, 65 (1961), 196–203.

921 PROCTOR, Samuel. "Jewish Life in New Orleans, 1718–1860." *La Hist Q*, 40 (1957), 110–132.

922 REZNIKOFF, Charles, and Uriah Z. ENGLEMAN. *The Jews of Charleston: A History of an American Jewish Community*. Philadelphia, Pa., 1950.

923 SIEMERLING, A. "Die Lateinische Ansiedlung in Texas" [The Latin Settlement in Texas]. Tr. C. W. Geue. *Texana*, 5 (1967), 126–131.

924 UNSTAD, Lyder L. "Norwegian Immigration to Texas: A Historic Resume with Four 'American Letters'." *SW Hist Q*, 43 (1939), 176–195.

925 WEAVER, Herbert. "Foreigners in Ante-Bellum Mississippi." *J Miss Hist*, 16 (1954), 151–163.

926 WEAVER, Herbert. "Foreigners in Ante-Bellum Savannah." *Ga Hist Q*, 37 (1953), 1–17.

927 WEAVER, Herbert. "Foreigners in Ante-Bellum Towns of the Lower South." *J S Hist*, 13 (1947), 62–73.

928 WISH, Harvey. "The French of Old Missouri (1804–1821): A Study in Assimilation." *Mid-Am*, 23 (1941), 167–189.

929 WOOSTER, Ralph A. "Foreigners in the Principal Towns of Ante-Bellum Texas." *SW Hist Q*, 66 (1962), 208–220.

930 YOUNGER, Edward, ed. "Yankee Reports on Virginia, 1842–1843: Letters of John Adam Kasson." *Va Mag Hist Biog*, 56 (1948), 408–430.

IX. The Movement for Social Reform

1. General

931 BOATWRIGHT, Eleanor M. "The Political and Civil Status of Women in Georgia, 1783–1860." See **893**.

932 CLEVELAND, Gordon B. "Social Conditions in Alabama as Seen by Travelers, 1840–1850." *Ala Rev*, 2 (1949), 3–23, 122–138.

933 KNIGHT, J. Stephen, Jr. "Discontent, Disunity, and Dissent in the Antebellum South: Virginia as a Test Case, 1844–1846." *Va Mag Hist Biog*, 81 (1973), 437–456.

934 KOCH, Adrienne. "Two Charlestonians in Pursuit of Truth: The Grimké Brothers." *S C Hist Mag*, 69 (1968), 159–170.

934a MITCHELL, Memory F., and Thornton W. MITCHELL. "The Philanthropic Bequests of John Rex of Raleigh." *N C Hist Rev*, 49 (1972), 254–279, 353–376.

935 THOMAS, John L. "Romantic Reform in America, 1819–1865." *Am Q*, 17 (1965), 656–681.

936 TURNER, Wallace B. "A Rising Social Consciousness in Kentucky during the 1850's." *Filson Club Hist Q*, 36 (1962), 18–31.

937 WEATHERSBY, Robert W., II. "J. H. Ingraham and Tennessee: A Record of Social and Literary Contributions." *Tenn Hist Q*, 34 (1975), 264–272.

938 WINDELL, Marie G. "The Background of Reform on the Missouri Frontier." *Mo Hist Rev*, 39 (1945), 155–183.

939 WINDELL, Marie G. "Reform in the Roaring Forties and Fifties." *Mo Hist Rev*, 39 (1945), 291–319.

2. Poor Relief

940 BROWN, Roy M. *Public Poor Relief in North Carolina*. New York, 1976.

941 COLL, Blanche D. "The Baltimore Society for the Prevention of Pauperism, 1820–1822." *Am Hist Rev*, 61 (1955), 77–87.

942 COLL, Blanche D. "Perspectives in Public Welfare: Colonial Times to 1860." *Wel Rev*, 5 (Nov.–Dec., 1967), 1–9; 6 (July–Aug., 1968), 12–22.

943 GRIFFIN, J. David. "Medical Assistance for the Sick Poor in Ante-Bellum Savannah." *Ga Hist Q*, 53 (1969), 463–469.

944 KENDALL, John S. "New Orleans' Miser Philanthropist: John McDonogh." *La Hist Q*, 26 (1943), 138–161.

945 KLEBANER, Benjamin J. "Public Poor Relief in Charleston, 1800–1860." *S C Hist Mag*, 55 (1954), 210–220.

946 KLEBANER, Benjamin J. "Some Aspects of North Carolina Public Poor Relief, 1700–1860." *N C Hist Rev*, 31 (1954), 479–492.

947 McCAMIC, Charles. "Administration of Poor Relief in the Virginias." *W Va Hist*, 1 (1940), 171–191.

948 MACKEY, Howard. "Social Welfare in Colonial Virginia: The Importance of the English Old Poor Law." *Hist Mag Prot Epis Church*, 36 (1967), 357–382.

949 WATSON, Alan D. "Public Poor Relief in Colonial North Carolina." *N C Hist Rev*, 54 (1977), 347–366.

950 WISNER, Elizabeth. *Social Welfare in the South from Colonial Times to World War I*. Baton Rouge, 1970.

3. The Mentally Ill

951 COCHRANE, Hortense S. "Early Treatment of the Mentally Ill in Georgia." *Ga Hist Q*, 32 (1948), 105–118.

952 DAIN, Norman. *Concepts of Insanity in the United States, 1789–1865*. New Brunswick, N. J., 1964.

953 DAIN, Norman. *Disordered Minds: The First Century of Eastern State Hospital in Williamsburg, Virginia, 1766–1866*. Williamsburg, Va., 1971.

954 McCULLOCH, Margaret C. "Founding the North Carolina Asylum for the Insane." *N C Hist Rev*, 13 (1936), 185–201.

955 MARSHALL, Helen E. *Dorothea L. Dix: Forgotten Samaritan.* New York, 1967.

956 THOMPSON, E. Bruce. "Reforms in the Care of the Insane in Tennessee, 1830–1850." *Tenn Hist Q*, 3 (1944), 319–334.

4. Legal and Penal Reform

957 BONNER, James C. "The Georgia Penitentiary at Milledgeville, 1817–1874." *Ga Hist Q*, 55 (1971), 303–328.

958 CROWE, Jesse C. "The Origin and Development of Tennessee's Prison Problems, 1831–1871." *Tenn Hist Q*, 15 (1956), 111–135.

959 GETTLEMAN, Marvin E. "The Maryland Penitentiary in the Age of Tocqueville, 1828–1842." *Md Hist Mag*, 56 (1961), 269–290.

960 HATCHER, William B. *Edward Livingston, Jeffersonian Republican and Jacksonian Democrat.* Magnolia, Mass., 1970.

961 LYONS, Grant. "Louisiana and the Livingston Criminal Codes." *La Hist*, 15 (1974), 243–272.

962 McKELVEY, Blake. *American Prisons, a History of Good Intentions.* Montclair, N.J., 1977.

963 MACKEY, Philip English. "Edward Livingston and the Origins of the Movement to Abolish Capital Punishment in America." *La Hist*, 16 (1975), 145–166.

964 MITTLEBEELER, Emmet V. "The Decline of Imprisonment for Debt in Kentucky." *Filson Club Hist Q*, 49 (1975), 169–189.

965 MOORE, Waddy W. "Some Aspects of Crime and Punishment on the Arkansas Frontier." *Ark Hist Q*, 23 (1964), 50–64.

966 NESHEIM, William C. "The Early Years of the Missouri State Penitentiary: 1833 to 1853." *Bul Mo Hist Soc*, 28 (1972), 246–263.

967 SAUNDERS, Robert M. "Crime and Punishment in Early National America: Richmond, Virginia, 1784–1820." *Va Mag Hist Biog*, 86 (1978), 33–44.

968 THOMPSON, E. Bruce. "Reforms in the Penal System of Mississippi, 1820–1850." *J Miss Hist*, 7 (1945), 51–74.

969 THOMPSON, E. Bruce. "Reforms in the Penal System of Tennessee, 1820–1850." *Tenn Hist Q*, 1 (1942), 291–308.

970 WHITE, Charles P. "Early Experiments with Prison Labor in Tennessee." *E Tenn Hist Soc Pub*, 12 (1940), 45–69.

971 WILLIAMS, Jack K. "Crime and Punishment in Alabama, 1819–1840." *Ala Rev*, 6 (1953), 14–30.

972 WILLIAMS, Jack K. "The Criminal Lawyer in Ante-Bellum South Carolina." *S C Hist Mag*, 56 (1955), 138–150.

973 WILLIAMS, Jack K. *Vogues in Villainy: Crime and Retribution in Ante-Bellum South Carolina.* Columbia, S. C., 1959.

974 WILLIAMS, Jack K. "White Lawbreakers in Ante-Bellum South Carolina." *J S Hist*, 21 (1955), 360–373.

5. The Physically Handicapped

975 COULTER, E. Merton. *John Jacobus Flournoy, Champion of the Common Man in the Ante-Bellum South.* Savannah, Ga., 1942.

976 SCHWARTZ, Harold. *Samuel Gridley Howe: Social Reformer, 1801–1876.* Cambridge, Mass., 1956.

6. Temperance

977 BEATTIE, Donald W. "Sons of Temperance: Pioneers in Total Abstinence and 'Contitutional' Prohibition." Doctoral dissertation, Boston University, 1966.

978 KROUT, John A. *The Origins of Prohibition.* New York, 1925.

979 PEARSON, Charles C., and J. Edwin HENDRICKS. *Liquor and Anti-Liquor in Virginia, 1619–1919.* Durham, N. C., 1967.

980 PULLEY, Raymond H. "General Cooke and the Temperance Crusade." *Va Cav*, 15 (Summer, 1965), 22–27.

981 SELLERS, James B. *The Prohibition Movement in Alabama, 1702 to 1943.* Chapel Hill, 1943.†

982 TANKERSLEY, Allen P. "Basil Hallam Overby: Champion of Prohibition in Ante-Bellum Georgia." *Ga Hist Q*, 31 (1947), 1–18.

983 WHITENER, Daniel J. *Prohibition in North Carolina, 1715–1945.* Chapel Hill, 1945.

984 WHITENER, Daniel J. "The Temperance Movement in North Carolina." *S Atl Q*, 34 (1935), 305–313.

7. The Peace Movement

985 BROCK, Peter. *Pacifism in the United States: From the Colonial Era to the First World War.* Princeton, 1968. (Paperback edition is entitled *Radical Pacifists in Antebellum America.*)†

986 GALPIN, W. Freeman. *Pioneering for Peace: A Study of American Peace Efforts to 1846.* 2nd ed. Syracuse, N.Y., 1933.

8. The Search for Utopia

987 ANDERSON, Russell H. "The Shaker Communities in Southeast Georgia." *Ga Hist Q*, 50 (1967), 162–172.

988 COOMBS, Elizabeth. "Brief History of the Shaker Colony at South Union, Kentucky." *Filson Club Hist Q*, 14 (1940), 154–173.

989 DAVIS, J. Treadwell. "Nashoba: Frances Wright's Experiment in Self-Emancipation." See **673**.

990 EMERSON, O. B. "Frances Wright and the Nashoba Experiment." See **675**.

991 GRANT, H. Roger. "Missouri's Utopian Communities." *Mo Hist Rev*, 66 (1971), 20–48.

992 HAM, F. Gerald. "Shakerism in the Old West." Doctoral dissertation, University of Kentucky, 1962.

993 KEITH, John M., Jr. "Ante-Bellum Agriculture of the South Union Shakers." *Filson Club Hist Q*, 51 (1977), 158–166.

994 MATTHEWS, Paul Aaron. "Frances Wright and the Nashoba Experiment: A Transitional Period in Antislavery Attitudes." See **679**.

995 NEAL, Julia. *The Kentucky Shakers*. Lexington, Ky., 1977.

996 PAYNE-GAPOSCHKIN, Cecilia Helena. "The Nashoba Plan for Removing the Evil of Slavery: Letters of Frances and Camilla Wright, 1820–1829." See **681**.

997 PEASE, William H., and Jane H. PEASE. "A New View of Nashoba." See **682**.

998 THOMAS, Samuel W., and Mary Lawrence YOUNG. "The Development of Shakertown at Pleasant Hill, Kentucky." *Filson Club Hist Q*, 49 (1975), 231–255.

999 TILLY, Bette B. "The Spirit of Improvement: Reformism and Slavery in West Tennessee." See **685**.

X. Agriculture

1. General

1000 ABBOTT, Richard H. "Yankee Farmers in Northern Virginia, 1840–1860." See **902**.

1001 ARNOW, Harriette S. *Flowering of the Cumberland*. New York, 1963.

1002 ARNOW, Harriette S. "The Pioneer Farmer and His Crops in the Cumberland Region." *Tenn Hist Q*, 19 (1960), 291–327.

1003 BARROW, Bennet H. *Plantation Life in the Florida Parishes of Louisiana*. See **110**.

1004 BATTALIO, Raymond C., and John KAGEL. "The Structure of Antebellum Southern Agriculture: South Carolina, a Case Study." *Ag Hist*, 44 (1970), 25–37.

1005 BLACKFORD, John. *Ferry Hill Plantation Journal, January 4, 1838–January 15, 1839.* See **844**.

1006 BONNER, James C. *A History of Georgia Agriculture, 1732–1860.* Athens, Ga., 1964.

1007 BOWERS, Douglas, comp.-ed. "A List of References for the History of Agriculture in the United States, 1790–1840." Davis, Cal., 1969. (Processed publication, issued by the University of California at Davis.)

1008 BROWN, Ralph M. "Agricultural Science and Education in Virginia before 1860." *Wm Mar Q*, 2nd ser., 19 (1939), 197–213.

1009 CATHEY, Cornelius O. *Agricultural Developments in North Carolina, 1783–1860.* Chapel Hill, 1956.

1010 COLE, Arthur H. "Agricultural Crazes, a Neglected Chapter in American Economic History." *Am Ec Rev*, 16 (1926), 622–639.

1011 COYNER, Martin B., Jr. "John Hartwell Cocke of Bremo: Agriculture and Slavery in the Ante-Bellum South." Doctoral dissertation, University of Virginia, 1961.

1012 CRAVEN, Avery O. *Soil Exhaustion as a Factor in the Agricultural History of Virginia and Maryland, 1806–1860.* Magnolia, Mass., 1926.

1013 FIELDS, Emmett B. "The Agricultural Population of Virginia, 1850–1860." See **877**.

1014 FLANDERS, Ralph B. "Planters' Problems in Ante-Bellum Georgia." *Ga Hist Q*, 14 (1930), 17–40.

1015 FOSCUE, Edwin J. "Agricultural History of the Lower Rio Grande Valley Region." *Ag Hist*, 8 (1934), 124–137.

1016 FOUST, James D., and Dale E. SWAN. "Productivity and Profitability of Antebellum Labor: A Micro-Approach." *Ag Hist*, 44 (1970), 39–62.

1017 GATES, Paul W. *The Farmer's Age: Agriculture, 1815–1860.* New York, 1960.†

1018 GEHRKE, William H. "The Ante-Bellum Agriculture of the Germans in North Carolina." *Ag Hist*, 9 (1935), 143–160.

1019 GENOVESE, Eugene D. "The Significance of the Slave Plantation for Southern Economic Development." *J S Hist*, 28 (1962), 422–437.

1020 GRANT, Hugh F. *Plantation Management and Capitalism in Ante-Bellum Georgia: The Journal of Hugh Fraser Grant, Rice Grower.* Ed. A. V. House. New York, 1954.

1021 GRAY, Lewis C. *History of Agriculture in the Southern United States to 1860.* 2 vols. Magnolia, Mass., 1958.

1022 HAGLER, Dorse H. "The Agrarian Theme in Southern History to 1860." Doctoral dissertation, Missouri University, 1968.

1023 HIRSCH, Arthur H. "French Influence on American Agriculture in the Colonial Period with Special Reference to the Southern Provinces." *Ag Hist*, 4 (1930), 1–9.

1024 HUTCHINSON, William T. *Cyrus Hall McCormick.* 2 vols. New York, 1968.

1025 JORDAN, Weymouth T. *Hugh Davis and His Alabama Plantation.* Westport, Conn., 1974.

1026 JORDAN, Weymouth T. "The Management Rules of an Alabama Black Belt Plantation, 1848–1862." *Ag Hist*, 18 (1944), 53–64.

1027 JORDAN, Weymouth T., ed. "System of Farming at Beaver Bend, Alabama, 1862." *J S Hist*, 7 (1941), 76–84.

1028 LEMMER, George F. "Farm Machinery in Ante-Bellum Missouri." *Mo Hist Rev*, 40 (1946), 467–480.

1029 LOEHR, Rodney C. "The Influence of English Agriculture on American Agriculture, 1715–1825." *Ag Hist*, 11 (1937), 3–15.

1030 McLENDON, James H. "The Development of Mississippi Agriculture, a Survey." *J Miss Hist*, 13 (1951), 75–87.

1031 MENDENHALL, Marjorie S. "A History of Agriculture in South Carolina, 1790–1860." Doctoral dissertation, University of North Carolina, 1940.

1032 MENDENHALL, Marjorie S. "The Rise of Southern Tenancy." *Yale Rev*, 27 (1937), 110–129.

1033 MOORE, John Hebron. *Agriculture in Ante-Bellum Mississippi*. New York, 1958.

1034 MOORE, John Hebron. "Mississippi's Search for a Staple Crop." *J Miss Hist*, 29 (1967), 371–385.

1035 MURRAY, Paul. "Agriculture in the Interior of Georgia, 1830–1860." *Ga Hist Q*, 19 (1935), 291–312.

1036 PARKER, William N. "The Slave Plantation in American Agriculture." *First International Conference of Economic History*. Stockholm, 1960.

1037 ROTHSTEIN, Morton. "The Ante-Bellum Plantation as a Business Enterprise: A Review of Scarborough's *The Overseer*." *Exp Ent Hist*, 2nd ser., 6 (1968), 128–133.

1038 SCARBOROUGH, William K. *The Overseer: Plantation Management in the Old South*. See **870**.

1039 SCARBOROUGH, William K. "The Southern Plantation Overseer: A Re-Evaluation." See **871**.

1040 SCHLEBECKER, John T. "Farmers in the Lower Shenandoah Valley, 1850." See **882**.

1041 SITTERSON, J. Carlyle. "Lewis Thompson, a Carolinian, and His Louisiana Plantation 1848–1888: A Study in Absentee Ownership." *Essays in Southern History*. Ed. Fletcher M. Green. Westport, Conn., 1976.

1042 SITTERSON, J. Carlyle. "The William J. Minor Plantations: A Study in Ante-Bellum Absentee Ownership." *J S Hist*, 9 (1943), 59–74.

1043 STEEL, Edward M., Jr. "A Pioneer Farmer in the Choctaw Purchase." See **840**.

1044 STEPHENSON, Wendell H. *Alexander Porter, Whig Planter of Old Louisiana*. New York, 1969.

1045 STEPHENSON, Wendell H. "A Quarter Century of a Mississippi Plantation: Eli J. Capell of 'Pleasant Hill'." *Miss Val Hist Rev*, 23 (1936), 355–374.

1046 TAYLOR, Paul S. "Plantation Laborer before the Civil War." *Ag Hist*, 28 (1954), 1–21.

1047 TROUTMAN, Richard L. "Aspects of Agriculture in the Ante-Bellum Bluegrass." *Filson Club Hist Q*, 45 (1979), 163–173.

1048 TROUTMAN, Richard L. "Henry Clay and His 'Ashland' Estate." *Filson Club Hist Q*, 30 (1956), 159–174.

1049 TROUTMAN, Richard L. "The Social and Economic Structure of Kentucky Agriculture, 1850–1860." Doctoral dissertation, University of Kentucky, 1958.

1050 WALL, Bennett H. "Ebenezer Pettigrew's Efforts to Control the Marketing of His Crops." *Ag Hist*, 27 (1953), 123–132.

1051 WALL, Bennett H. "The Founding of the Pettigrew Plantations."*N C Hist Rev*, 27 (1950), 395–418.

2. Reform and Reformers

1052 ALLMOND, C. M., ed. "The Agricultural Memorandums of Samuel H. Black: 1815–1820." *Ag Hist*, 32 (1958), 56–61.

1053 BIERCK, Harold A., Jr. "Spoils, Soils, and Skinner." *Md Hist Mag*, 49 (1954), 21–40, 143–155.

1054 BONNER, James C. "Advancing Trends in Southern Agriculture, 1840–1860." *Ag Hist*, 22 (1948), 248–259.

1055 BONNER, James C. "Agricultural Adjustment in Ante-Bellum Georgia." *Studies in Georgia History and Government*. Ed. James C. Bonner and Lucien E. Roberts. Spartanburg, S.C., 1974.

1056 BONNER, James C. "Genesis of Agricultural Reform in the Cotton Belt." *J S Hist*, 9 (1943), 475–500.

1057 BRUCE, Kathleen. "Virginia Agricultural Decline to 1860: A Fallacy." *Ag Hist*, 6 (1932), 3–13.

1058 CATHEY, Cornelius O. "Agricultural Implements in North Carolina, 1783–1860." *Ag Hist*, 25 (1951), 128–135.

1059 CATHEY, Cornelius O. "Sidney Weller: Ante-Bellum Promoter of Agricultural Reform." *N C Hist Rev*, 31 (1954), 1–17.

1060 CLEMENS, Paul G. E. "From Tobacco to Grain: Economic Development on Maryland's Eastern Shore, 1660–1750." *J Ec Hist*, 35 (1975), 256–259.

1061 COULTER, E. Merton. *Daniel Lee, Agriculturist: His Life, North and South.* Athens, Ga., 1972.

1062 COULTER, E. Merton. *Thomas Spalding of Sapelo.* Baton Rouge, 1940.

1063 CRAVEN, Avery O. "Agricultural Reforms of the Ante-Bellum South." *Am Hist Rev*, 33 (1928), 302–314.

1064 CRAVEN, Avery O. "John Taylor and Southern Agriculture." *J S Hist*, 4 (1938), 137–147.

1065 DESTLER, Chester M. "David Dickson's 'System of Farming' and the Agricultural Revolution in the Deep South, 1850–1860." *Ag Hist*, 31 (July, 1957), 30–39.

1066 ESSLER, Elizabeth M. "The Agricultural Reform Movement in Alabama, 1850–1860." *Ala Rev*, 1 (1948), 243–260.

1067 GOOD, H. G. "Early Attempts to Teach Agriculture in Old Virginia." *Va Mag Hist Biog*, 48 (1940), 341–351.

1068 HALL, Arthur R. *Early Erosion-Control Practices in Virginia.* Washington, D. C., 1937. (USDA, *Misc Pub*, no. 256)

1069 HALL, Arthur R. "Soil Erosion and Agriculture in the Southern Piedmont: A History." Doctoral dissertation, Duke University, 1948.

1070　HALL, Arthur R. *The Story of Soil Conservation in the South Carolina Piedmont, 1800–1860.* Washington, D. C., 1940. (USDA, *Misc Pub,* no. 407).

1071　HALL, Arthur R. "Terracing in the Southern Piedmont." *Ag Hist,* 23 (1949), 96–109.

1072　HAMILTON, William B. "The Planters Society in Claiborne County: The First Incorporated Cooperative and the First Farmers' Purchasing Cooperative." *J Miss Hist,* 11 (1949), 67–70.

1073　HOLMES, Francis S. *The Southern Farmer and Market Gardener: Being a Compilation of Useful Articles on these Subjects from the Most Approved Writers.* . . . New and enl. ed. Charleston, S. C., 1852.

1074　JORDAN, Weymouth T. "Noah B. Cloud's Activities on Behalf of Southern Agriculture." *Ag Hist,* 25 (1951), 53–58.

1075　JORDAN, Weymouth T. "The Peruvian Guano Gospel in the Old South.' *Ag Hist,* 24 (1950), 211–221.

1076　LEMMER, George F. "Agitation for Agricultural Improvement in Central Missouri Newspapers Prior to the Civil War." *Mo Hist Rev,* 37 (1943), 371–385.

1077　RANGE, Willard. "The Prince of Southern Farmers." *Ga Rev,* 2 (1948), 92–97.

1078　RUBIN, Julius. "The Limits of Agricultural Progress in the Nineteenth–Century South." *Ag Hist,* 49 (1975), 362–373.

1079　RUFFIN, Edmund. *An Essay on Calcareous Manures.* Ed. J. Carlyle Sitterson. Cambridge, Mass., 1961.

1080　TAYLOR, John. *The Arator.* Ed. M. E. Bradford. Indianapolis, Ind., 1978.†

1081　TAYLOR, Rosser H. "Commercial Fertilizers in South Carolina." *S Atl Q,* 29 (1930), 179–189.

1082　TAYLOR, Rosser H. "Fertilizers and Farming in the Southeast, 1840–1950: Part I, 1840–1900." *N C Hist Rev,* 30 (1953), 305–328.

1083　TAYLOR, Rosser H. "The Sale and Application of Commercial Fertilizers in the South Atlantic States to 1900."*Ag Hist,* 21 (1947), 46–52.

1084　TRUE, Rodney H. "The Virginia Board of Agriculture, 1841–1843." *Ag Hist,* 14 (1940), 97–103.

1085　TURNER, Charles W. "Virginia Agricultural Reform, 1815–1860." *Ag Hist,* 26 (1952), 80–89.

1086　WARD, James E. " 'Monticello': An Experimental Farm." *Ag Hist,* 19 (1945), 183–185.

1087　WILLIAMS, Robert W., Jr. "The Mississippi Career of Thomas Affleck." Doctoral dissertation, Tulane University, 1954.

1088　WILLIAMS, Robert W. "Thomas Affleck: Missionary to the Planter, the Farmer, and the Gardener." *Ag Hist,* 31 (July, 1957), 40–48.

1089　WISER, Vivian. "Improving Maryland's Agriculture, 1840–1860." *Md Hist Mag,* 64 (1969), 105–132.

1090　WISER, Vivian. "The Movement for Agricultural Improvement in Maryland, 1785–1865." Doctoral dissertation, University of Maryland, 1963.

1091　WOODALL, Clyde E., and William H. FAVER. "Famous South Carolina Farmers." *Ag Hist,* 33 (1959), 138–141.

3. Agricultural Journals, Societies, Fairs, and Conventions

1092 BARDOLPH, Richard. "A North Carolina Farm Journal of the Middle 'Fifties'." *N C Hist Rev*, 25 (1948), 57–89.

1093 DEMAREE, Albert L. *The American Agricultural Press, 1819–1860.* Philadelphia, Pa., 1974.

1094 GOVAN, Thomas P. "An Ante-Bellum Attempt to Regulate the Price and Supply of Cotton." *N C Hist Rev*, 17 (1940), 302–312.

1095 JORDAN, Weymouth T. "Agricultural Societies in Ante-Bellum Alabama." *Ala Rev*, 4 (1951), 241–253.

1096 JORDAN, Weymouth T. "Cotton Planters' Conventions in the Old South." *J S Hist*, 19 (1953), 321–345.

1097 JORDAN, Weymouth T. "The Florida Plan', an Ante-Bellum Effort to Control Cotton Sales." *Fla Hist Q*, 35 (1957), 205–218.

1098 JORDAN, Weymouth T. "Noah B. Cloud and the *American Cotton Planter*." *Ag Hist*, 31 (October, 1957), 44–49.

1099 JORDAN, Weymouth T. *Rebels in the Making: Planters' Conventions and Southern Propaganda.* Tuscaloosa, Ala., 1958.†

1100 LEMMER, George F. "Early Agricultural Editors and Their Farm Philosophies." *Ag Hist*, 31 (October, 1957), 3–22.

1101 LEMMER, George F. "The Early Agricultural Fairs of Missouri." *Ag Hist*, 17 (1943), 145–152.

1102 NEELY, Wayne C. *The Agricultural Fair.* New York, 1967.

1103 NORSE, Clifford C. *"The Southern Cultivator*, 1843–1861." Doctoral dissertation, Florida State University, 1969.

1104 PINKETT, Harold T. "The American Farmer, a Pioneer Agricultural Journal, 1819–1834." *Ag Hist*, 24 (1950), 146–151.

1105 TRUE, Rodney H. "Early Days of the Albemarle Agricultural Society." *Ann Rept Am Hist Assn*, (1918), I, 241–259.

1106 TRUE, Rodney H. "The Early Development of Agricultural Societies in the United States." *Ann Rept Am Hist Assn*, (1920), 293–306.

1107 TURNER, Charles W. "Virginia State Agricultural Societies, 1811–1860." *Ag Hist*, 38 (1964), 167–177.

1108 WALLACE, Wesley H. "North Carolina's Agricultural Journals, 1838–1861: A Crusading Press." *N C Hist Rev*, 36 (1959), 275–306.

1109 WARD, Hortense W. "The First State Fair of Texas." *SW Hist Q*, 57 (1953), 163–174.

1110 WOODALL, Clyde E., and George E. AULL. "The Pendleton Farmer's Society." *Ag Hist*, 31 (April, 1957), 36–37.

4. *Staple Crops*

A. Indigo

1111 COON, David L. "Eliza Lucas Pinckney and the Reintroduction of Indigo Culture in South Carolina." *J S Hist*, 42 (1976), 61–76.

B. Tobacco

1112 CLEMENS, Paul G. E. "The Operation of an Eighteenth-Century Chesapeake Tobacco Plantation." *Ag Hist*, 49 (1975), 517–531.

1113 ROBERT, Joseph C. *The Tobacco Kingdom: Plantation, Market, and Factory in Virginia and North Carolina, 1800–1860.* Magnolia, Mass., 1965.

C. Cotton

1114 COOPER, William J., Jr. "The Cotton Crisis in the Antebellum South: Another Look." *Ag Hist*, 49 (1975), 381–391.

1115 DAVIS, Charles S. *The Cotton Kingdom in Alabama.* Philadelphia, Pa., 1974.

1116 FITE, Gilbert C. "Development of the Cotton Industry by the Five Civilized Tribes in Indian Territory." *J S Hist*, 15 (1949), 342–353.

1117 GALLMAN, Robert E. "Self-Sufficiency in the Cotton Economy of the Antebellum South." *Ag Hist*, 44 (1970), 5–23.

1118 GENOVESE, Eugene D. "Cotton, Slavery and Soil Exhaustion in the Old South." *Cot Hist Rev*, 2 (1961), 3–17.

1119 HAMILTON, William B. "Early Cotton Regulations in the Lower Mississippi Valley." *Ag Hist*, 15 (1941), 20–25.

1120 HOLBROOK, Abigail C. "Cotton Marketing in Antebellum Texas." *SW Hist Q*, 73 (1970), 431–455.

1121 MOORE, John Hebron. "Cotton Breeding in the Old South." *Ag Hist*, 30 (1956), 95–104.

1122 PATTERSON, Ernest F. "Cotton, the First Problem of United States Agriculture." *Cot Hist Rev*, 1 (1960), 151–174.

1123 ROTHSTEIN, Morton. "The Cotton Frontier of the Antebellum United States: A Methodological Battleground." *Ag Hist*, 44 (1970), 149–165.

1124 SHOFNER, Jerrell H., and William W. ROGERS. "Sea Island Cotton in Ante-Bellum Florida." *Fla Hist Q*, 40 (1962), 373–380.

1125 SMITH, Julia F. "Cotton and the Factorage System in Antebellum Florida." *Fla Hist Q*, 49 (1970), 36–48.

1126 *The Structure of the Cotton Economy in the Antebellum South*. Ed. William N. Parker. See **434**.

1127 THOMAS, Daniel H. "Pre-Whitney Cotton Gins in French Louisiana." *J S Hist*, 31 (1965), 135–148.

1128 WILLIAMSON, Edward C. "Cotton as a Cause of the Florida Seminole War." *Textile Hist Rev*, 4 (1963), 79–84.

1129 WOODMAN, Harold D. "Itinerant Cotton Merchants of the Antebellum South." *Ag Hist*, 40 (1966), 79–90.

D. Rice

1130 CLIFTON, James M., ed. "The Ante-Bellum Rice Planter as Revealed in the Letterbook of Charles Manigault, 1846–1848." *S C Hist Mag*, 74 (1973), 119–127, 300–310.

1131 CLIFTON, James M. "Golden Grains of White: Rice Planting on the Lower Cape Fear." *N C Hist Rev*, 50 (1973), 365–393.

1132 CLIFTON, James M. "A Half-Century of a Georgia Rice Plantation." *N C Hist Rev*, 47 (1970), 388–415.

1133 CLIFTON, James M., ed. *Life and Labor on Argyle Island: Letters and Documents of a Savannah River Rice Plantation, 1833–1867*. Savannah, Ga., 1978.

1134 DUNCAN, Bingham. "Diplomatic Support of the American Rice Trade, 1835–1845." *Ag Hist*, 23 (1949), 92–96.

1135 EASTERBY, J. Harold. "The South Carolina Rice Factor as Revealed in the Papers of Robert F. W. Allston." *J S Hist*, 7 (1941), 160–172.

1136 EASTERBY, J. Harold. *The South Carolina Rice Plantation as Revealed in the Papers of Robert F. W. Allston.*. Fairfield, N.J., [n. d.].

1137 GRANT, Hugh F. *Plantation Management and Capitalism in Ante-Bellum Georgia: The Journal of Hugh Fraser Grant, Rice Grower*. See **1020**.

1138 HOUSE, Albert V., Jr., ed. "Charles Manigault's Essay on the Open Planting of Rice." *Ag Hist*, 16 (1942), 184–193.

1139 HOUSE, Albert V., Jr. "Labor Management Problems on Georgia Rice Plantations, 1840–1860." *Ag Hist*, 28 (1954), 149–155.

1140 HOUSE, Albert V., Jr. "The Management of a Rice Plantation in Georgia, 1834–1861, as Revealed in the Journal of Hugh Fraser Grant." *Ag Hist*, 13 (1939), 208–217.

E. Sugar

1141 PRICHARD, Walter. "Routine on a Louisiana Sugar Plantation under the Slave Regime." *Miss Val Hist Rev*, 14 (1927), 168–178.

1142 SIEBERT, Wilbur. "The Early Sugar Industry in Florida." *Fla Hist Q*, 35 (1957), 312–319.

1143 SITTERSON, J. Carlyle. "Ante-Bellum Sugar Culture in the South Atlantic States." *J S Hist*, 3 (1937), 175–187.

1144 SITTERSON, J. Carlyle. "Financing and Marketing the Sugar Crop of the Old South." *J S Hist*, 10 (1944), 188–199.

1145 SITTERSON, J. Carlyle. "Hired Labor on Sugar Plantations of the Ante-Bellum South." *J S Hist*, 14 (1948), 192–205.

1146 SITTERSON, J. Carlyle. "Magnolia Plantation, 1852–1862: A Decade of a Louisiana Sugar Estate." *Miss Val Hist Rev*, 25 (1938), 197–210.

1147 SITTERSON, J. Carlyle. *Sugar Country: The Cane Sugar Industry in the South, 1753–1950.* Westport, Conn., 1973.

F. Hemp

1148 ADERMAN, Ralph M. "David Myerle and Kentucky Hemp." *Filson Club Hist Q*, 35 (1961), 11–27.

1149 CLARK, Thomas D. "The Ante-Bellum Hemp Trade of Kentucky with the Cotton Belt." *Reg Ky Hist Soc*, 27 (1929), 538–544.

1150 EATON, Miles W. "The Development and Later Decline of the Hemp Industry in Missouri." *Mo Hist Rev*, 43 (1949), 344–359.

1151 HOPKINS, James F. *History of the Hemp Industry in Kentucky.* Lexington, Ky., 1951.

5. Minor Crops, Fruits, and Vegetables

1152 BONNER, James C. "The Georgia Wine Industry on the Eve of the Civil War." *Ga Hist Q*, 41 (1957), 19–30.

1153 BONNER, James C. "The Peach Industry in Ante-Bellum Georgia." *Ga Hist Q*, 31 (1947), 241–248.

1154 BONNER, James C. "Silk Growing in the Georgia Colony." *Ag Hist*, 43 (1969), 143–147.

1155 DAVIS, T. Frederick. "Early Orange Culture in Florida and the Epochal Cold of 1835." *Fla Hist Soc Q*, 15 (1937), 232–241.

1156 KEMMERER, Donald L. "The Pre-Civil War South's Leading Crop, Corn." *Ag Hist*, 23 (1949), 236–239.

1157 STEPHENS, Pauline T. "Pecans in Georgia." *Ga Rev*, (1948), 352–361.

1158 TABOR, Paul. "The Early History of Annual Lespedeza in the United States." *Ag Hist*, 35 (1961), 85–89.

1159 TABOR, Paul. "Home Grown Coffee in the South in 1835." *Ga Hist Q*, 54 (1970), 87–90.

1160 TRAFTON, Spalding. "Silk Culture in Herndon County, Kentucky." *Filsor Club Hist Q*, 4 (1930), 184–189.

6. Livestock

1161 ARNADE, Charles W. "Cattle Raising in Spanish Florida, 1513–1763." *Ag Hist*, 35 (1961), 116–124.

1162 ATKINSON, J. H. "Cattle Drives from Arkansas to California Prior to the Civil War." *Ark Hist Q*, 28 (1969), 275–281.

1163 BONNER, James C. "The Angora Goat: A Footnote in Southern Agricultural History." *Ag Hist*, 21 (1947), 42–46.

1164 BONNER, James C. "Open Range Livestock Industry in Colonial Georgia." *Ga Rev*, 17 (1963), 85–92.

1165 BURNETT, Edmund C. "Hog Raising and Hog Driving in the Region of the French Broad River." *Ag Hist*, 20 (1946), 86–103.

1166 CARPENTER, Clifford D. "The Early Cattle Industry in Missouri." *Mo Hist Rev*, 47 (1953), 201–215.

1167 CLARK, Thomas D. "Livestock Trade between Kentucky and the South, 1840–1860." *Reg Ky Hist Soc*, 27 (1929), 569–581.

1168 CONNOR, L. G. "A Brief History of the Sheep Industry in the United States." *Ann Rept Am Hist Assn*, (1918), I, 89–197.

1169 CULMER, Frederjc A., ed. "Selling Missouri Mules Down South in 1835." *Mo Hist Rev*, 24 (1930), 537–549.

1170 DORAN, Michael F. "Antebellum Cattle Herding in the Indian Territory." *Geog Rev*, 66 (1976), 48–58.

1171 DUNBAR, Gary S. "Colonial Carolina Cowpens." *Ag Hist*, 35 (1961), 125–130.

1172 DUNBAR, Gary S. "Deer-Keeping in Early South Carolina." *Ag Hist*, 36 (1962), 108–109.

1173 ESTES, Worth. "Henry Clary as a Livestock Breeder." *Filson Club Hist Q*, 32 (1958), 350–355.

1174 FUGATE, Francis L. "Origins of the Range Cattle Era in South Texas." *Ag Hist*, 35 (1961), 155–158.

1175 GALENSON, David. "Origins of the Long [Cattle] Drive [from Texas]." *J West*, 14 (July, 1975), 3–14.

1176 GENOVESE, Eugene D. "Livestock in the Slave Economy of the Old South—A Revised View." *Ag Hist*, 36 (1962), 143–149.

1177 GOFF, John H. "Cow Punching in Old Georgia." *Ga Rev*, 3 (1949), 341–348.

1178 HENLEIN, Paul C. *The Cattle Kingdom in the Ohio Valley, 1783–1860.* Lexington, Ky., 1959.

1179 HILLIARD, Sam B. *Hogmeat and Hoecake: Food Supply in the Old South, 1840–1860.* Carbondale, Ill., 1972.

1180 HILLIARD, Sam B. "Pork in the Ante-Bellum South: The Geography of Self-Sufficiency." *Ann Assn Am Geog*, 59 (1969), 461–480.

1181 HOPKINS, James F., ed. "Henry Clay, Farmer and Stockman." *J S Hist*, 15 (1949), 89–96.

1182 JORDAN, Terry G. "The Origin of Anglo-American Cattle Ranching in Texas: A Documentation of Diffusion from the Lower South." *Econ Geog*, 45 (1969), 63–87.

1183 LAMB, Robert B. *The Mule in Southern Agriculture*. Berkeley and Los Angeles, Cal., 1963. (University of California, Publications in Geography, vol. 15)

1184 LEAVITT, Charles T. "Attempts to Improve Cattle Breeds in the United States, 1790–1860." *Ag Hist*, 7 (1933), 51–67.

1185 LEMMER, George F. "Early Leaders in Livestock Improvement in Missouri." *Mo Hist Rev*, 37 (1942), 29–39.

1186 LEMMER, George F. "The Spread of Improved Cattle through the Eastern United States to 1850." *Ag Hist*, 21 (1947), 79–93.

1187 McDONALD, Forrest, and Grady McWHINEY. "The Antebellum Southern Herdsman: A Reinterpretation." See **789**.

1188 PURSELL, Carroll W., Jr. "E. I. DuPont and the Merino Mania in Delaware, 1805–1815." *Ag Hist*, 36 (1962), 91–100.

1189 THOMPSON, James Westfall. *A History of Livestock Raising in the United States, 1607–1860*. Washington, D. C., 1942. (USDA, Agricultural History Series, no. 5)

1190 TROUTMAN, Richard L. "Stock Raising in the Antebellum Bluegrass." *Reg Ky Hist Soc*, 55 (1957), 15–28.

XI. Commerce and Business

1. Transportation and Communication

A. Internal Improvements

1191 ANDREASSEN, John C. L. "Internal Improvements in Louisiana, 1824–1837." *La Hist Q*, 30 (1947), 5–119.

1192 BOYD, William K. "The North Carolina Fund for Internal Improvements." *S Atl Q*, 15 (1916), 52–67.

1193 BREWSTER, Lawrence F. "Ante-Bellum Planters and Their Means of Transportation." *Proc S C Hist Assn*, 18 (1948), 15–25.

1194 FOLMSBEE, Stanley J. *Sectionalism and Internal Improvements in Tennessee, 1796–1845*. Knoxville, Tenn., 1939.

1195 GREEN, Fletcher M. "Georgia's Board of Public Works, 1817–1826." *Ga Hist Q*, 22 (1938), 117–137.

1196   KANAREK, Harold. "The U. S. Army Corps of Engineers and Early Internal Improvements in Maryland." *Md Hist Mag*, 72 (1977), 99–109.

1197   KOHN, David, and Bess GLENN, eds. *Internal Improvements in South Carolina, 1817–1828*. Washington, D. C., 1938.

1198   LAMMONS, Frank B. "Operation Camel: An Experiment in Animal Transportation in Texas, 1857–1860." *SW Hist Q*, 61 (1957), 20–50.

1199   MEYER, Balthasar H., ed. *History of Transportation in the United States before 1860*. New York, 1948.

1200   MOFFATT, Walter. "Transportation in Arkansas, 1819–1840." *Ark Hist Q*, 15 (1956), 187–201.

1201   PHILLIPS, Ulrich B. *History of Transportation in the Eastern Cotton Belt to 1860*. New York, 1968.

1202   RICE, Philip M. "International Improvements in Virginia, 1775–1860." Doctoral dissertation, University of North Carolina, 1949.

1203   SCRIBNER, Robert L. "Virginia Transit, Ante-Bellum Style." *Va Cav*, 4 (Summer, 1954), 34–38.

1204   TAYLOR, George R. *The Transportation Revolution, 1815–1860*. New York, 1951.†

1205   WOODWARD, Earl F. "Texas's Internal Improvement Crisis of 1856: Four Remedial Plans Considered." *E Tex Hist J*, 13 (Spring, 1975), 13–22.

B. Rivers and Canals

1206   BAUGHMAN, James P. *Charles Morgan and the Development of Southern Transportation*. Nashville, Tenn., 1968.

1207   BAUGHMAN, James P. "The Evolution of Rail-Water Systems of Transportation in the Gulf Southwest, 1836–1860." *J S Hist*, 34 (1968), 357–381.

1208   BENNETT, Charles E. "Early History of the Cross-Florida Barge Canal." *Fla Hist Q*, 45 (1966), 132–144.

1209   BROWN, Alexander C. "The Canal Boat, *Governor McDowell*, Virginia's Pioneer Iron Steamer." *Va Mag Hist Biog*, 74 (1966), 336–345.

1210   BROWN, Alexander C. "The *John Randolph*: America's First Commercially Successful Iron Steamboat." *Ga Hist Q*, 36 (1952), 32–45.

1211   BROWN, Mattie. "River Transportation in Arkansas, 1819–1890." *Ark Hist Q*, 1 (1942), 342–354.

1212   COLEMAN, J. Winston, Jr. "Kentucky River Steamboats." *Reg Ky Hist Soc*, 63 (1965), 299–322.

1213   CRANE, Verner W. "The Tennessee River as the Road to Carolina: The Beginnings of Exploration and Trade." *Miss Val Hist Rev*, 3 (1916), 3–18.

1214   DUNAWAY, Wayland F. *History of the James River and Kanawha Company*. New York, 1969.

1215   GAMBLE, J. Mack. "Steamboats in West Virginia." *W Va Hist*, 15 (1954), 124–138.

1216   GOFF, John H. "The Steamboat Period in Georgia." *Ga Hist Q*, 12 (1928), 236–254.

1217 HANDLEY, Harry E. "The James River and the Kanawha Canal." *W Va Hist,* 25 (1964), 92–101.

1218 HARRISON, Robert W. "Levee Building in Mississippi before the Civil War." *J Miss Hist,* 12 (1950), 63–97.

1219 HINSHAW, Clifford R., Jr. "North Carolina Canals before 1860." *N C Hist Rev,* 25 (1948), 1–56.

1220 HOLLIS, Daniel W. "Costly Delusion: Inland Navigation in the South Carolina Piedmont." *Proc S C Hist Assn,* 38 (1968), 29–43.

1221 HUNTER, Louis C. *Steamboats on the Western Rivers.* New York, 1969.

1222 IRONS, George V. "River Ferries in Alabama before 1861." *Ala Rev,* 4 (1951), 22–37.

1223 MUELLER, Edward A. "East Coast Florida Steamboating, 1831–1861." *Fla Hist Q,* 40 (1962), 241–260.

1224 OWENS, Harry P. "Sail and Steam Vessels Serving the Apalachicola-Chattahoochee Valley." *Ala Rev,* 21 (1968), 195–210.

1225 RICE, Philip M. "The Early Development of the Roanoke Waterway—A Study in Interstate Relations." *N C Hist Rev,* 31 (1954), 50–74.

1226 SANDERLIN, Walter S. "The Maryland Canal Project—An Episode in the History of Maryland's Internal Improvements." *Md Hist Mag,* 41 (1946), 51–65.

1227 SHERWOOD, Diana. "Clearing the Channel: The Snagboat in Arkansas." *Ark Hist Q,* 3 (1944), 53–62.

1228 TENNESSEE VALLEY AUTHORITY. *History of Navigation on the Tennessee River System.* Washington, D.C., 1937. (House Doc. 254, 75th Cong., 1st Ses.)

1229 TRESCOTT, Paul B. "The Louisville and Portland Canal Company, 1825–1874." *Miss Val Hist Rev,* 44 (1958), 686–708.

C. Turnpikes, Roads, and Plank Roads

1230 ALLEN, Turner W. "The Turnpike System in Kentucky: A Review of State Road Policy in the Nineteenth Century." *Filson Club Hist Q,* 28 (1954), 239–259.

1231 BOYD, S. G. "The Louisville and Nashville Turnpike." *Reg Ky Hist Soc,* 24 (1926), 163–174.

1232 COTTERILL, Robert S. "The Natchez Trace." *La Hist Q,* 6 (1923), 259–268.

1233 FOLMSBEE, Stanley J. "The Turnpike Phase of Tennessee's Internal Improvement System of 1836–1838." *J S Hist,* 3 (1937), 453–477.

1234 GENTRY, North T. "Plank Roads in Missouri." *Mo Hist Rev,* 31 (1937), 272–287.

1235 HUNTER, Robert F. "Turnpike Construction in Antebellum Virginia." *Tech Cult,* 4 (1963), 177–200.

1236 HUNTER, Robert F. "The Turnpike Movement in Virginia, 1816–1860." *Va Mag Hist Biog,* 69 (1961), 278–289. See also, Doctoral dissertation, Columbia University, 1957, bearing the same title.

1237 KINCAID, Robert L. "The Wilderness Road in Tennessee." *E Tenn Hist Soc Pub*, 20 (1948), 37–48.

1238 STARLING, Robert B. "The Plank Road Movement in North Carolina." *N C Hist Rev*, 16 (1939), 1–22, 147–173.

1239 WOOD, Walter K. "Henry Edmundson, the Alleghany Turnpike, and 'Fotheringay' Plantation, 1805–1847." *Va Mag Hist Biog*, 83 (1975), 304–320.

D. Railroads

1240 ALVAREZ, Eugene. *Travel on Southern Antebellum Railroads, 1828–1860.* University, Ala., 1974.

1241 BAUGHMAN, James P. *Charles Morgan and the Development of Southern Transportation.* See **1206**.

1242 BROOKS, Addie Lou. "The Building of the Trunk Line Railroads in West Tennessee, 1852–1861." *Tenn Hist Q*, 1 (1942), 99–124.

1243 BROWN, Cecil K. *A State Movement in Railroad Development: The Story of North Carolina's First Effort to Establish an East and West Trunk Line Railroad.* Chapel Hill, 1928.

1244 CLARK, Thomas D. "The Building of the Memphis and Charleston Railroad." *E Tenn Hist Soc Pub*, 8 (1936), 9–25.

1245 CLARK, Thomas D. "The Lexington and Ohio Railroad—a Pioneer Venture." *Reg Ky Hist Soc*, 31 (1933), 9–28.

1246 CLARK, Thomas D. *A Pioneer Southern Railroad from New Orleans to Cairo.* Chapel Hill, 1936.

1247 COTTERILL, Robert S. "The Beginnings of Railroads in the Southwest." *Miss Val Hist Rev*, 8 (1922), 318–326.

1248 COTTERILL, Robert S. "Southern Railroads, 1850–1860." *Miss Val Hist Rev*, 10 (1924), 396–405.

1249 COTTERILL, Robert S. "Southern Railroads and Western Trade, 1840–1850." *Miss Val Hist Rev*, 3 (1917), 427–441.

1250 DAVIS, T. Frederick. "Pioneer Florida: The First Railroads." *Fla Hist Q*, 23 (1945), 177–183.

1251 DIXON, Max. "Building the Central Railroad of Georgia." *Ga Hist Q*, 45 (1961), 1–21.

1252 FENLON, Paul E. "The Florida, Atlantic and Gulf Central Railroad: The First Railroad in Jacksonville." *Fla Hist Q*, 32 (1953), 71–80.

1253 FOLMSBEE, Stanley J. "The Beginnings of the Railroad Movement in East Tennessee." *E Tenn Hist Soc Pub*, 5 (1933), 81–104.

1254 FOLMSBEE, Stanley J. "The Origins of the Nashville and Chattanooga Railroad." *E Tenn Hist Soc Pub*, 6 (1934), 81–95.

1255 HEATH, Milton S. "Public Cooperation in Railroad Construction in the Southern United States to 1861." Doctoral dissertation, Harvard University, 1937.

1256 HEATH, Milton S. "Public Railroad Construction and the Development of Private Enterprise in the South before 1861."*J Ec Hist*, supplement 10 (1950),

40–53. This supplementary issue, published separately, is entitled *The Task of Economic History*, and its contents are the papers read at the 10th Ann Meeting of the Ec Hist Assn.

1257 HOLLAND, James W. "The Building of the East Tennessee and Virginia Railroad." *E Tenn Hist Soc Pub*, 4 (1932), 83–101.

1258 HOLLAND, James W. "The East Tennessee and Georgia Railroad, 1836–1860."*E Tenn Hist Soc Pub*, 3 (1931), 89–107.

1259 JOHNSON, Charles R. "Railroad Legislation and Building in Mississippi, 1830–1840." *J Miss Hist*, 4 (1942), 195–206.

1260 LIVINGOOD, James W. "Chattanooga: A Rail Junction of the Old South." *Tenn Hist Q*, 6 (1947), 230–250.

1261 MEHRLING, John C. "The Memphis and Charleston Railroad." *W Tenn Hist Soc Pap*, 19 (1965), 21–35.

1262 MEHRLING, John C. "The Memphis and Ohio Railroad." *W Tenn Hist Soc Pap*, 22 (1968), 52–61.

1263 MUIR, Andrew F. "Railroad Enterprise in Texas, 1836–1841."*SW Hist Q*, 47 (1944), 339–370.

1264 PORTER, Eugene O. "Railroad Enterprises in the Republic of Texas." *SW Hist Q*, 59 (1956), 363–371.

1265 REED, Merl E. "Government Investment and Economic Growth: Louisiana's Ante Bellum Railroads."*J S Hist*, 28 (1962), 183–201.

1266 REED, Merl E. *New Orleans and the Railroads: The Struggle for Commercial Empire, 1830–1860*. Baton Rouge, 1966.

1267 ROBERSON, Jere W. "The South and the Pacific Railroad, 1845–1855." *W Hist Q*, 5 (1974), 163–186.

1268 SPRAGUE, Stuart Seely. "Kentucky and the Cincinnati-Charleston Railroad, 1835–1839." *Reg Ky Hist Soc*, 73 (1975), 122–135.

1269 TURNER, Charles W. "The Early Railroad Movement in Virginia." *Va Mag Hist Biog*, 55 (1947), 350–371.

1270 TURNER, Charles W. "Early Virginia Railroad Entrepreneurs and Personnel." *Va Mag Hist Biog*, 59 (1950), 325–334.

1271 TURNER, Charles W. "Railroad Service to Virginia Farmers, 1828–1860." *Ag Hist*, 22 (1948), 239–248.

1272 TURNER, Charles W. "Virginia Ante-Bellum Railroad Disputes and Problems." *N C Hist Rev*, 27 (1950), 314–335.

1273 TURNER, Charles W. "Virginia Railroad Development, 1845–1860." *Historian*, 10 (1947), 43–62.

1274 WARD, James A. "A New Look at Antebellum Southern Railroad Development." *J S Hist*, 39 (1973), 409–420.

E. The Telegraph

1275 CARLETON, Eleanor B. "The Establishment of the Electric Telegraph in Louisiana and Mississippi." *La Hist Q*, 31 (1948), 425–490.

1276 COTTERILL, Robert S. "The Telegraph in the South, 1845–1850." *S Atl Q*, 16 (1971), 149–154.

1277 SUNDER, John E. "Arkansas' First 'Wonder Working Wire'." *Ark Hist Q*, 16 (1957), 231–242.

1278 SUNDER, John E. "The Early Telegraph in Rural Missouri, 1847–1859." *Mo Hist Rev*, 51 (1956), 42–53.

1279 SUNDER, John E. "St. Louis and the Early Telegraph, 1847–1857." *Mo Hist Rev*, 50 (1956), 248–258.

1280 THOMPSON, Robert L. *Wiring a Continent: The History of the Telegraph Industry in the United States from 1832 to 1866.* New York, 1972.

2. Commercial Conventions

1281 COTTERILL, Robert S. "Memphis Railroad Convention, 1849." *Tenn Hist Mag*, 4 (1918), 83–94.

1282 DAVIS, William W. "Ante-Bellum Southern Commercial Conventions." *Trans Ala Hist Soc*, 5 (1904), 153–202.

1283 EASTERBY, J. Harold. "The Charleston Commercial Convention of 1854." *S Atl Q*, 25 (1926), 181–197.

1284 ROBERSON, Jere W. "The Memphis Commercial Convention of 1853: Southern Dreams and 'Young America'." *Tenn Hist Q*, 33 (1974), 279–296.

1285 ROBERSON, Jere W. "To Build a Pacific Railroad: Congress, Texas, and the Charleston Convention of 1854."*SW Hist Q*, 78 (1974), 117–139.

1286 VAN DEUSEN, John G. *The Ante-Bellum Southern Commercial Conventions.* New York, 1970.

1287 WENDER, Herbert. "The Southern Commercial Convention at Savannah, 1856." *Ga Hist Q*, 15 (1931), 173–191.

1288 WENDER, Herbert. *Southern Commercial Conventions, 1837–1859.* Baltimore, Md., 1930.

3. Economic Development—General

1289 DIAMOND, William. "Nathaniel A. Ware, National Economist."*J S Hist*, 5 (1939), 501–526.

1290 DORFMAN, Joseph. *The Economic Mind in American Civilization, 1606–1865.* New York, 1966.

1291 ENGERMAN, Stanley L. "The Antebellum South: What Probably Was and What Should Have Been." See **407**.

1292 ENGERMAN, Stanley L. "A Reconsideration of Southern Economic Growth, 1770–1860." *Ag Hist*, 49 (1975), 343–361.

1293 FISHLOW, Albert. "Antebellum Interregional Trade Reconsidered."*Am Ec Rev*, 54 (1964), 352–364.

1294 FORD, John V. "Economic Philosophy of John Taylor." *Wm Mar Q*, 2nd ser., 9 (1929), 221–235.

1295 GRAMPP, William D. "John Taylor: Economist of Southern Agrarianism." *S Ec J*, 11 (1945), 255–268.

1296 HEATH, Milton S. *Constructive Liberalism: The Role of the State in Economic Development in Georgia to 1860.* Cambridge, Mass., 1954.

1297 HEATH, Milton S. "Laissez Faire in Georgia, 1732–1860."J Ec Hist, 3 (1943), 78–100. This is a supplement to the December 1943 issue, and the contents of the issue are the papers read at the 3rd Ann Meeting of the Ec Hist Assn.

1298 KETTELL, Thomas P. *Southern Wealth and Northern Profits.* Ed. Fletcher M. Green. University, Ala., 1965.

1299 LEIMAN, Melvin M. *Jacob N. Cardozo: Economic Thought in the Antebellum South.* New York, 1966.

1300 LINDSTROM, Diane. "Southern Dependence upon Interregional Grain Supplies: A Review of the Trade Flows, 1840–1860." *Ag Hist*, 44 (1970), 101–113.

1301 MURRAY, Paul. "Economic Sectionalism in Georgia Politics, 1825–1855." *J S Hist*, 10 (1944), 293–307.

1302 ROTHSTEIN, Morton. "The Ante-Bellum South as a Dual Economy: A Tentative Hypothesis." *Ag Hist*, 41 (1967), 373–382.

1303 RUSSEL, Robert R. *Economic Aspects of Southern Sectionalism, 1840–1861.* New York, 1973.

1304 SITTERSON, J. Carlyle. "Economic Sectionalism in Ante-Bellum North Carolina." *N C Hist Rev*, 16 (1939), 134–146.

1305 SKIPPER, Otis C. "J. D. B. DeBow." *Trans Huguenot Soc S C*, 44 (1939), 23–32.

1306 SKIPPER, Otis C. *J. D. B. DeBow, Magazinist of the Old South.* Athens, Ga., 1958.

1307 SKIPPER, Otis C. "J. D. B. DeBow, Statistician of the Old South." *Proc S C Hist Assn*, 8 (1938), 3–15.

1308 SKIPPER, Otis C. "J. D. B. DeBow, the Man." *J S Hist*, 10 (1944), 404–423.

1309 SNAVELY, Tipton R. *George Tucker as Political Economist.* Charlottesville, Va., 1964.

1310 STANDARD, Diffee W. *"DeBow's Review*, 1846–1880, a Magazine of Southern Opinion." Doctoral dissertation, University of North Carolina, 1970.

1311 TURNER, Frederick J. "The South, 1820–1830." See **805**.

1312 VAN DEUSEN, John G. *Economic Bases of Disunion in South Carolina.* New York, 1970.

1313 WOODMAN, Harold D. "New Perspectives on Southern Economic Development: A Comment."*Ag Hist*, 49 (1975), 374–380.

4. Efforts toward Direct Trade with England and the Continent

1314 HASKINS, Ralph W. "The Cotton Factor, 1800–1860: A Study in Southern Economic and Social History." Doctoral dissertation, University of California, Berkeley, 1950.

1315 HASKINS, Ralph W. "Planter and Cotton Factor in the Old South: Some Areas of Friction." *Ag Hist*, 29 (1955), 1–14.

1316 KILLICK, John R. "The Cotton Operations of Alexander Brown and Sons in the Deep South, 1820–1860." *J S Hist*, 43 (1977), 169–194.

1317 MARTIN, Thomas P. "Conflicting Cotton Interests at Home and Abroad, 1848–1857." *J S Hist*, 7 (1941), 173–194.

1318 MARTIN, Thomas P. "Cotton and Wheat in Anglo-American Trade and Politics, 1846–1852." *J S Hist*, 1 (1935), 293–319.

1319 PERKINS, Edwin J. "Financing Antebellum Importers: The Role of Brown Bros. and Co. in Baltimore." *Bus Hist Rev*, 45 (1971), 421–451.

1320 ROTHSTEIN, Morton. "Antebellum Wheat and Cotton Exports: A Contrast in Marketing Organization and Economic Development." *Ag Hist*, 40 (1966), 91–100.

5. Investments, Banking, and the Southern Economy

1321 ABERNETHY, Thomas P. "The Early Development of Commerce and Banking in Tennessee." *Miss Val Hist Rev*, 14 (1927), 311–325.

1322 ATHERTON, Lewis E. "The Problem of Credit Rating in the Ante-Bellum South." *J S Hist*, 12 (1946), 534–556.

1323 CAMPBELL, Claude A. "Banking and Finance in Tennessee during the Depression of 1837." *E Tenn Hist Soc Pub*, 9 (1937), 19–30.

1324 CAMPBELL, Claude A. "Branch Banking in Tennessee Prior to the Civil War." *E Tenn Hist Soc Pub*, 11 (1939), 34–46.

1325 GALLMAN, Robert E. "Self-Sufficiency in the Cotton Economy of the Antebellum South." See **1117**.

1326 GATES, Paul W. "Southern Investments in Northern Lands before the Civil War." *J S Hist*, 5 (1939), 155–185.

1327 GLEICK, Harry S. "Banking in Early Missouri." *Mo Hist Rev*, 61 (1967), 427–443; 62 (1967), 30–44.

1328 GOVAN, Thomas P. "The Banking and Credit System in Georgia, 1810–1860." *J S Hist*, 4 (1938), 164–184.

1329 GREEN, George D. *Finance and Economic Development in the Old South: Louisiana Banking, 1804–1861.* Stanford, Cal., 1972.

1330 GREEN, George D. "The Louisiana Bank Act of 1842: Policy Making during Financial Crisis." *Exp Ec Hist*, 7 (1970), 399–412.

1331 GRIFFIN, Richard W. "The Fisher Committee Report to the North Carolina General Assembly, 1828." *Cot Hist Rev*, 2 (1961), 52–67.

1332 GUNDERSON, Gerald. "Southern Income Reconsidered: A Reply." *Exp Ec Hist*, 12 (1975), 101–102.

1333 HOYT, Elizabeth S. "Reactions in North Carolina to Jackson's Banking Policy, 1829–1832." *N C Hist Rev*, 25 (1948), 167–178.

1334 HUFF, Archie V., Jr. *Langdon Cheves of South Carolina*. Columbia, S. C., 1977.

1335 LESESNE, John M. *The Bank of the State of South Carolina: A General and Political History*. Columbia, S. C., 1970.

1336 McGRANE, Reginald C. "Some Aspects of American State Debts in the Forties." *Am Hist Rev*, 38 (1933), 673–686.

1337 MOORE, John Hebron. "Economic Conditions in Mississippi on the Eve of the Civil War." *J Miss Hist*, 22 (1960), 167–178.

1338 NEU, Irene D. "Edmond Jean Forstall and Louisiana Banking." *Exp Ec Hist*, 7 (1970), 383–398.

1339 PHIFER, Edward W. "Money, Banking, and Burke County in the Ante-Bellum Era." *N C Hist Rev*, 37 (1960), 22–37.

1340 RAIFORD, Norman G. "South Carolina and the Second Bank of the United States: Conflict in Political Principle or Economic Interest?" *S C Hist Mag*, 72 (1971), 30–43.

1341 ROCKOFF, Hugh T. "Varieties of Banking and Regional Economic Development in the United States, 1840–1860."*J Ec Hist*, 35 (1975), 160–181. The contents of this issue represent papers read at the 34th Ann Meeting of the Ec Hist Assn.

1342 ROYALTY, Dale. "James Prentiss and the Failure of the Kentucky Insurance Company, 1813–1818." *Reg Ky Hist Soc*, 73 (1975), 1–16.

1343 SELLERS, Charles G., Jr. "Banking and Politics in Jackson's Tennessee, 1817–1827." *Miss Val Hist Rev*, 41 (1954), 61–84.

1344 SPRATT, John S. "Banking Phobia in Texas [1835–45]." *SW Rev*, 60 (1975), 341–354.

1345 WEEMS, Robert C., Jr. "Mississippi's First Banking System." *J Miss Hist*, 29 (1967), 386–408.

1346 WORLEY, Ted R. "Arkansas and the Money Crisis of 1836–1837." *J S Hist*, 15 (1949), 178–191.

1347 WORLEY, Ted R. "The Control of the Real Estate Bank of the State of Arkansas, 1836–1855." *Miss Val Hist Rev*, 37 (1950), 403–426.

6. Business—Wholesale and Retail

1348 ATHERTON, Lewis E. "Itinerant Merchandising in the Ante-Bellum South." *Bul Bus Hist Soc*, 19 (1945), 35–59.

1349 ATHERTON, Lewis E. "John McDonogh—New Orleans Mercantile Capitalist." *J S Hist*, 7 (1941), 451–481.

1350 ATHERTON, Lewis E. "Missouri's Society and Economy in 1821." See **811**.

1351 ATHERTON, Lewis E. *The Southern Country Store, 1800–1860*. Westport, Conn., 1968.

1352 BACON, H. Phillip. "Nashville's Trade at the Beginning of the Nineteenth Century." *Tenn Hist Q*, 15 (1956), 30–36.

1353 CHILDS, William T. *John McDonogh, His Life and Work*. See **672**.

1354 CLARK, John G. "The Antebellum Grain Trade of New Orleans: Changing Patterns in the Relation of New Orleans with the Old Northwest." *Ag Hist*, 39 (1964), 131–142.

1355 EATON, Clement. *The Mind of the Old South*. See **286**.

1356 EISTERHOLD, John A. "Lumber and Trade in the Lower Mississippi Valley and New Orleans, 1800–1860." *La Hist*, 13 (1972), 71–91.

1357 GALLMAN, Robert E. "Southern Ante-Bellum Income Reconsidered." *Exp Ec Hist*, 12 (1975), 89–99.

1358 GALPIN, W. Freeman. "The Grain Trade of Alexandria, Virginia, 1801–1815." *N C Hist Rev*, 4 (1927), 404–427.

1359 GALPIN, W. Freeman. "The Grain Trade of New Orleans, 1804–1814." *Miss Val Hist Rev*, 14 (1928), 496–507.

1360 GIBSON, George H., ed. "The Mississippi Market for Woolen Goods: An 1822 Analysis." *J S Hist*, 31 (1965), 80–90.

1361 GRONERT, Theodore G. "Trade in the Blue-Grass Region, 1810–1820." *Miss Val Hist Rev*, 5 (1918), 313–323.

1362 HALSELL, Willie D. "A Country Merchant's Stock of Goods in 1860." *J Miss Hist*, 12 (1950), 46–48.

1363 HERBST, Lawrence A. Interregional Commodity Trade from the North to the South and American Economic Development in the Antebellum Period." *J Ec Hist*, 35 (1975), 264–270.

1364 KILLICK, John. "Risk, Specialization and Profit in the Mercantile Sector of the Nineteenth Century Cotton Trade: Alexander Brown and Sons [of Baltimore], 1820–80." *Bus Hist*, 16 (1974), 1–16.

1365 LEWIS, Elsie M. "Economic Conditions in Ante-Bellum Arkansas, 1850–1861." *Ark Hist Q*, 6 (1947), 256–274.

1366 MABRY, William A. "Ante-Bellum Cincinnati and Its Southern Trade." *American Studies in Honor of William Kenneth Boyd*. Duke University. Americana Club. Freeport, N. Y., 1968.

1367 MARKWALDER, Donald. "The Ante-Bellum South as a Market for Food—Myth or Reality?" *Ga Hist Q*, 54 (1970), 408–418.

1368 METZER, Jacob. "Rational Management, Modern Business Practices, and Economics of Scale in the Ante-Bellum Southern Plantation." *Exp Ec Hist*, 12 (1975), 123–150.

1369 MORRIS, Wayne. "Traders and Factories on the Arkansas Frontier, 1805–1822." *Ark Hist Q*, 28 (1969), 28–48.

1370 PARR, Elizabeth L. "Kentucky's Overland Trade with the Ante-Bellum South." *Filson Club Hist Q*, 2 (1928), 71–81.

1371 REED, Merl E. "Boom or Bust—Louisiana's Economy during the 1830's." *La Hist*, 4 (1963), 35–53.

1372 ROBERT, Joseph C. "Rise of the Tobacco Warehouse Auction System in Virginia, 1800–1860." *Ag Hist*, 7 (1933), 170–182.

1373 ROEDER, Robert E. "Merchants of Ante-Bellum New Orleans." *Exp Ent Hist*, 10 (1958), 113–122.

1374 SCHENE, Michael G. "Robert and John Grattan Gamble: Middle Florida Entrepreneurs [1827–1852]." *Fla Hist Q*, 54 (1975), 61–73.

1375 SMITH, Alfred G. *Economic Readjustment of an Old Cotton State: South Carolina, 1820–1860*. Columbia, S. C., 1958.

1376 SMITH, George W. "Ante-Bellum Attempts of Northern Business Interests to 'Redeem' the Upper South." *J S Hist*, 11 (1945), 177–213.

1377 STONE, Alfred H. "The Cotton Factorage System of the Southern States." *Am Hist Rev*, 20 (1915), 557–565.

1378 *The Structure of the Cotton Economy of the Antebellum South*. Ed. William N. Parker. See **434**.

1379 SUAREZ, Raleigh A. "Bargains, Bills, and Bankruptcies: Business Activity in Rural Antebellum Louisiana." *La Hist*, 7 (1966), 189–206.

1380 TRUETT, Randle B. *Trade and Travel around the Southern Appalachians before 1830*. Chapel Hill, 1935.

1381 WINSTON, James E. "Notes on the Economic History of New Orleans, 1803–1836." *Miss Val Hist Rev*, 11 (1924), 200–226.

1382 WOODMAN, Harold D. "Itinerant Cotton Merchants of the Antebellum South." *Ag Hist*, 40 (1966), 79–90.

1383 WOODMAN, Harold D. *King Cotton and His Retainers: Financing and Marketing the Cotton Crop of the South, 1800–1925*. Lexington, Ky., 1968.

1384 WRIGHT, Gavin. "'Economic Democracy' and the Concentration of Agricultural Wealth in the Cotton South, 1850–1860." *Ag Hist*, 44 (1970), 63–93; plus a "Note on the Manuscript Census Samples . . . ," 95–99.

7. *Labor*

1385 MARKS, George P., III. "The New Orleans Screwmen's Benevolent Association, 1850–1861." *Lab Hist*, 14 (1973), 259–263.

1386 REESE, James V. "The Early History of Labor Organizations in Texas, 1838–1876." *SW Hist Q*, 72 (1968), 1–20.

XII. Industrial Development

1. General

1387 ATACK, Jeremy. "Returns to Scale in Antebellum United States Manufacturing." *Exp Ec Hist*, 14 (1977), 337–359.

1388 BATEMAN, Fred, and Thomas WEISS. "Comparative Regional Development in Ante-Bellum Manufacturing." *J Ec Hist*, 35 (1975), 182–208.

1389 BATEMAN, Fred, James FOUST, and Thomas WEISS. "The Participation of Planters in Manufacturing in the Antebellum South." *Ag Hist*, 48 (1974), 277–297.

1390 BATEMAN, Fred, James FOUST, and Thomas WEISS. "Profitability in Southern Manufacturing: Estimates for 1860." *Exp Ec Hist*, 12 (1975), 211–231.

1391 BELISSARY, Constantine S. "Industry and Industrial Philosophy in Tennessee, 1850–1860." *E Tenn Hist Soc Pub*, 23 (1951), 46–57.

1392 BOUCHER, Chauncey S. "The Ante-Bellum Attitude of South Carolina towards Manufacturing and Agriculture." *Washington Univ Stud*, 3, pt. 2 (1916), 243–270.

1393 CHILDS, Arney, R., ed. *Planters and Businessmen: The Guignard Family of South Carolina, 1795–1930.* Columbia S. C., 1957.

1394 CLARK, Victor S. *History of Manufactures in the United States, 1607–1860.* 3 vols. Magnolia, Mass., 1949.

1395 COLLINS, Herbert. "The Southern Industrial Gospel before 1860." *J S Hist*, 12 (1946), 386–402.

1396 DAVIDSON, Philip G. "Industrialism in the Ante-Bellum South." *S Atl Q*, 27 (1928), 404–425.

1397 GREEN, Fletcher M. "Duff Green: Industrial Promoter." *J S Hist*, 2 (1936), 29–42.

1398 GRIFFIN, Richard W. "Manufacturing Interests of Mississippi Planters, 1810–1832." *J Miss Hist*, 22 (1960), 110–122.

1399 HERRING, Harriet L. "Early Industrial Development in the South." *Ann Am Acad Pol Soc Sci*, 153 (1931), 1–10.

1400 JOHNSON, J. G. "Notes on Manufacturing in Ante-Bellum Georgia." *Ga Hist Q*, 16 (1932), 214–231.

1401 LANDER, Ernest M., Jr. "Charleston: Manufacturing Center of the Old South." *J S Hist*, 26 (1960), 330–351.

1402 LINDEN, Fabian. "Repercussions of Manufacturing in the Ante-Bellum South." *N C Hist Rev*, 17 (1940), 313–331.

1403 MARMOR, T. R. "Anti-Industrialism and the Old South: The Agrarian Perspective of John C. Calhoun." *Comp Stud Soc Hist*, 9 (1967), 377–406.

1404 PRATT, Merrill E. "Daniel Pratt, Alabama's First Industrialist." *Cot Hist Rev*, 2 (1961), 18–29.

1405 PREYER, Norris W. "Why Did Industrialization Lag in the Old South?" *Ga Hist Q*, 55 (1971), 378–396.

1406 SMILEY, David L. "Cassius M. Clay and Southern Industrialism." *Filson Club Hist Q*, 28 (1954), 315–327.

1407 STAVISKY, Leonard P. "Industrialism in Ante-Bellum Charleston." *J Neg Hist*, 36 (1951), 302–322.

1408 STEADMAN, E. "A Brief Treatise on Manufacturing in the South (1851)." *Cot Hist. Rev*, 2 (1961), 103–118.

1409 WINSTON, James E. "Notes on Commercial Relations between New Orleans and Texan Ports, 1838–1839." *SW Hist Q*, 34 (1930), 91–105.

1410 WYATT, Edward A., IV. "Rise of Industry in Ante-Bellum Petersburg." *Wm Mar Q*, 2nd ser., 17 (1937), 1–36.

2. *Cotton Textiles*

1411 BLICKSILVER, Jack. *Cotton Manufacturing in the Southeast: An Historical Analysis.* Atlanta, Ga., 1959.

1412 FRIES, Adelaide L. "One Hundred Years of Textiles in Salem." *N C Hist Rev*, 27 (1950), 1–19.

1413 GRIFFIN, Richard W. "Cotton Manufacture in Alabama to 1865." *Ala Hist Q*, 18 (1956), 289–307.

1414 GRIFFIN, Richard W. "The Cotton Mill Campaign in Florida, 1828–1863." *Fla Hist Q*, 40 (1962), 261–274.

1415 GRIFFIN, Richard W. "An Origin of the Industrial Revolution in Maryland: The Textile Industry, 1789–1826." *Md Hist Mag*, 61 (1966), 24–36.

1416 GRIFFIN, Richard W. "An Origin of the New South: The South Carolina Homespun Company, 1808–1815." *Bus Hist Rev*, 35 (1961), 402–414.

1417 GRIFFIN, Richard W. "The Origins of Southern Cotton Manufacture, 1807–1816." *Cot Hist Rev*, 1 (1960), 5–12.

1418 GRIFFIN, Richard W. "The Origins of the Industrial Revolution in Georgia: Cotton Textiles, 1810–1865." *Ga Hist Q*, 42 (1958), 353–375.

1419 GRIFFIN, Richard W. "Poor White Laborers in Southern Cotton Factories, 1789–1865." *S C Hist Mag*, 61 (1960), 26–40. The author is obviously referring to the yeoman farmer group, rather than to the poor white.

1420 GRIFFIN, Richard W. "Pro-Industrial Sentiment and Cotton Factories in Arkansas, 1820–1863." *Ark Hist Q*, 15 (1956), 125–139.

1421 HAMMOND, Seth. "The Ante-Bellum Kentucky Cotton Industry, 1790–1860." *Cot Hist Rev*, 1 (1960), 47–55.

1422 JONES, Charles C., Jr. "Pioneer Manufacturing in Richmond County, Georgia." *Text Hist Rev*, 5 (1964), 69–83.

1423 LANDER, Ernest M., Jr. "The Development of Textiles in the South Carolina Piedmont before 1860." *Cot Hist Rev*, 1 (1960), 88–100.

1424 LANDER, Ernest M., Jr. "The South Carolina Textile Industry before 1845." *Proc S C Hist Assn*, 21 (1951), 19–28.

1425 LANDER, Ernest M., Jr. *Textile Industry in Antebellum South Carolina.* Baton Rouge, 1969.

1426 MARTIN, Thomas P., ed. "The Advent of William Gregg and the Graniteville Company." *J S Hist*, 11 (1945), 389–423.

1427 MILLER, Randall M. "Daniel Pratt's Industrial Urbanism: The Cotton Mill Town in Antebellum Alabama." *Ala Hist Q*, 34 (1972), 5–35.

1428 MILLER, Randall M., ed. "Love of Labor: A Note on Daniel Pratt's [Cotton Factory] Employment Practices." *Ala Hist Q*, 37 (1975), 146–150.

1429 MITCHELL, Broadus. *William Gregg, Factory Master of the Old South.* New York, 1966.

1430 MOORE, John Hebron. "Mississippi's Ante-Bellum Textile Industry." *J Miss Hist*, 16 (1954), 81–98.

1431 O'CONNOR, Thomas H. "Young Mr. Lawrence Views the South." *Text Hist Rev*, 3 (1962), 59–67.

1432 PHILLIPS, Ulrich B. "The Overproduction of Cotton and a Possible Remedy." *Ag Hist*, 13 (1939), 118–125.

1433 STANDARD, Diffie W., and Richard W. GRIFFIN. "The Cotton Textile Industry in Ante-Bellum North Carolina." *N C Hist Rev*, 34 (1957), 15–35, 131–164.

1434 TAYLOR, James H. "Manufactures in South Carolina." *Cot Hist Rev*, 1 (1960), 131–137.

1435 TERRILL, Tom E. "Eager Hands: Labor for Southern Textiles, 1850–1860." *J Ec Hist*, 36 (1976), 84–99.

1436 THOMAS, Daniel H. "Pre-Whitney Cotton Gins in French Louisiana." *J S Hist*, 31 (1965), 135–148.

1437 WALLACE, David Duncan. "The Founding of Graniteville." *Cot Hist Rev*, 1 (1960), 19–25.

1438 WHITE, Raymond E. "Cotton Ginning in Texas to 1861." *SW Hist Q*, 61 (1957), 257–269.

3. Tobacco

1439 PRICE, Jacob M. "The Beginnings of Tobacco Manufacture in Virginia." *Va Mag Hist Biog*, 64 (1956), 3–29.

1440 ROBERT, Joseph C. "The Tobacco Industry in Ante-Bellum North Carolina." *N C Hist Rev*, 15 (1938), 119–130.

1141 ROBERT, Joseph C. *The Tobacco Kingdom: Plantation, Market, and Factory in Virginia and North Carolina, 1800–1860.* See **1113**.

4. Iron and Steel

1442 BRADFORD, S. Sidney. "The Negro Ironworker in Ante Bellum Virginia." *J S Hist*, 25 (1959), 194–206.

1443 BRUCE, Kathleen. "Slave Labor in the Virginian Iron Industry."*Wm Mar Q*, 2nd ser., 6 (1926), 289–302; 7 (1927), 21–31.

1444 Bruce, Kathleen. *Virginia Iron Manufacture in the Slave Era*. Fairfield, N. J., 1968.

1445 CAPPON, Lester J. "History of the Southern Iron Industry to the Close of the Civil War." Doctoral dissertation, Harvard University, 1928.

1446 CAPPON, Lester J. "Iron-Making—A Forgotten Industry of North Carolina." *N C Hist Rev*, 9 (1932), 331–348.

1447 COLEMAN, J. Winston, Jr. "Old Kentucky Iron Furnaces." *Filson Club Hist Q*, 31 (1957), 227–242.

1448 COZZENS, Arthur B. "The Iron Industry of Missouri." *Mo Hist Rev*, 35 (1941), 509–538; 36 (1941), 48–59.

1449 CROCKER, Les. "An Early Iron Foundry in Northern Mississippi." *J Miss Hist*, 35 (1973), 113–126.

1450 DALTON, Robert E. "Montgomery Bell and the Narrows of the Harpeth." *Tenn Hist Q*, 35 (1976), 3–28.

1451 DEW, Charles B. *Ironmaker to the Confederacy: Joseph R. Anderson and the Tredegar Iron Works*. New Haven, Conn., 1966.

1452 HARVEY, Katherine A. "Building a Frontier Ironworks [George's Greek Coal and Iron Co., Md.]: Problems of Transport and Supply, 1837–1840." *Md Hist Mag*, 70 (1975), 149–166.

1453 HUNT, Raymond F., Jr. "The Pactolus Ironworks." *Tenn Hist Q*, 25 (1966), 176–196.

1454 JOHNSON, Keach. "The Genesis of the Baltimore Ironworks." *J S Hist*, 19 (1953), 157–179.

1455 LANDER, Ernest M., Jr. "The Iron Industry in Ante-Bellum South Carolina." *J S Hist*, 20 (1954), 337–355.

1456 PHELPS, Dawson A., and John T. WILLETT. "Iron Works on the Natchez Trace." *Tenn Hist Q*, 12 (1953), 309–322.

1457 QUENZEL, Carrol H. "The Manufacture of Locomotives and Cars in Alexandria in the 1850's." *Va Mag Hist Biog*, 62 (1954), 181–189.

1458 WILLIAMS, Samuel C. "Early Iron Works in Tennessee Country." *Tenn Hist Q*, 6 (1947), 39–46.

5. The Lesser Industries

1459 ALLMOND, Charles M., III. "The Great Silk Bubble." *Del Hist*, 11 (1965), 208–228.

1460 BERRY, Thomas S. 'The Rise of Flour Milling in Richmond." *Va Mag Hist Biog*, 78 (1970), 387–408.

1461 CARSON, Gerald. "Bourbon: Amber Waves of Grain—100 Proof." *Am Heritage*, 25 (February, 1974), 60–63, 95.

1462 COLEMAN, J. Winston, Jr. "John W. Coleman: Early Kentucky Hemp Manufacturer." *Filson Club Hist Q*, 24 (1950), 34–48.

1463 COULTER, E. Merton. "Note on a Georgia Paper Mill." *Ga Hist Q*, 48 (1964), 239–242.

1464 CROWGEY, Henry G. *Kentucky Bourbon: The Early Years of Kentucky Whiskey-Making.* Lexington, Ky., 1971.

1465 EISTERHOLD, John A. "Charleston: Lumber and Trade in a Declining Southern Port." *S C Hist Mag*, 74 (1973), 61–72.

1466 EISTERHOLD, John A. "Lumber and Trade in Pensacola and West Florida: 1800–1860."*Fla Hist Q*, 51 (1973), 267–280.

1467 EISTERHOLD, John A. "Lumber and Trade in the Seaboard Cities of the Old South, 1607–1860." Doctoral dissertation, University of Mississippi, 1970.

1468 EISTERHOLD, John A. "Mobile: Lumber Center of the Gulf Coast." *Ala Rev*, 26 (1973), 83–104.

1469 EISTERHOLD, John A. "Savannah: Lumber Center of the South Atlantic." *Ga Hist Q*, 57 (1973), 526–543.

1470 ELLSWORTH, Lucius F. "Raiford and Abercrombie: Pensacola's Premier Manufacturer." *Fla Hist Q*, 54 (1974), 247–260.

1471 HAMER, Marguerite B. "The Foundation and Failure of the Silk Industry in Provincial Georgia." *N C Hist Rev*, 12 (1935), 125–148.

1472 HERNDON, G. Melvin. "Naval Stores in Colonial Georgia." *Ga Hist Q*, 52 (1968), 426–433.

1473 HERNDON, G. Melvin. "A War-Inspired Industry: The Manufacture of Hemp in Virginia during the Revolution." *Va Mag Hist Biog*, 74 (1966), 301–311.

1474 HOPKINS, James F. *History of the Hemp Industry in Kentucky.* See **1151**.

1475 HOPKINS, James F. "The Production of Hemp in Kentucky for Naval Use." *Filson Club Hist Q*, 23 (1949), 34–51.

1476 LANDER, Ernest M., Jr. "Ante-Bellum Milling in South Carolina." *S C Hist Gen Mag*, 52 (1951), 125–132.

1477 LANDER, Ernest M., Jr. "Paper Manufacturing in South Carolina before the Civil War." *N C Hist Rev*, 29 (1952), 220–227.

1478 LANMON, Dwight P. "The Baltimore Glass Trade, 1780–1820." *Winterthur Port*, 5 (1969), 15–48.

1479 MOORE, John Hebron. *Andrew Brown and Cypress Lumbering in the Old Southwest.* Baton Rouge, 1967.

1480 PERRY, Percival. "The Naval-Stores Industry in the Old South, 1790–1860." *J S Hist*, 34 (1968), 509–526.

1481 PETERSON, Arthur G. "Flour and Grist Milling in Virginia: A Brief History." *Va Mag Hist Biog*, 43 (1935), 97–108.

1482 SNOW, Sinclair. "Naval Stores in Colonial Virginia." *Va Mag Hist Biog*, 72 (1964), 75–93.

1483 STEPHENS, Pauline T. "The Silk Industry in Georgia." *Ga Rev*, 7 (1953), 39–49.

1484 STONE, J. William. "The Hope Distillery Company." *Filson Club Hist Q*, 27 (1953), 29–35.

6. Mining and Minerals

1485 CLARK, Thomas D. "Salt, a Factor in the Settlement of Kentucky." *Filson Club Hist Q*, 12 (1938), 42–52.

1486 CONLEY, Phil. "Early Coal Development in Kanawha Valley." *W Va Hist*, 8 (1947), 207—215.

1487 COULTER, E. Merton. *Auraria: The Story of a Georgia Gold-Mining Town.* Athens, Ga., 1956.

1488 FAUST, Burton. "The History of Saltpetre Mining in Mammoth Cave, Kentucky." *Filson Club Hist Q*, 41 (1967), 5–20, 127–140, 227–262, 323–352.

1489 GIBSON, A. M. "Lead Mining in Southwest Missouri to 1865." *Mo Hist Rev*, 53 (1959), 197–205.

1490 GOODALL, Elizabeth J. "The Manufacture of Salt—Kanawha's First Commercial Enterprise." *W Va Hist*, 26 (1965), 234–250.

1491 GREEN, Fletcher M. "Georgia's Forgotten Industry: Gold Mining." *Ga Hist Q*, 19 (1935), 93–111, 210–228.

1492 GREEN, Fletcher M. "Gold Mining: A Forgotten Industry of Ante-Bellum North Carolina." *N C Hist Rev*, 14 (1937), 1–19, 135–155.

1493 GREEN, Fletcher M. "Gold Mining in Ante-Bellum Virginia." *Va Mag Hist Biog*, 45 (1937), 227–235, 357–366.

1494 KNAPP, Richard F. "Golden Promise in the Piedmont: The Story of John Reed's Mine." *N C Hist Rev*, 52 (1975), 1–19.

1495 LAING, James T. "The Early Development of the Coal Industry in the Western Counties of Virginia, 1800–1865." *W Va Hist*, 27 (1966), 144–155.

1496 LITTLEFIELD, Daniel F., Jr. "The Salt Industry in Arkansas Territory, 1819–1836." *Ark Hist Q*, 32 (1973), 312–336.

1497 LUCKINGHAM, Brad. "A Note on the Lead Mines of Missouri: Henry R. Schoolcraft to William H. Crawford, 1820." *Mo Hist Rev*, 59 (1965), 344–348.

1498 McGEE, Mrs. C. M. "The Great American Oil Well, Burkeville, Kentucky." *Filson Club Hist Q*, 33 (1959), 318–326.

1499 PEARRE, Nancy C. "Mining for Copper and Related Minerals in Maryland." *Md Hist Mag,* 59 (1964), 15–33.

1500 PEASE, Louise M. "The Great Kanawha in the Old South, 1671–1861: A Study in Contradictions." Doctoral dissertation, West Virginia University, 1959.

1501 REED, Louis. "First Oil Lease South of the Mason and Dixon Line." *W Va Hist*, 25 (1964), 150–155.

1502 RICE, Otis K. "Coal Mining in the Kanawha Valley to 1861: A View of Industrialization in the Old South." *J S Hist*, 31 (1965), 393–416.

1503 RUSSELL, Robert A. "Gold Mining in Alabama before 1860." *Ala Rev*, 10 (1957), 5–14.

1504 STEALEY, John E., III. "The Salt Industry of the Great Kanawha Valley of Virginia: A Study in Ante-Bellum Internal Commerce." Doctoral dissertation, West Virginia University, 1970.

1505 STEALEY, John E., III. "Slavery and the Western Virginia Salt Industry." See **490a**.

1506 SWARTZLOW, Ruby Johnson. "The Early History of Lead Mining in Missouri." *Mo Hist Rev*, 28 (1934), 184–194, 287–295; 29 (1934), 27–34, (1935), 109–114, 195–205.

1507 TALLEY, William M. "Salt Lick Creek and Its Salt Works." *Reg Ky Hist Soc*, 64 (1966), 85–109.

XIII. Education

1. General

1508 BETTS, Leonidas. "George Frederick Holmes, Nineteenth-Century Virginia Educator." *Va Mag Hist Biog*, 76 (1968), 472–484.

1509 DesCHAMPS, Margaret Burr. "Presbyterians and Southern Education." *J Presb Hist Soc*, 31 (1953), 113–124.

1510 EZELL, John S. "A Southern Education for Southrons." *J S Hist*, 17 (1951), 303–327.

1511 FAUST, Drew Gilpin. *A Sacred Circle: The Dilemma of the Intellectual in the Old South*. Baltimore, Md., 1977.

1512 HAUNTON, Richard H. "Education and Democracy: The Views of Philip Lindsley." *Tenn Hist Q*, 21 (1962), 131–139.

1513 HONEYWELL, Roy J. *The Educational Work of Thomas Jefferson*. New York, 1964.

1514 HONEYWELL, Roy J. "A Note on the Educational Work of Thomas Jefferson." *Hist Ed Q*, 9 (1969), 64–72.

1515 INSKO, W. Robert. "Benjamin Bosworth Smith, Kentucky Pioneer Clergyman and Educator." *Reg Ky Hist Soc*, 69 (1971), 37–86.

1516 KNIGHT, Edgar W., ed. *Documentary History of Education in the South before 1860*. 5 vols. Chapel Hill, N. C., 1949–1953.

1517 KNIGHT, Edgar W. "Interest in the South in Lancasterian Methods." *N C Hist Rev*, 25 (1948), 377–402.

1518 KRUMPELMANN, John T. *Southern Scholars in Goethe's Germany*. Chapel Hill, N. C., 1965.

1519 LONGTON, William H. "Some Aspects of Intellectual Activity in Ante-Bellum South Carolina, 1830–1860: An Introductory Study." Doctoral dissertation, University of North Carolina, 1969.

1520 McGROARTY, William B. "Alexandria's Lancasterian Schools." *Wm Mar Q*, 2nd ser., 21 (1941), 111–118.

1521 REINDERS, Robert C. "New England Influences on the Formation of Public Schools in New Orleans." *J S Hist*, 30 (1964), 181–195.

1522 WELTER, Rush, ed. *American Writings on Popular Education*. Indianapolis, Ind., 1941.

2. Plantation Tutors

1523 CARROLL, Rosemary F. "Margaret Clark Griffis, Plantation Teacher." *Tenn Hist Q*, 26 (1967), 295–303.

1524 COPELAND, J. Isaac. "The Tutor in the Ante-Bellum South." *Proc S C Hist Assn*, 35 (1965), 36–47.

1525 FITHIAN, Philip Vickers. *Journal and Letters*. Ed. Hunter Dickinson Farish. See **122**.

1526 HALL, D. D., ed. "A Yankee Tutor in the Old South." *N Eng Q*, 33 (1960), 82–91.

1527 McLEAN, Robert C., ed. "Yankee Tutor in the Old South." *N C Hist Rev*, 47 (1970), 51–85.

1528 PADGETT, James A., ed. "Yankee School Teacher in Louisiana, 1835–1837: The Diary of Carolina B. Poole." *La Hist Q*, 20 (1937), 651–679.

1529 PATTON, James W., ed. "New England Tutors in Granville County, North Carolina, 1845–1850." *N C Hist Rev*, 37 (1960), 544–567.

3. Private Schools, Academies, and Old Field Schools

1530 BAILEY, Hugh C. "The Up-Country Academies of Moses Waddel."*Proc S C Hist Assn*, 29 (1959), 36–43.

1531 CAMPBELL, Helen J. "The Symes and Eaton Schools and Their Successor." *Wm Mar Q*, 2nd ser., 20 (1940), 1–61.

1532 COIT, Margaret L. "Moses Waddel: A Light in the Wilderness." *Ga Rev*, 5 (1951), 34–47.

1533 COON, Charles L., ed. *North Carolina Schools and Academies, 1790–1840: A Documentary History*. Raleigh, N. C., 1915.

1534 COULTER, E. Merton. "The Ante-Bellum Academy Movement in Georgia." *Ga Hist Q*, 5 (December, 1921), 11–42.

1535 CRABB, Alfred L. "James Priestly, Pioneer Schoolmaster." *Tenn Hist Q*, 12 (1953), 129–134.

1536 JOHNSTON, Richard M. "Early Educational Life in Middle Georgia." U. S. Bureau of Education. *Report of the Commissioner ... 1894/1895*, vol. 2, 1699–1733. Washington, D. C., 1896.

1537 KNIGHT, Edgar W. "The Academy Movement in the South." *High Sch J*, 2 (1919), 199–204, 235–240; 3 (1920), 6–11.

1538 KNIGHT, Edgar W. "Manual Labor Schools in the South." *S Atl Q*, 16 (1917), 209–221.

1539 LYON, Ralph M. "Moses Waddel and the Willington Academy." *N C Hist Rev*, 8 (1931), 284–299.

1540 McCAUL, Robert L. "Education in Georgia during the Period of Royal Government, 1752–1776."*Ga Hist Q*, 40 (1956), 103–112, 248–259.

1541 MOBLEY, James W. "The Academy Movement in Louisiana." *La Hist Q*, 30 (1947), 737–978.

1542 NEWCOMER, Lee N., ed. "Two New England Teachers in Nashville, 1818." *Tenn Hist Q*, 19 (1960), 74–79.

1543 UTLEY, Buford C. "The Early Academies of West Tennessee." *W Tenn Hist Soc Pap*, 8 (1954), 5–38.

1544 WALSH, Richard. "The South Carolina Academy, 1800–1811." *Proc S C Hist Assn*, 25 (1955), 5–14.

4. The Beginnings of City and State School Systems

1545 AMBLER, Charles H. "Poor Relief Education (Kanawha County, Virginia, 1818–1847)." *W Va Hist*, 3 (1942), 285–304.

1546 AMBLER, Charles H. "Public Education in Monroe County, (West) Virginia, 1819–1861." *W Va Hist*, 4 (1942), 25–36.

1547 ANDERSON, J. Perrin. "Public Education in Ante-Bellum South Carolina." *Proc S C Hist Assn*, 3 (1933), 3–11.

1548 ARROWOOD, Charles F., ed. *Thomas Jefferson and Education in a Republic.* St. Clair Shores, Mich., 1970.

1549 BERGER, Max. "Stephen F. Austin and Education in Early Texas, 1821–1835." *SW Hist Q*, 48 (1945), 387–394.

1550 BOYD, William K. "The Finances of the North Carolina Literary Fund." *S Atl Q*, 13 (1914), 270–279, 361–370.

1551 BRAVERMAN, Howard. "Calvin Henderson Wiley, North Carolina Educator and Writer." Doctoral dissertation, Duke University, 1951.

1552 COLTON, David L. "Lawyers, Legislation and Educational Localism: The Missouri School Code of 1825." *Mo Hist Rev*, 69 (1975), 121–146.

1553 COON, Charles L., ed. *The Beginnings of Public Education in North Carolina: A Documentary History.* 2 vols. Raleigh, N. C., 1908.

1554 COULTER, E. Merton. "A Georgia Educational Movement during the Eighteen Hundred Fifties." *Ga Hist Q*, 9 (1925), 1–33.

EDUCATION

1555 DABNEY, Charles W. *Universal Education in the South.* 2 vols. Chapel Hill, 1936.

1556 DAVIS, T. Frederick, ed. "Pioneer Florida: A Free Public School in St. Augustine, 1832." *Fla Hist Q,* 22 (1944), 201–207.

1557 EAVES, Robert W. "A History of the Educational Developments of Alexandria, Virginia, Prior to 1860." *Wm Mar Q,* 2nd ser., 16 (1936), 111–161.

1558 FORD, Paul H. M. "Calvin H. Wiley and the Common Schools of North Carolina, 1850–1869." Doctoral dissertation, Harvard University, 1960.

1559 GILLIAM, Will D. "Robert Jefferson Breckenridge, 1800–1871."*Reg Ky Hist Soc,* 72 (1974), 207–223, 319–336.

1560 HARRISON, Lowell. "South Carolina's Educational System in 1822." *S C Hist Gen Mag,* 51 (1950), 1–9.

1561 KNIGHT, Edgar W. *Public Education in the South.* Boston, 1922.

1562 KNIGHT, Edgar W. "Some Fallacies Concerning the History of Public Education in the South." *S Atl Q,* 13 (1914), 371–381.

1563 LEWIS, Frank G. "Education in St. Augustine, 1821–1845." *Fla Hist Q,* 30 (1952), 237–260.

1564 LOCKEY, Joseph B. "Public Education in Spanish St. Augustine." *Fla Hist Soc Q,* 15 (1937), 147–168.

1565 McCAIN, William D. "Education in Mississippi (in 1860)." *J Miss Hist,* 22 (1960), 153–166.

1566 McVEY, Frank L. *The Gates Open Slowly: A History of Education in Kentucky.* Lexington, Ky., 1949.

1567 MADDOX, William A. *The Free School Idea in Virginia before the Civil War.* New York, 1918.

1568 MAYO, A. D. "The Common School in the Southern States beyond the Mississippi River, from 1830 to 1860." U. S. Bureau of Education. *Report of the Commissioner. . .1900/1901,* vol. 1, 357–401. Washington, D. C., 1902.

1569 MAYO, A. D. "The Organization and Development of the American Common School in the Atlantic and Central States of the South, 1830 to 1860." U. S. Bureau of Education. *Report of the Commissioner . . . 1899/1900,* vol. 1, 427–561. Washington, D. C., 1901.

1570 MOFFATT, Walter. "Arkansas Schools, 1819–1840." *Ark Hist Q,* 12 (1953), 91–105.

1571 NAGY, J. Emerick. "The South Nashville Institute [1851–54]." *Tenn Hist Q,* 36 (1977), 180–196.

1572 NAGY, J. Emerick. "Wanted: A Teacher for the Nashville English School." *Tenn Hist Q,* 21 (1962), 171–186.

1573 NOBLE, Stuart G. "Schools of New Orleans during the First Quarter of the Nineteenth Century." *La Hist Q,* 14 (1931), 65–78.

1574 ORR, Dorothy. *A History of Education in Georgia.* Chapel Hill, 1950.

1575 PIPPIN, Kathryn A. "The Common School Movement in the South, 1840–1860." Doctoral dissertation, University of North Carolina, 1977.

1576 PYBURN, Nita K., ed. "John Westcott's Plan for Public Education in Florida, 1844." *Fla Hist Q,* 27 (1949), 300–307.

1577 PYBURN, Nita K. "Mobile Public Schools before 1860." *Ala Rev,* 11 (1958), 177–188.

1578 PYBURN, Nita K. "The Public School System of Charleston before 1860." *S C Hist Mag*, 61 (1960), 86–98.

1579 PYBURN, Nita K. "Public Schools in Mississippi before 1860." *J Miss Hist*, 21 (1959), 113–130.

1580 ROBERTS, L. E. "Educational Reform in Ante-Bellum Georgia." *Ga Rev*, 16 (1961), 68–82.

1581 "Some Historical Documents Bearing Upon Common School Education in Virginia and South Carolina Previous to the Civil War: (1) Henry Ruffner's Proposed Plan, (2) Governor Wise's Address to His Constituents, and (3) J. H. Thornwell's Letter to Governor Manning." U. S. Bureau of Education. *Report of the Commissioner . . . 1899/1900,* vol. 1, 381–426. Washington, D. C., 1901.

1582 SUAREZ, Raleigh A. "Chronicle of a Failure: Public Education in Antebellum Louisiana." *La Hist*, 12 (1971), 109–122.

1583 SWIFT, David E. "Thomas Jefferson, John Holt Rice, and Education in Virginia, 1815–25." *J Presb Hist*, 49 (1971), 32–58.

1584 WEATHERSBY, William H. *A History of Educational Legislation in Mississippi from 1798 to 1860.* Chicago, 1921.

1585 WEEKS, Stephen B. "Calvin Henderson Wiley and the Organization of the Common Schools of North Carolina." U. S. Bureau of Education. *Report of the Commissioner . . . 1896/1897,* vol. 2, 1379–1474.

1586 WILLIAMS, Virginia. "Tennessee Public School Lands." *Tenn Hist Q*, 3 (1944), 335–348.

5. *Colleges and Universities*

1587 ADAMS, O. Burton. "Yale Influence on the Formation of the University of Georgia." *Ga Hist Q*, 51 (1967), 175–185.

1588 BORROWMAN, Merle. "The False Dawn of the State University." *Hist Ed Q*, 1 (June, 1961), 6–22.

1589 BRUCE, Philip A. *History of the University of Virgina, 1819–1919.* 5 vols. New York, 1920–1922.

1590 BRUGGER, Robert J. *Beverley Tucker: Heart over Head in the Old South.* Baltimore, Md., 1978.

1591 CALLCOTT, George H. *A History of the University of Maryland.* Baltimore, Md., 1966.

1592 CHAFFIN, Nora C. *Trinity College, 1839–1892: The Beginnings of Duke University.* Durham, N. C., 1950.

1593 CHUTE, William J. "The Life of Frederick A. P. Barnard to His Election as President of Columbia in 1864." Doctoral dissertation, Columbia University, 1951.

1594 COME, Donald R. "The Influence of Princeton on Higher Education in the South before 1825." *Wm Mar Q*, 3rd ser., 2 (1945), 359–396.

1595 CONNOR, R. D. W. "The Genesis of Higher Education in North Carolina." *N C Hist Rev*, 28 (1951), 1–14 .

1596 COULTER, E. Merton. *College Life in the Old South.* Athens, Ga., 1951.

1597 COULTER, E. Merton. "Why John and Joseph LeConte Left the University of Georgia, 1855–1856." *Ga Hist Q*, 53 (1969), 18–40.

1598 COUPER, William. *One Hundred Years at V. M. I.* 4 vols. Richmond, Va., 1939.

1599 CROWSON, E. T. "George Frederick Holmes." *Va Cav*, 17 (Spring, 1968), 18–29.

1600 DAVIS, Richard Beale. *Francis Walker Gilmer: Life and Learning in Jefferson's Virginia.* Richmond, Va., 1939.

1601 EASTERBY, J. Harold. *History of the College of Charleston.* Charleston, S. C., 1935.

1602 FOERSTER, Alma P. "The State University of the Old South: A Study of Social and Intellectual Influence in State University Education." Doctoral dissertation, Duke University, 1939.

1603 FOLMSBEE, Stanley J. "Blount College and East Tennessee College, 1794–1840: The First Predecessors of the University of Tennessee." *East Tenn Hist Soc Pub*, 17 (1945), 22–50.

1604 FOLMSBEE, Stanley J. "East Tennessee University, Pre-War Years, 1840–1861." *E Tenn Hist Soc Pub*, 22 (1950), 60–93.

1605 GEER, William M. "Francis Lieber at the South Carolina College." *Proc S C Hist Assn*, 13 (1943), 3–22.

1606 GILLESPIE, Neal C. "Ole Miss: A New Look at Her First President." *J Miss Hist*, 30 (1968), 275–290.

1607 GODBOLD, Albea. *The Church College in the Old South.* Durham, N. C., 1944.

1608 GRIFFIN, Richard W., ed. "Student Days at Davidson College: 1838–1857, in Letters to the Reverend G. H. W. Petrie." *J Presb Hist Soc*, 40 (1962), 181–186.

1609 GRIFFIN, Richard W. "Wesleyan College: Its Genesis, 1835–1840." *Ga Hist Q*, 50 (1966), 54–73.

1610 GROVES, Walter A. "Centre College—The Second Phase, 1830–1857." *Filson Club Hist Q*, 24 (1950), 311–334.

1611 GUERRY, Moultrie. "Leonidas Polk and the University of the South." *Hist Mag Prot Epis Church*, 7 (1938), 378–388.

1612 HAMILTON, William B. "Jefferson College and Education in Mississippi, 1798–1817." *J Miss Hist*, 3 (1941), 259–276.

1613 HANCOCK, J. Harrison. "Life and Thought in a Student Organization of the Old South." *Va Mag Hist Biog*, 47 (1939), 315–329.

1614 HEWLETT, James H. "Centre College of Kentucky, 1819–1830." *Filson Club Hist Q*, 19 (1944), 173–191.

1615 HOFSTADTER, Richard, and Wilson SMITH, eds. *American Higher Education: A Documentary History.* 2 vols. Chicago, 1961.

1616 HOLLAND, Lynwood H. "Georgia Military Institute, the West Point of Georgia, 1851–1864." *Ga Hist Q*, 43 (1959), 225–247.

1617 HOLLIS, Daniel W. "James H. Thornwell and the South Carolina College." *Proc S C Hist Assn*, 23 (1953), 17–36.

1618 HOLLIS, Daniel W. *University of South Carolina*. 2 vols. Columbia, S. C., 1951, 1956.

1619 JUDD, Romie D. *The Educational Contributions of Horace Holley*. Nashville, Tenn., 1936.

1620 KNIGHT, Edgar W., ed. "Henry Harisse on Collegiate Education." *N C Hist Rev*, 24 (1947), 58–111.

1621 McGLOTHLIN, William J. "Rev. Horace Holley: Transylvania's Unitarian President, 1818–1827." *Filson Club Hist Q*, 51 (1977), 234–248.

1622 MALONE, Dumas. *The Public Life of Thomas Cooper, 1783–1839*. New York, 1976.

1623 MANSFIELD, Stephen. "Thomas Roderick Dew at William and Mary: 'A Main Prop of that Venerable Institution'." *Va Mag Hist Biog*, 75 (1967), 429–442.

1624 MILLER, James L., Jr. "Transylvania University as the Nation Saw It, 1818–1828." *Filson Club Hist Q*, 34 (1960), 305–318.

1625 MITCHELL, Enoch L. "College Life in Ante-Bellum Tennessee." *W Tenn Hist Soc Pap*, 12 (1958), 5–40.

1626 MORRISON, John L. "Alexander Campbell: Moral Educator of the Middle Frontier." *W Va Hist*, 36 (1975), 187–201.

1627 PATTERSON, Giles J. *Journal of a Southern Student, 1846–1848*. Nashville, Tenn., 1944.

1628 SELLERS, James B. *History of the University of Alabama*. University, Ala., 1953.

1629 SELLERS, James B. "Student Life at the University of Alabama before 1860." *Ala Rev*, 2 (1949), 269–293.

1630 SHAW, Arthur M., Jr. "Rampant Individualism in an Ante-Bellum Southern College." *La Hist Q*, 31 (1949), 877–896.

1631 SONNE, Niels H. *Liberal Kentucky, 1780–1828*. Lexington, Ky., 1939.†

1632 SWINT, Henry L. "Higher Education in the Tennessee-Kentucky Region a Century Ago." *Tenn Hist Q*, 2 (1943), 129–143.

1633 THOMSON, Robert P. "Colleges in the Revolutionary South: The Shaping of A Tradition." *Hist Ed Q*, 10 (1970), 399–412.

1634 WILLS, Elbert V. "Basil Manly, Frederick A. P. Barnard, and the University of Alabama Curriculum Inquiry, 1852–1854." *S Assn Q*, 9 (1954), 306–311.

1635 WOOLVERTON, John F. "Philip Lindsley and the Cause of Education in the Old Southwest." *Tenn Hist Q*, 19 (1960), 3–22.

6. *Education of Women*

1636 BLAIR, Marian H. "Contenporary Evidence—Salem Boarding School, 1834–1844." *N C Hist Rev*, 27 (1950), 142–161.

1637 COHEN, Hennig, ed. *A Barhamville Miscellany: Notes and Documents Concerning the South Carolina Female Collegiate Institute, 1826–1865*. Columbia, S. C., 1956.†

1638 OWSLEY, Frank L. "The Education of a Southern Frontier Girl." *Ala Rev*, 6 (1953), 268–288; 7 (1954), 66–74.

1639 STOKES, Allen. "Education in Young Arkansas: Spring Hill Female Academy." *Ark Hist Q*, 27 (1968), 105–112.

1640 TAYLOR, A. Elizabeth. "Regulations Governing Student Life at the Judson Female Institute during the Decade Preceding the Civil War." *Ala Hist Q*, 3 (1941), 23–29.

1641 UNDERWOOD, Betsy Swint. "The Life of a Young Girl in a Female Academy, 1848–1850." *Tenn Hist Q*, 21 (1962), 162–170.

1642 WOODY, Thomas. *A History of Women's Education in the United States*. 2 vols. New York, 1966.

7. Education of Blacks and Indians

1643 BIRNIE, C. W. "The Education of the Negro in Charleston, South Carolina, before the Civil War." *J Neg Hist*, 12 (1927), 13–21.

1644 BRIGHAM, R. I. "Negro Education in Ante Bellum Missouri." *J Neg Hist*, 30 (1945), 405–420.

1645 KLINGBERG, Frank J. "Early Attempts at Indian Education in South Carolina: A Documentary." *S C Hist Mag*, 61 (1960), 1–10.

1646 PILCHER, George W. "Samuel Davies and the Instruction of Negroes in Virginia." *Va Mag Hist Biog*, 74 (1966), 293–300.

1647 WOODSON, Carter G. *The Education of the Negro Prior to 1861*. Washington D. C., 1919.

8. Trade, Professional, and Adult Education

1648 ATHERTON, Lewis E. "Mercantile Education in the Ante-Bellum South." *Miss Val Hist Rev*, 39 (1953), 623–640.

1649 BAUGHN, Milton L. "An Early Experiment in Adult Education: The Nashville Lyceum, 1830–1832." *Tenn Hist Q*, 11 (1952), 235–245.

1650 DUFFY, John. "Sectional Conflict and Medical Education in Louisiana." *J S Hist*, 23 (1959), 289–306.

1651 EATON, Clement. "A Law Student at Transylvania University, 1810–1812." *Filson Club Hist Q*, 31 (1957), 267–273.

1652 FARMER, Fannie Memory. "The Bar Examination and Beginning Years of Legal Practice in North Carolina, 1820–1860." *N C Hist Rev*, 29 (1952), 159–170.

1653 FARMER, Fannie Memory. "Legal Education in North Carolina, 1820–1860." *N C Hist Rev*, 28 (1951), 271–297.

1654 FARMER, Fannie Memory. "Legal Practice and Ethics in North Carolina, 1820–1860." *N C Hist Rev*, 30 (1953), 329–353.

1655 GRAF, LeRoy P. "The Greeneville Legal Association (1858)." *E Tenn Hist Soc Pub*, 24 (1954), 155–160.

1656 HARRELL, Laura D. S. "The Development of the Lyceum Movement in Mississippi." *J Miss Hist*, 31 (1969), 187–201.

1657 HOLLEY, Howard L. "Medical Education in Alabama." *Ala Rev*, 7 (1954), 245–264.

1658 SCAFIDEL, J. R. "A Georgian in Connecticut: A. B. Longstreet's Legal Education." *Ga Hist Q*, 61 (1977), 222–232.

9. Libraries, Bookstores, and Reading Interests

1659 BRADEN, Waldo M. "Three Southern Readers and Southern Oratory." *S Speech J*, 32 (1966), 31–40.

1660 BRIDGES, Hal. "D. H. Hill's Anti-Yankee Algebra." *J S Hist*, 22 (1956), 220–222.

1661 CANTRELL, Clyde H. "The Reading Habits of Ante-Bellum Southerners." Doctoral dissertation, University of Illinois, 1960.

1662 COMETTI, Elizabeth. "Some Early Best Sellers in Piedmont, North Carolina." *J S Hist*, 16 (1950), 324–337.

1663 DAVIS, Richard Beale. "Literary Tastes in Virginia before Poe." *Wm Mar Q*, 2nd ser., 19 (1939), 55–68.

1664 GOUDEAU, John M. "Booksellers and Printers in New Orleans, 1764–1885." *J Lib Hist*, 5 (1970), 5–19.

1665 GREGORIE, Anne King. "The First Decade of the Charleston Library Society." *Proc S C Hist Assn*, 5 (1935), 3–10.

1666 HOULETTE, William D. "Plantation and Parish Libraries in the Old South." Doctoral dissertation, State University of Iowa, 1933.

1667 HOULETTE, William D. "Sources of Books for the Old South." *Lib Q*, 28 (1959), 194–201.

1668 JONES, James P. " 'I Have Been Reading,' a Literary Journal, 1861." *Ga Rev*, 17 (1963), 173–180.

1669 KASER, David. "A Directory of the Book and Printing Industries in Ante-Bellum Nashville." *Bul N Y Pub Lib*, 70 (1966), 209–217.

1670 McCUTCHEON, Roger P. "Books and Booksellers in New Orleans, 1730–1833." *La Hist Q*, 20 (1937), 606–618.

1671 McCUTCHEON, Roger P. "Libraries in New Orleans, 1771–1833." *La Hist Q*, 20 (1937), 152–158.

1672 McMULLEN, Haynes. "Social Libraries in Ante-Bellum Kentucky." *Reg Ky Hist Soc*, 58 (1960), 97–128.

1673 MUMFORD, Richard L., and Rodney F. ALLEN. "The New Castle Library Company: The Founding and Early History of a Subscription Library, 1811 to 1850." *Del Hist*, 11 (1965), 282–300.

1674 PATRICK, Walton R. "A Circulatory Library of Ante-Bellum Louisiana." *La Hist Q*, 23 (1940), 131–140.

1675 POWELL, William S. "Patrons of the Press: Subscription Book Purchases in North Carolina, 1733–1850." *N C Hist Rev*, 39 (1962), 423–499.

1676 PURCELL, James S. "A Book Pedlar's Progress in North Carolina." *N C Hist Rev*, 29 (1952), 8–23.

1677 SHERMAN, Stuart C. "The Library Company of Baltimore, 1795–1854." *Md Hist Mag*, 39 (1944), 6–24.

1678 SILVER, Rollo G. "The Baltimore Book Trade, 1800–1825." *Bul N Y Pub Lib*, 57 (1953), 114–125, 182–201, 297–305, 349–357.

1679 SPAIN, Frances L. "Early Libraries in Pendleton." *S C Hist Gen Mag*, 50 (1949), 115–126.

1680 SPAIN, Frances L. "Libraries of South Carolina: Their Origins and Early History, 1700–1830." See also Doctoral dissertation, University of Chicago, 1945, bearing the same title.

1681 SPRUILL, Julia C. "The Southern Lady's Library, 1700–1776." *S Atl Q*, 34 (1935), 23–41.

1682 STEINER, Bernard C. "Rev. Thomas Bray and His American Libraries." *Am Hist Rev*, 2 (1896), 59–75.

1683 STERN, Madeleine B. "John Russell: 'Lord John' of Charleston." *N C Hist Rev*, 26 (1949), 285–299.

1684 STEWART, David Marshall. "William T. Berry and His Fabulous Bookstore: An Early Nashville Literary Emporium without Parallel." *Tenn Hist Q*, 37 (1978), 36–48.

1685 STREET, T. Watson. "Thomas Smith: Presbyterian Bookman." *J Presb Hist Soc*, 37 (1959), 1–14.

1686 WHEELER, Joseph T. "Thomas Bray and the Maryland Parochial Libraries." *Md Hist Mag*, 34 (1939), 246–265.

XIV. Scientific Interests

1. Health and Medical Practice

1687 BAIRD, Nancy D. "Asiatic Cholera's First Visit to Kentucky [1832]: A Study in Panic and Fear." *Filson Club Hist Q*, 48 (1974), 228–240.

1688 BREEDEN, James O. "Body Snatchers and Anatomy Professors: Medical Education in Nineteenth-Century Virginia." *Va Mag Hist Biog*, 83 (1975), 321–345.

1689 BREWER, Paul W. "Voluntarism on Trial: St. Louis' Response to the Cholera Epidemic of 1849." *Bul Hist Med*, 49 (1975), 102–122.

1690 CARRIGAN, Jo Ann. "Privilege, Prejudice, and the Strangers' Disease in Nineteenth-Century New Orleans." *J S Hist*, 36 (1970), 568–578.

1691 CARRIGAN, Jo Ann. "The Saffron Scourge: A History of Yellow Fever in Louisiana, 1796–1905." Doctoral dissertation, Louisiana State University, 1961.

1692 CARRIGAN, Jo Ann. "Yellow Fever in New Orleans, 1853: Abstractions and Realities." *J S Hist*, 25 (1959), 339–355.

1693 CHILDS, St. Julien Ravenel. "Notes on the History of Public Health in South Carolina, 1670–1800." *Proc S C Hist Assn*, 2 (1932), 13–22.

1694 COWEN, David L. "Louisiana, Pioneer in the Regulation of Pharmacy." *La Hist Q*, 26 (1943), 330–340.

1695 DUFFY, John. "Eighteenth-Century Carolina Health Conditions." *J S Hist*, 18 (1952), 289–302.

1696 DUFFY, John. "Medical Practice in the Ante Bellum South."*J S Hist*, 25 (1959), 53–72.

1697 DUFFY, John. "A Note on Ante-Bellum Southern Nationalism and Medical Practice." *J S Hist*, 34 (1968), 266–276.

1698 DUFFY, John. *Sword of Pestilence: The New Orleans Yellow Fever Epidemic of 1853*. Baton Rouge, 1966.

1699 DUFFY, John. "Yellow Fever in Colonial Charleston." *S C Hist Gen Mag*, 52 (1951), 189–197.

1700 EVERETT, Donald E. "The New Orleans Yellow Fever Epidemic of 1853." *La Hist Q*, 33 (1950), 380–405.

1701 FARLEY, M. Foster. "The Mighty Monarch of the South: Yellow Fever in Charleston and Savannah." *Ga Rev*, 27 (1973), 56–70.

1702 FOSSIER, A. E. "Charles Aloysius Luzenberg, 1805–1848: A History of Medicine in New Orleans during the Years 1830–1848." *La Hist Q*, 26 (1943), 49–137.

1703 FOSSIER, A. E. "History of Yellow Fever in New Orleans." *La Hist Q*, 34 (1951), 205–215.

1704 GIFFORD, G. E. Jr. "John George F. Wurdemann: A Forgotten Southern Physician-Naturalist." *J Hist Med Al Sc*, 24 (1969), 44–64.

1705 GILLSON, Gordon. "Louisiana, Pioneer in Public Health." *La Hist*, 4 (1963), 207–232.

1706 GRAY, Laman A. "Ephraim McDowell, Father of Abdominal Surgery, Biographical Data." *Filson Club Hist Q*, 43 (1969), 216–229.

1707 HAGGARD, J. Villasana. "Epidemic Cholera in Texas, 1833–1834." *SW Hist Q*, 40 (1937), 216–230.

1708 HAMMOND, E. Ashby. "Notes on the Medical History of Key West, 1822–1832." *Fla Hist Q*, 46 (1967), 93–110.

1709 HARRIS, Seale, and Frances W. BROWIN. *Woman's Surgeon: The Life of J. Marion Sims*. New York, 1950.

1710 HUNTER, John M. "Geophagy in Africa and in the United States: A Culture-Nutrition Hypothesis." *Geog Rev*, 63 (1973), 170–195.

1711 JORDAN, Weymouth T. "Plantation Medicine in the Old South." See **390**.

1712 KIPLE, Kenneth F., and Virginia H. KIPLE. "Black Tongue and Black Men: Pellagra and Slavery in the Antebellum South." See **391**.

1713 LEWIS, Carl P., Jr. "The Baltimore College of Dental Surgery and the Birth of Professional Dentistry, 1840." *Md Hist Mag*, 59 (1964), 268–285.

1714 McCORMACK, Mrs. Arthur T. "Our Pioneer Heroine of Surgery—Mrs. Jane Todd Crawford." *Filson Club Hist Q*, 6 (1932), 109–123.

1715 McLEAR, Patrick E. "The St. Louis Cholera Epidemic of 1849." *Mo Hist Rev*, 63 (1969), 171–181.

1716 MATAS, Rudolph. *The Rudolph Matas History of Medicine in Louisiana*. Ed. John Duffy. 2 vols. Baton Rouge, 1958–1962.

1717 MILNE, John A. "Early Mississippi Physicans." *J Miss Hist*, 18 (1965), 157–174.

1718 MITCHELL, Martha Carolyn. "Health and the Medical Profession in the Lower South, 1845–1860." *J S Hist*, 10 (1944), 424–446.

1719 MORRIS, James P. "An American First: Blood Transfusion in New Orleans in the 1850's." *La Hist*, 16 (1975), 341–360.

1720 PHIFER, Edward W. "Certain Aspects of Medical Practice in Ante-Bellum Burke County." *N C Hist Rev*, 36 (1959), 28–46.

1721 PODOLSKY, Edward. "A Pioneer Southern Surgeon: Ephraim McDowell." *Sew Rev*, 48 (1940), 36–45.

1722 POSTELL, William D. "The Doctor in the Old South." *S Atl Q*, 51 (1952), 393–400.

1723 POSTELL, William D. *The Health of Slaves on Southern Plantations*. See **393**.

1724 RIESS, Karlem. "The Rebel Physiologist—Bennet Dowler." *J Hist Med Al Sci*, 16 (1961), 39–48.

1725 SHRYOCK, Richard H. "Medical Practice in the Old South." *S Atl Q*, 29 (1930), 160–178.

1726 SIKES, Lewright. "Medical Care for Slaves: A Preview of the Welfare State." See **396**.

1727 SIMS, J. Marion. *The Story of My Life*. New York, 1968.

1728 STEPHENS, Lester D. "Of Mercury, Moses, and Medicine: Views of Dr. John M. B. Harden." *Ga Hist Q*, 59 (1975), 402–415.

1729 SUAREZ, Raliegh A. "Health in Rural Ante Bellum Louisiana." *McNeese Rev*, 8 (1956), 84–91.

1730 SWADOS, Felice. "Negro Health on the Ante Bellum Plantations." *Bul Hist Med*, 10 (1941), 460–472.

1731 TAYLOR, Frances Long. *Crawford W. Long and the Discovery of Ether Anesthetic*. New York, 1928.

1732 TWYMAN, Robert W. "The Clay Eater: A New Look at an Old Southern Enigma." *J S Hist*, 37 (1971), 439–448.

1733 WARING, Joseph I. "Asiatic Cholera in Southern Carolina." *Bul Hist Med*, 40 (1966), 459–466.

1734 WARING, Joseph I. "The Yellow Fever Epidemic of Savannah in 1820, with a Sketch of William Coffee Daniell." *Ga Hist Q*, 52 (1968), 398–404.

1735 WHITE, Robert H. "Beginnings of Health and Medical Legislation in Tennessee." *Tenn Hist Q*, 2 (1943), 43–51.

2. *Science and Scientists*

1736 ALLEN, Elsa G. "John Abbot, Pioneer Naturalist of Georgia." *Ga Hist Q*, 41 (1957), 143–157.

1737 BALL, Brenda. "Arkansas Weatherman: Dr. Nathan D. Smith." *Ark Hist Q*, 24 (1965), 67–81.

1738 BERKELEY, Edmund, and Dorothy S. BERKELEY. *Dr. Alexander Garden of Charles Town*. Chapel Hill, 1969.

1739 BOZEMAN, Theodore D. "Joseph LeConte: Organic Science and a 'Sociology for the South'." *J S Hist*, 39 (1973), 565–582.

1740 BROWN, Bahngrell W. "The First Hundred Years of Geology in Mississippi." *S Q*, 13 (1975), 295–302.

1741 CHRISTIAN, Schuyler M. "A Sketch of the History of Science in Georgia." *Ga Rev*, 2 (1948), 415–427; 3 (1949), 57–69.

1742 COBBS, Nicholas H. "The Night the Stars Fell on Alabama." *Ala Rev*, 22 (1939), 147–157.

1743 DAVIES, P. Albert. "Charles Wilkins Short, 1794–1863, Botanist and Physician." *Filson Club Hist Q*, 19 (1945), 131–155, 208–249.

1744 DAVIS, Richard Beale. "Forgotten Scientists in Georgia and South Carolina." *Ga Hist Q*, 27 (1943), 271–284.

1745 DAVIS, Richard Beale. "Forgotten Scientists in Old Virginia." *Va Mag Hist and Biog*, 46 (1938), 97–111.

1746 DUPRÉ, Huntley, *Rafinesque in Lexington, 1819–1826*. Lexington, Ky., 1945.

1747 EATON, Clement. *The Mind of the Old South*. See **286**.

1748 ERNST, William. "William Barton Rogers: Ante Bellum Virginia Geologist." *Va Cav*, 24 (1974), 12–21.

1749 HENDRICKSON, Walter B. "David Dale Owen, Pioneer Geologist of the Middle West." Doctoral dissertation, Harvard University, 1941.

1750 JELLISON, Richard M., and Phillip S. SWARTZ. "The Scientific Interest of Robert W. Gibbes." *S C Hist Mag*, 66 (1965), 77–97.

1751 JOHNSON, Thomas C. *Scientific Interests in the Old South*. Wilmington, Del., 1973.

1752 KLOSE, Nelson. "Dr. Henry Perrine, Tropical Plant Enthusiast." *Fla Hist Q*, 27 (1948), 198–201.

1753 LeCONTE, Joseph. *The Autobiography of Joseph LeConte*. Ed. W. D. Armes. St. Clair Shores, Mich., [1972?].

1754 LEDIN, R. Bruce. "John Loomis Blodgett (1809–1853), a Pioneer Botanist of South Florida." *Tequesta*, 13 (1953), 23–33.

1755 LONGTON, William H. "The Carolina Ideal World: Natural Science and Social Thought in Ante Bellum South Carolina." *Civ War Hist*, 20 (1974), 118–134.

1756 LONGTON, William H. "Some Aspects of Intellectual Activity in Ante-Bellum South Carolina, 1830–1860: An Introductory Study." See **1519**.

1757 MOFFAT, Charles H. "Charles Tait, Planter, Politician, and Scientist of the Old South." *J S Hist*, 14 (1948), 206–233.

1758 PIERS, Ellen. "Girard Troost, Pioneer Scientist." *Peabody J Ed*, 30 (1953), 265–274.

1759 ROBINSON, T. Ralph. "Henry Perrine, Pioneer Horticulturist of Florida." *Tequesta*, 1 (August, 1942), 16–24.

1760 ROGERS, William B. *Life and Letters of William Barton Rogers*. Ed. Emma S. Rogers. 2 vols. New York, [n. d.].

1761 ROSS, Margaret. "The New Madrid Earthquake." *Ark Hist Q*, 27 (1969), 83–104.

1762 STANTON, William. The Leopard's Spots: Scientific Attitudes Toward Race in America. Chicago, 1966.†

1763 STEEDMAN, Marguerite. "John Lining: Pioneer Southern Scientist." *Ga Rev*, 10 (1956), 334–345.

1764 SYDNOR, Charles. *A Gentleman of the Old Natchez Region: Benjamin L. C. Wailes*. Westport, Conn., 1970.

1765 SNYDOR, Charles S. "State Geological Surveys in the Old South." *American Studies in Honor of William Kenneth Boyd*. Duke University. Americana Club. Freeport, N. Y., 1968.

1766 WILLIAMS, Frances Leigh. *Matthew Fontaine Maury, Scientist of the Sea*. New Brunswick, N. J., 1963.

XV. Life in the Old South

1. Recreation and Amusements

1767 ANDERSON, John Q. "Drinking, Fighting, and Fooling—Sidelights of the Social History of Antebellum Louisiana." *La Hist*, 5 (1964), 29–40.

1768 ARRINGTON, Joseph E. "George Brewer's Moving Panorama of the Mammoth Cave and Other Natural Wonders of America." *Filson Club Hist Q*, 39 (1965), 22–45, 151–169.

1769 BERKELEY, Edmund, Jr. "Quoits, the Sport of Gentlemen." *Va Cav*, 15 (Summer 1965), 11–21.

1770 BLANCHARD, Elizabeth A. Cameron, and Manly Wade WELLMAN. *The Life and Times of Sir Archie: The Story of America's Greatest Thoroughbred, 1805–1833.* Chapel Hill, 1958.

1771 BONNER, James C. "The Historical Basis of Southern Military Tradition." *Ga Hist Q,* 9 (1955), 74–85.

1772 BOWEN, Elbert R. "Amusements and Entertainments in Early Missouri." *Mo Hist Rev,* 47 (1953), 307–317.

1773 BOWEN, Elbert R. "The Circus in Early Rural Missouri." *Mo Hist Rev,* 47 (1952), 1–17.

1774 BROWN, Sara Shallenberger. "The Kentucky Thoroughbred." *Filson Club Hist Q,* 25 (1951), 3–23.

1775 CALDWELL, Dorothy J. "Christmas in Early Missouri." *Mo Hist Rev,* 65 (1971), 125–138.

1776 CARPENTER, Charles, ed. "Henry Dana War: Early Diary Keeper of the Kanawha Valley." See **774**.

1777 CHANCE, Elbert. "Fast Horses and Sporting Blood." *Del Hist,* 11 (1964), 149–181.

1778 COULTER, E. Merton. "Boating as a Sport in the Old South." *Ga Hist Q,* 27 (1943), 231–247.

1779 CROOKS, Esther J., and Ruth W. CROOKS. *The Ring Tournament in the United States.* Richmond, Va., 1936.

1780 DAVIS, Edwin A., ed. "A Northern Sojourner's Remembrances of the Mississippi." See **909**.

1781 DODD, Dorothy. Florida in 1845." See **778**.

1782 ELLIOTT, William. *Carolina Sports by Land and Water.* Greenwood, S. C., 1977.

1783 FRANKLIN, John Hope. *The Militant South, 1800–1860.* Cambridge, Mass., 1970.

1784 GOHDES, Clarence, ed. *Hunting in the Old South.* Baton Rouge, 1967.

1785 GREEN, Fletcher M. "Listen to the Eagle Scream: One Hundred Years of the Fourth of July in North Carolina (1776–1876)." *N C Hist Rev,* 31 (1954), 295–320, 529–549.

1786 HARRELL, Laura D. S. "Horse Racing in the Old Natchez District, 1783–1830." *J Miss Hist,* 13 (1951), 123–137.

1787 HARRELL, Laura D. S. "Jockey Clubs and Race Tracks in Antebellum Mississippi." *J Miss Hist,* 28 (1966), 304–318.

1788 HAY, Robert. "Freedom's Jubilee: The Fourth of July in Charleston, 1826–1876." *W Va Hist,* 26 (1965), 207–219.

1789 HAY, Robert P. "A Jubilee for Freeman: The Fourth of July in Frontier Kentucky, 1788–1816." *Reg Ky Hist Soc,* 64 (1966), 169–195.

1790 HOGAN, William R. "Amusements in the Republic of Texas." *J S Hist,* 3 (1937), 397–421.

1791 JOHNSON, Guion Griffis. "Recreational and Cultural Activities in the Ante-Bellum Town of North Carolina." *N C Hist Rev,* 6 (1929), 17–37.

1792 LEWIS, Henry W. "Horses and Horsemen in Northampton before 1900." *N C Hist Rev,* 51 (1974), 125–148.

1793 MILLS, W. H. "The Thoroughbred in South Carolina." *Proc S C Hist Assn*, 7 (1937), 13–24.

1794 MOFFATT, Walter. "Cultural and Recreational Activities in Pioneer Arkansas." *Ark Hist Q*, 13 (1954), 372–385.

1795 ORIONS, H. Harrison. "The Origin of the Ring Tournament in the United States." *Md Hist Mag*, 36 (1941), 263–277.

1796 POSEY, Walter B. "The Public Manners of Ante-Bellum Southerners." See **798**.

1797 PRIOR, Granville T. "Charleston Pastime and Culture during the Nullification Decade, 1822–1832." *Proc S C Hist Assn*, 10 (1940), 36–44.

1798 ROBERTS, B. W. C. "Cockfighting: An Early Entertainment in North Carolina." *N C Hist Rev*, 42 (1965), 306–314.

1799 ROBERTSON, James I., Jr. "Frolics, Fights and Firewater in Frontier Tennessee." *Tenn Hist Q*, 17 (1958), 97–111.

1800 TEDFORD, Harold C. "Circuses in Northwest Arkansas before the Civil War." *Ark Hist Q*, 26 (1967), 244–256.

2. *Travellers, Vacationers, Inns, and Hotels*

1801 BAUGHMAN, James P. "A Southern Spa: Ante-Bellum Lake Ponchartrain." *La Hist*, 3 (1962), 5–32.

1802 BOX, Mrs. Eugene. "Ante-Bellum Travelers in Mississippi." *J Miss Hist*, 17 (1955), 110–126.

1803 BREWSTER, Lawrence F. *Summer Migrations and Resorts of South Carolina Low-Country Planters.* Durham N. C., 1947.

1804 COKER, Robert E. "Springville: A Summer Village of Darlington District." *S C Hist Mag*, 53 (1952), 190–211.

1805 COLEMAN, Kenneth. "Social Life in Georgia in the 1780's." *Ga Rev*, 9 (1955), 217–277.

1806 COULTER, E. Merton. "Madison Springs, Georgia Watering Place." *Ga Hist Q*, 47 (1963), 375–407.

1807 EASTERBY, J. Harold. "South Carolina through New England Eyes: Almira Coffin's Visit to the Low Country in 1851." *S C Hist Gen Mag*, 45 (1944), 127–136.

1808 FRANKLIN, John Hope. *A Southern Odyssey: Travelers in the Antebellum North.* Baton Rouge, 1976.

1809 GARWOOD, Ellen. "Early Texas Inns: A Study in Social Relationships." *SW Hist Q*, 60 (1956), 219–244.

1810 GRIFFITH, Lucille. "Anne Royall in Alabama." *Ala Rev*, 21 (1968), 53–63.

1811 JONES, Ruth I. "Ante-Bellum Watering Places of the Mississippi Gulf Coast." *J Miss Hist*, 18 (1936), 268–301.

1812 JONES, Ruth I. "Hot Springs: Ante-Bellum Watering Place." *Ark Hist Q*, 14 (1955), 3–31.

1813 KIDD, James R. "The History of Salt Sulphur Springs." *W Va Hist*, 15 (1954), 187–257.

1814 KING, Doris E. "The First-Class Hotel and the Age of the Comman Man." *J S Hist*, 23 (1957), 173–188.

1815 KING, Doris E. "Hotels of the Old South, 1793–1860: A Study of the Origin and Development of the First-Class Hotels." Doctoral dissertation, Duke University, 1952.

1816 LATHROP, Barnes F., ed. "A Southern Girl at Saratoga Springs, 1834." *N C Hist Rev*, 15 (1938), 159–161.

1817 McKISSICK, J. Rion. "Some Observations of Travelers on South Carolina, 1800–1860." *Proc S C Hist Assn*, 2 (1932), 44–51.

1818 MATHEWS, Maxine. "Old Inns of East Tennessee." *E Tenn Hist Soc Pub*, 2 (1930), 22–33.

1819 OLDEN, Samuel B., Jr. "Hotels, Inns, and Taverns in Mississippi, 1830–1860." *J Miss Hist*, 5 (1943), 171–184.

1820 PATTON, James W. "Glimpses of North Carolina in the Writings of Northern and Foreign Travelers, 1783–1860." See **919**.

1821 PETERS, Martha A. "The St. Charles Hotel: New Orleans Social Center, 1837–1860." *La Hist*, 1 (1960), 191–211.

1822 PHELPS, Dawson A. "Stands and Travel Accommodations on the Natchez Trace." *J Miss Hist*, 11 (1949), 1–54.

1823 RENIERS, Percival. *The Springs of Virginia*. Chapel Hill, 1941.

1824 ROGERS, Benjamin F. "Florida Seen through the Eyes of Nineteenth Century Travellers." See **799**.

1825 ROGERS, William W., ed. "Florida on the Eve of the Civil War as Seen by a Southern Reporter." *Fla Hist Q*, 39 (1960), 145–158.

1826 SIBLEY, Marilyn M. *Travelers in Texas, 1761–1860*. Austin, Tex., 1967.

1827 STONEY, Samuel G., ed. "Pendleton in the Eighteen Thirties: Selections from the Langdon Cheves Papers." *S C Hist Gen Mag*, 47 (1946), 69–75.

1828 SULZBY, James F., Jr. "Blount Springs: Alabama's Foremost Watering Place of Yesteryear." *Ala Rev*, 2 (1949), 163–175.

1829 WILLIAMS, Jack K. "An Evaluation of Seventeen British Travelers to Ante-Bellum Georgia." *Ga Hist Q*, 35 (1951), 307–318.

1830 WILLIAMS, Jack K. "Georgians as Seen by Ante-Bellum English Travelers." *Ga Hist Q*, 31 (1948), 158–174.

1831 WILLIAMS, Jack K. "Travel in Ante-Bellum Georgia as Recorded by English Visitors." *Ga Hist Q*, 33 (1949), 191–205.

3. Town and City Life

1832 BACON, H. Phillip. "Some Problems of Adjustment to Nashville's Site and Situation, 1780–1860." *Tenn Hist Q*, 15 (1956), 322–329.

1833 BECK, Lewis H. "Griffin: Early Cultural and Military Center of Georgia." *Ga Rev*, 4 (1950), 331–339.

1834 BOMAN, Martha. "A City of the Old South: Jackson, Mississippi, 1850–1860." *J Miss Hist*, 15 (1953), 1–32.

1835 BONNER, James C. *Milledgeville, Georgia's Antebellum Capital*. Athens, Ga., 1978.

1836 BONNER, James C. "Profile of a Late Ante-Bellum Community." *Am Hist Rev*, 49 (1944), 663–680.

1837 BRANNON, Peter A. "Old Glenville: An Early Center of East Alabama Culture." *Ala Rev*, 11 (1958), 255–266.

1838 CAPERS, Gerald M., Jr. *Biography of a River Town: Memphis, Its Heroic Age*. Chapel Hill, 1939.

1839 CAPERS, Gerald M., Jr. "The Rural Lag on Southern Cities." *Miss Q*, 21 (1968), 253–261.

1840 CLARK, John G. *New Orleans, 1718–1812: An Economic History*. Baton Rouge, 1970.

1841 CLINTON, Thomas P. "Early History of Tuscaloosa." *Ala Hist Q*, 1 (1930), 139–147, 169–178.

1842 CURRY, Leonard P. "Urbanization and Urbanism in the Old South: A Comparative View." *J S Hist*, 40 (1974), 43–60.

1843 DAVENPORT, F. Garvin. *Cultural Life in Nashville on the Eve of the Civil War*. Chapel Hill, 1941.

1844 DOHERTY, Herbert J., Jr. "Ante-Bellum Pensacola: 1821–1860." *Fla Hist Q*, 37 (1959), 337–356.

1845 DORSETT, Lyle W., and Arthur H. SHAFFER. "Was the Antebellum South Antiurban? A Suggestion." *J S Hist*, 38 (1972), 93–100.

1846 EARNEST, Grace E. "City Life in the Old South: The British Travelers' Image." Doctoral dissertation, Florida State University, 1966.

1847 EISTERHOLD, John A. "Commercial, Financial and Industrial Macon, Georgia, during the 1840's." *Ga Hist Q*, 53 (1969), 424–441.

1848 FARLEY, M. Foster. "John Elliott Webb, Mayor of Savannah, 1853–1854." *Ga Hist Q*, 53 (1969), 68–77.

1849 FISCHER, Roger A. "Racial Segregation in Ante Bellum New Orleans." *Am Hist Rev*, 74 (1969), 926–937.

1850 FOLMSBEE, Stanley J., and Lucile DEADRICK, "The Founding of Knoxville." *E Tenn Hist Soc Pub*, 13 (1941), 3–20.

1851 GOLDFIELD, David R. "Friends and Neighbors: Urban-Rural Relations in Antebellum Virginia." *Va Cav*, 25 (1975), 14–27.

1852 GOLDFIELD, David R. "Pursuing the American Dream: Cities in the Old South." *The City in Southern History*. Eds. Blaine A. Brownell and David R. Goldfield. Port Washington, N. Y., 1977.

1852a GOLDFIELD, David R. *Urban Growth in the Age of Sectionalism: Virginia, 1847–1861*. Baton Rouge, 1977.

1853 GOLDFIELD, David R. "Urban-Rural Relations in the Old South: The Example of Virginia." *J Urban Hist*, 2 (1976), 146–168.

1854 GREEN, Mary Fulton. "A Profile of Columbia in 1850." *S C Hist Mag*, 70 (1969), 104–121.

1855 GRIFFIN, J. David. "Savannah's City Income Tax." *Ga Hist Q*, 50 (1966), 173–176.

1856 GROENE, Bertram H. "Ante-Bellum Tallahassee: It Was A Gay Time Then." Doctoral dissertation, Florida State University, 1967.

1857 GROTH, Philip. "Plantation Agriculture and the Urbanization of the South." *Rur Soc*, 42 (1977), 206–219.

1858 HAUNTON, Richard H. "Savannah in the 1850's." Doctoral dissertation, Emory University, 1968.

1859 HEARN, Walter C. "Towns in Antebellum Mississippi." Doctoral dissertation, University of Mississippi, 1969.

1860 HENDRICKSON, Walter B. "Culture in Early Arkansas: The Antiquarian and Natural History Society of Little Rock." *Ark Hist Q*, 17 (1858), 21–32.

1861 JAMES, D. Clayton. *Antebellum Natchez*. Baton Rouge, 1968.

1862 JENKINS, William T. "Ante-Bellum Macon and Bibb County, Georgia." Doctoral dissertation, University of Georgia, 1966.

1863 JOHNSON, Guion Griffis. "The Ante-Bellum Town in North Carolina." *N C Hist Rev*, 5 (1928), 372–389.

1864 JORDON, Weymouth T. *Ante-Bellum Alabama: Town and Country*. Tallahassee, Fla., 1957.

1865 JORDAN, Weymouth T. "Early Ante-Bellum Marion: A Black Belt Town." *Ala Hist Q*, 5 (1943), 12–31.

1866 MAHONEY, Nell S. "William Strickland's Introduction to Nashville, 1845." *Tenn Hist Q*, 9 (1950), 46–63.

1867 MALLALIEU, William C. "Origins of Louisville Culture." *Filson Club Hist Q*, 38 (1964), 149–156.

1868 MATTHEWS, James S. "Sequent Occupance in Memphis, Tennessee, 1819–1860." *W Tenn Hist Soc Pap*, 11 (1957), 112–134.

1869 OLIPHANT, Mary C. Simms. "The Genesis of an Up-Country Town." *Proc S C Hist Assn*, 3 (1933), 50–62.

1870 OWENS, Harry P. "Apalachicola: The Beginning." *Fla Hist Q*, (1969), 276–291.

1871 OWENS, Harry P. "Port of Aplachicola." *Fla Hist Q*, 48 (1969), 1–25.

1872 POSEY, Walter B. "The Public Manners of Ante-Bellum Southerners." See **798**.

1873 SMITH, Clarence M. "William Porcher Miles, Progressive Mayor of Charleston, 1855–1857." *Proc S C Hist Assn*, 12 (1942), 30–39.

1874 SPRAGUE, Stuart Seely. "Town Making in the Era of Good Feelings: Kentucky, 1814–1820." *Reg Ky Hist Soc*, 72 (1974), 337–341.

1875 STEEL, Edward M., Jr. "Flush Times in Brunswick, Georgia in the 1830's." *Ga Hist Q*, 39 (1955), 221–339.

1876 STEEN, Ivan D. "Charleston in the 1850's: As Described by British Travelers." *S C Hist Mag*, 71 (1970), 36–45.

1877 STEPHENSON, Wendell H. "Ante-Bellum New Orleans as an Agricultural Focus." *Ag Hist*, 15 (1941), 161–174.

1878 STONE, James H. "Economic Conditions in Macon, Georgia in the 1830's." *Ga Hist Q*, 54 (1970), 209–225.

1879 STONE, James H. "The Economic Development of Holly Springs during the 1840's." *J Miss Hist*, 32 (1970), 341–361.

1880 SUMMERSELL, Charles G. *Mobile, History of a Seaport Town.* University, Ala., 1949.

1881 TREGLE, Joseph G., Jr. "Early New Orleans Society: A Reappraisal." *J S Hist*, 18 (1952), 20–36.

1882 WHEELER, Kenneth W. *To Wear a City's Crown: The Beginning of Urban Growth in Texas, 1836–1865.* Cambridge, Mass., 1968.

1883 WILLIAMS, Clanton W. "Early Ante-Bellum Montgomery: A Black Belt Constituency." *J S Hist*, 7 (1941), 495–525.

1884 WILSON, Charles R. "Cincinnati, a Southern Outpost in 1860–1861." *Miss Val Hist Rev*, 24 (1937), 473–482.

1885 WORLEY, Ted R. "Glimpses of an Old Southwestern Town." *Ark Hist Q*, 8 (1948), 132–159.

1886 YATES, Bowling C. "Macon, Georgia, Inland Trading Center, 1826–1836." *Ga Hist Q*, 55 (1971), 365–377.

4. Law Enforcement

1887 EATON, Clement. "Mob Violence in the Old South." *Miss Val Hist Rev*, 29 (1942), 351–370.

1888 HAYNES, Robert V. "Law Enforcement in Frontier Mississippi." *J Miss Hist*, 22 (1960), 27–42.

1889 HOWINGTON, Arthur F. "Violence in Alabama: A Study of Late Ante-Bellum Montgomery." *Ala Rev*, 27 (1974), 213–231.

1890 SYDNOR, Charles S. "The Southerner and the Laws." *J S Hist*, 6 (1940), 3–23.

1891 WILLIAMS, Jack K. Vogues in Villainy: Crime and Retribution in Ante-Bellum South Carolina. Columbia, S. C., 1959.

5. Fires and Fire Protection

1892 CLARK, John B., Jr. "Fire Protection in Old Knoxville." *E Tenn Hist Soc Pap*, 31 (1959), 32–42.

1893 CLARK, John B., Jr. "Fire Protection in the Old South." Doctoral dissertation, University of Kentucky, 1957.

1894 CLARK, John B., Jr. "From Bucket Brigade to Steam Fire Engine: Fire Fighting in Old Louisville through 1865." *Filson Club Hist Q*, 27 (1955), 103–118.

1895 COULTER, E. Merton. "The Great Savannah Fire of 1820." *Ga Hist Q*, 23 (1939), 1–27.

1896 GAINES, William H., Jr. "The Fatal Lamp, or Panic at the Play." *Va Cav*, 2 (Summer, 1952), 4–8.

1897 LAMPE, Anthony B. "St Louis Volunteer Fire Department, 1820–1850: A Study in the Volunteer Age." *Mo Hist Rev*, 62 (1968), 253–259.

1898 WAGANDT, Charles L. "Fighting Fires the Baltimore Way—A British View of 1862." *Md Hist Mag*, 61 (1966), 257–261.

6. *Dueling*

1899 CARDWELL, Guy A. "The Duel in the Old South: Crux of a Concept." *S Atl Q*, 66 (1967), 50–69.

1900 COLEMAN, J. Winston, Jr. "The Code Duello in Ante-Bellum Kentucky." *Filson Club Hist Q*, 30 (1956), 125–140.

1901 CORTS, Paul R. "Randolph vs Clay: A Duel of Words and Bullets." *Filson Club Hist Q*, 42 (1969), 151–157.

1902 CUMMING, Joseph B. "The Cumming-McDuffie Duels." *Ga Hist Q*, 44 (1969), 18–40.

1903 DOHERTY, Herbert J., Jr. "Code Duello in Florida." *Fla Hist Q*, 29 (1951), 243–252.

1904 EVANS, Richard Xavier. "Smith-Holmes Duel, 1809." *Wm Mar Q*, 2nd ser., 15 (1935), 413–423.

1905 HOWISON, Robert Reid. "Dueling in Virgina." *Wm Mar Q*, 2nd ser., 4 (1924), 217–244.

1906 KENDALL, John S. "According to Code." *La Hist Q*, 23 (1940), 141–161.

1907 KENDALL, John S. "The Humors of the Duello." *La Hist Q*, 23 (1940), 445–470.

1908 LEWIS, Henry W. "The Dugger-Dromgoole Duel." *N C Hist Rev*, 34 (1957), 327–345.

1909 LORD, C. W. "Young Louis Wigfall: South Carolina Politician and Duelist." *S C Hist Mag*, 59 (1958), 96–112.

1910 OSTHAUS, Carl R. "The Ritchie-Pleasants Duel and the Press." *Va Cav*, 26 (1977), 110–123.

1911 RUTLEDGE, Wilmuth S. "Dueling in Ante-Bellum Mississippi." *J Miss Hist*, 26 (1964), 181–191.

1912 SCRIBNER, Robert L. "The Code Duello in Virginia." *Va Cav*, 3 (Autumn, 1953), 28–31.

1913 SHERWOOD, Diana. "The Code Duello in Arkansas." *Ark Hist Q*, 6 (1947), 186–197.

1914 ULMER, S. Sidney. "Some Eighteenth Century South Carolinians and the Duel." *S C Hist Mag*, 60 (1959), 1–9.

1915 WALKER, William C. "The South Carolina College Duel of 1833." *S C Hist Gen Mag*, 52 (1951), 140–142.

1916 WILLIAMS, Jack K. "The Code of Honor in Ante-Bellum South Carolina." *S C Hist Mag*, 54 (1954), 113–128.

XVI. Literature

1. General

1917 BENTLEY, George F. "Printers and Printing in the Southwest Territory, 1790–1796." *Tenn Hist Q*, 8 (1949), 332–344.

1918 BROOKS, Van Wyck. "The South, 1850." *Am Sch*, 16 (1947), 407–417.

1919 BROOKS, Van Wyck. *The World of Washington Irving.* New York, 1950.

1920 CURRENT-GARCIA, Eugene. 'Southern Literary Criticism and the Sectional Dilemma." *J S Hist*, 15 (1949), 325–341.

1921 HOLMAN, C. Hugh. "The Southern as American Writer." *The Southerner as American.* Ed. Charles G. Sellers, Jr. New York, 1966.†

1922 HUBBELL, Jay B. "Literary Nationalism in the Old South." *American Studies in Honor of William Kenneth Boyd.* Duke University. Americana Club. Freeport, N. Y., 1968.

1923 HUBBELL, Jay B. "The Old South Literary Histories." *S Atl Q*, 48 (1949), 452–467.

1924 HUBBELL, Jay B. *The South in American Literature, 1607–1900.* Durham, N. C., 1954.

1925 KORN, BERTRAM W. *Benjamin Levy: New Orleans Printer and Publisher.* Portland, Maine, 1961.

1926 LANDRUM, Grace W. "Sir Walter Scott and His Literary Rivals in the Old South." *Am Lit*, 2 (1930), 256–276.

1927 McMURTRIE, Douglas C. "The Beginning of Printing in Florida." *Fla Hist Q*, 23 (1944), 63–96.

1928 McMURTRIE, Douglas C. *Early Printing in New Orleans, 1764–1810, with a Bibliography of the Issues of the Louisiana Press.* New Orleans, 1929.

1929 McMURTRIE, Douglas C. "A Note on P. Joseph Forster: Pioneer Alabama Printer." *Ala Hist Q*, 5 (1943), 234–239.

1930 McMURTRIE, Douglas C. "A Note on Printing in Kentucky in the Eighteenth Century, with Special Reference to Thomas Parvin . . . ." *Filson Club Hist Q*, 10 (1936), 261–280.

1931 McMURTRIE, Douglas C. "Pioneer Printing in Georgia." *Ga Hist Q*, 16 (1932), 77–113.

1932 McMURTRIE, Douglas C. "Pioneer Printing in Texas." *SW Hist Q*, 35 (1932), 173–193.

1933 OSTERWEIS, Rollin G. *Romanticism and Nationalism in the Old South.* Baton Rouge, 1971.†

1934 PARKS, Edd Winfield. *Ante-Bellum Southern Literary Critics.* Westport, Conn., 1978.

1935 PARKS, Edd Winfield. "Legaré and Grayson: Types of Classical Influence on Criticism in the Old South." *SW Rev*, 22 (1937), 354–365.

1936 PARKS, Edd W. *William Gilmore Simms as Literary Critic.* Athens, Ga., 1961.†

1937 PARRINGTON, Vernon L. *The Romantic Revolution in America, 1800–1860.* New York, 1955. This is vol. 2 of *Main Currents in American Thought.*†

1938 RICE, Otis K. "West Virginia Printers and Their Works, 1790–1830." *W Va Hist*, 14 (1953), 297–338.

1939 SCHMIDT, Martin F. "The Early Printers in Louisville, 1800–1860." *Filson Club Hist Q*, 40 (1966), 307–334.

1940 SIMMS, William G. *The Letters of William Gilmore Simms.* Eds. Mary C. Simms Oliphant, Alfred T. Odell, and T. C. Duncan Eaves. 5 vols. Columbia, S. C., 1952–1956.

1941 SIMMS, William G. *Views and Reviews in Amercian Literature, History and Fiction.* Ed. C. Hugh Holman. Cambridge, Mass., 1962.†

1942 SYDNOR, Charles S. "The Beginning of Printing in Mississippi." *J S Hist*, 1 (1935), 49–55.

1943 TAYLOR, William R. *Cavalier and Yankee: The Old South and American National Character.* New York, 1969.†

1944 TAYLOR, William R. "William Wirt and the Legend of the Old South." *Wm Mar Q*, 3rd ser., 14 (1957), 477–494.

1945 THORNTON, Mary L. "Public Printing in North Carolina, 1749–1815." *N C Hist Rev*, 21 (1944), 181–202.

1946 TRYON, Warren S. "The Publications of Ticknor and Fields in the South, 1840–1865." *J S Hist*, 14 (1948), 305–330.

1947 WELSH, John R. "William Gilmore Simms, Critic of the South." *J S Hist*, 26 (1960), 201–214.

2. *Journals, Newspapers, and Their Editors*

1948 AMBLER, Charles H. *Thomas Ritchie: A Study in Virginia Politics.* New York, 1970.

1949 ANDERSON, John Q. "The Richmond *Compiler*, 1841–1844." *La Hist Q*, 39 (1956), 417–441. Study of a rural antebellum newspaper.

1950 BACARISSE, Charles A. "The Texas *Gazette*, 1829–1831." *SW Hist Q*, 56 (1952), 239–253.

1951 BAKER, Thomas H. "The Early Newspapers of Memphis, Tennessee, 1827–1860." *W Tenn Hist Soc Pap*, 17 (1963), 20–46.

1952 BROWN, Walter L. "Albert Pike, Arkansas Editor." *Ark Hist Q*, 10 (1951), 393–408.

1953 CALHOUN, Richard J. "The Ante-Bellum Literary Twilight: *Russell's Magazine*." *S Lit J*, 3 (Fall, 1970), 89–110.

1954 CARDWELL, Guy A. "Charleston Periodicals, 1795–1860: A Study in Literary Influences." Doctoral dissertation, University of North Carolina, 1936.

LITERATURE

1955 CARSON, Clements. "Four Magazine Centers of the Old South." Master's thesis, Vanderbilt University, 1933.

1956 COHEN, Hennig. *The South Carolina Gazette, 1732–1775.* Columbia, S. C., 1953.

1957 CONGLETON, Betty C. "George D. Prentice: Nineteenth Century Southern Editor." *Reg Ky Hist Soc,* 65 (1967), 94–119.

1958 CONGLETON, Betty C. "The Louisville *Journal:* Its Origin and Early Years." *Reg Ky Hist Soc,* 62 (1964), 87–103.

1959 EATON, Clement. "The Freedom of the Press in the Upper South." *Miss Val Hist Rev,* 18 (1932), 479–499.

1960 ELLIOTT, Robert N. *The Raleigh Register, 1799–1863.* Chapel Hill, 1955.†

1961 ETHRIDGE, Harrison. "Alexander Moseley: Political Editor Extraordinaire." *Va Cav,* 18 (Winter, 1969), 41–47.

1962 FLANDERS, Bertram H. *Early Georgia Magazines.* Athens, Ga., 1944.

1963 FOLK, Edgar E. "W. W. Holden and the North Carolina *Standard,* 1843–1848." *N C Hist Rev,* 19 (1942), 22–47.

1964 FORNELL, Earl W. "Ferdinand Flake: German Pioneer Journalist of the Southwest." *Am-Ger Rev,* 21 (Feb.–Mar., 1955), 25–28.

1965 GRAHAM, Thomas S. "Florida Politics and the Tallahassee Press, 1845–1861." *Fla Hist Q,* 46 (1968), 234–242.

1966 GREEN, Fletcher M. "Duff Green, Militant Journalist of the Old School." *Am Hist Rev,* 52 (1947), 247–264.

1967 GUILDS, John C. "Simms as Editor and Prophet: The Flowering and Early Death of the Southern *Magnolia.*" *S Lit J,* 4 (Spring, 1972), 69–92.

1968 HARRISON, Lowell. "Cassius Marcellus Clay and the *True American.*" *Filson Club Hist Q,* 22 (1948), 30–49.

1969 HOOLE, William Stanley. "The Gilmans and the *Southern Rose.*" *N C Hist Rev,* 11 (1934), 116–128.

1970 JACKSON, David K. *Poe and the Southern Literary Messenger.* New York, 1970.

1971 JACOBS, Robert D. "Campaign for a Southern Literature: The *Southern Literary Messenger.*" *S Lit J,* 2 (Fall, 1969), 66–98.

1972 LOWE, Richard G. "Republican Newspapers in Ante-Bellum Virginia." *W Va Hist,* 28 (1967), 282–284.

1973 LUXON, Norval Neil. "H. Niles, the Man and the Editor." *Miss Val Hist Rev,* 28 (1941), 27–40.

1974 LUXON, Norval Neil. *Niles' Weekly Register: News Magazine of the Nineteenth Century.* Westport, Conn., 1970.

1975 LYON, William H. *The Pioneer Editor in Missouri, 1808–1860.* Columbia, Mo., 1965.

1976 McFARLAND, Daniel M. "North Carolina Newspapers, Editors, and Journalistic Politics, 1815–1835." *N C Hist Rev,* 30 (1953), 376–414.

1977 MILES, Edwin A. "The Mississippi Press in the Jackson Era, 1824–1841." *J Miss Hist,* 19 (1957), 1–20.

1978 MOTT, Frank L. *A History of American Magazines.* 5 vols. Cambridge, Mass., 1938–1968.

1979 NIXON, Herman Clarence. "*DeBow's Review*." *Sew Rev*, 39 (1931), 54–61.

1980 PRIOR, Granville T. "A History of the Charleston *Mercury*, 1822–1852." Doctoral dissertation, Harvard University, 1947.

1981 RHEA, Linda. *Hugh Swinton Legaré, a Charleston Intellectual*. Chapel Hill, 1934.

1982 RILEY, Susan B. "The Hazards of Periodical Publishing in the South during the Nineteenth Century." *Tenn Hist Q*, 21 (1962), 365–376.

1983 RILEY, Susan B. "The Southern Literary Magazine of the Mid-Nineteenth Century." *Tenn Hist Q*, 23 (1964), 221–236.

1984 ROSS, Margaret. *Arkansas Gazette: The Early Years, 1819–1866*. Little Rock, Ark., 1969.

1985 RYAN, Frank W., Jr. "The *Southern Quarterly Review*, 1842–1857: A Study in Thought and Opinion in the Old South." Doctoral dissertation, University of North Carolina, 1956.

1986 SKIPPER, Otis Clark. *J. D. B. DeBow: Magazinist of the Old South*, See **1306**.

1987 STAMPER, James C. "Felix K. Zollicoffer: Tennessee Editor and Politician." *Tenn Hist Q*, 28 (1969), 356–376.

1988 STANDARD, Diffee W. "De Bow's Review, 1846–1880: A Magazine of Southern Opinion." Doctoral dissertation, University of North Carolina, 1970.

1989 STEARNS, Bertha-Monica. "Southern Magazines for Ladies, 1819–1860." *S Atl Q*, 31 (1932), 70–87.

1990 STROUPE, Henry S. "The Religious Press in the South Atlantic States, 1802–1865." Doctoral dissertation, Duke University, 1942.

1991 TALMADGE, John E. "The Barritt Mystery: Partisan Journalism in Ante-Bellum Georgia." *Ga Rev*, 8 (1954), 332–340. Publication of Walker's *Appeal* and the controversy surrounding it.

1992 WALLACE, Wesley H. "Cultural and Social Advertising in Early North Carolina Newspapers." *N C Hist Rev*, 33 (1956), 281–309.

1993 WALLACE, Wesley H. "Property and Trade: Main Themes of Early North Carolina Newspaper Advertisements." *N C Hist Rev*, 32 (1955), 451–482.

1994 WATSON, Harry L. "Early Newspapers of Abbeville District, 1812–1834." *Proc S C Hist Assn*, 10 (1940), 18–35.

1995 WELSH, John R. "An Early Pioneer: Legaré's *Southern Review*." *S Lit J*, 3 (Spring, 1971), 79–97.

3. *Novelists, Short Story and Sketch Writers*

1996 BOHNER, Charles H. *John Pendleton Kennedy: Gentleman from Baltimore*. Baltimore, Md., 1961.

1997 BOHNER, Charles H. "*Swallow Barn*: John P. Kennedy's Chronicle of Virginia Society." *Va Mag Hist Biog*, 68 (1960), 317–330.

LITERATURE

1998 BOYLE, Regis Louise. "Mrs. E. D. E. N. Southworth, Novelist." Doctoral dissertation, Catholic University, 1939.

1999 BRATTON, Mary Jo J. "John Esten Cooke: The Young Writer and the Old South, 1830–1861." Doctoral dissertation, University of North Carolina, 1969.

2000 BRAVERMAN, Howard. "An Unusual Characterization by a Southern Ante-Bellum Writer." *Phylon*, 19 (1958), 171–179. Calvin H. Wiley's novel, *Roanoke*, gives a sympathetic protrayal of a liberty-loving, articulate, and highly intelligent escaped slave.

2001 BRUGGER, Robert J. *Beverly Tucker: Heart over Head in the Old South.* See **1590**.

2002 CARTER, Maude. "A Study of Caroline Lee Hentz, Sentimentalist of the Fifties." Master's thesis, Duke University, 1942.

2003 CURRENT-GARCIA, Eugene. "Alabama Writers in the *Spirit.*" *Ala Rev*, 10 (1957), 243–269.

2004 CURRENT-GARCIA, Eugene. " 'York's Tall Son' and His Southern Correspondents." *Am Q*, 7 (1955), 371–384.

2005 DAVIS, Curtis C. *Chronicler of the Cavaliers: A Life of the Virginia Novelist, Dr. William A. Caruthers.* Richmond, Va., 1953.

2006 EATON, Clement. *The Mind of the Old South.* See **286**.

2007 EBY, Cecil D. *"Porte Crayon": The Life of David Hunter Strother.* Westport, Conn., 1973.

2008 FRENCH, Warren G. "A Sketch of the Life of Joseph Holt Ingraham." *J Miss Hist*, 11 (1949), 155–171.

2009 HOLMAN, C. Hugh. "William Gilmore Simms's Theory and Practice of Historical Fiction." Doctoral dissertation, University of North Carolina, 1950.

2010 JULIAN, Grace L. "Southern Novels, 1850–1855: A Study in Culture." Master's thesis, Tulane University, 1942. Emphasis is upon the writings of Caroline Lee Hentz and Mrs. E. D. E. N. Southworth.

2011 KENNEDY, John Pendleton. *Horse-Shoe Robinson.* Ed. Ernest E. Leisy. New York, 1962.

2012 McLEAN, Robert C. *George Tucker: Moral Philosopher and Man of Letters.* Chapel Hill, 1961.

2013 PAINE, Gregory L., ed. *Southern Prose Writers.* Freeport, N. Y., 1969.

2014 PREBLE, Jack. "Introducing Porte Crayon."*W Va Hist*, 31 (1970), 125–130.

2015 RIDGELY, Joseph Vincent. *John Pendleton Kennedy.* Boston, 1966.

2016 SIMMS, William Gilmore. *The Yemassee: A Romance of Carolina.* Ed. C. Hugh Holman. Boston, 1961.

2017 [STROTHER, David Hunter]. *The Old South, Illustrated.* Ed. Cecil D. Eby. Chapel Hill, 1969.

2018 TUCKER, Nathaniel Beverley. *The Partisan Leader: A Tale of the Future.* Ed. C. Hugh Holman. Chapel Hill, 1971.

2019 TURRENTINE, Percy W. "Life and Works of Nathaniel Beverley Tucker." Doctoral dissertation, Harvard University, 1952.

2020 WAKELYN, Jon L. "William Gilmore Simms, the Artist as Public Man: A Political Odyssey, 1830–1860." Doctoral dissertation, Rice University, 1966.

2021 WALKER, William E. "John Esten Cooke: A Critical Biography." Doctoral dissertation, Vanderbilt University, 1957.

2022 WEATHERSBY, Robert W., II. "Joseph Holt Ingraham: A Critical Introduction to the Man and His Works." Doctoral dissertation, University of Tennessee, 1974.

4. Poets

2023 ALLEN, John D. *Philip Pendleton Cooke.* Chapel Hill, 1942.

2024 DAMON, S. Foster. *Thomas Holley Chivers: Friend of Poe.* New York, 1930.

2025 MABBOTT, T. O., and Frank Lester PLEADWELL. *The Life and Works of Edward Coote Pinkney.* New York, 1926.

2026 MOORE, Rayburn S. "Paul Hamilton Hayne." *Ga Rev,* 22 (1968), 106–124.

2027 NIXON, Herman Clarence. *Alexander Beaufort Meek: Poet, Orator, Journalist, Historian, Statesman.* Auburn, Ala., 1910.

2028 PARKS, Edd Winfield. *Southern Poets.* New York, 1936.

2029 QUINN, Arthur H. *Edgar Allen Poe: A Critical Biography.* New York, 1969.

2030 RICHARDSON, Edgar P. *Washington Allston: A Study of the Romantic Artist in America.* Chicago, 1948.

2031 RILEY, Susan B. *The Life and Works of Albert Pike to 1860.* Nashville, Tenn., 1934.

2032 STARKE, Aubrey H. *Sidney Lanier.* Chapel Hill, 1933.

2033 WATTS, Charles H. *Thomas Holley Chivers: His Literary Career and His Poetry.* Athens, Ga., 1956.

2034 WAUCHOPE, George A. *Henry Timrod: Man and Poet.* Columbia, S. C., 1915.

2035 WELSH, John R. "Washington Allston, Cosmopolite and Early Romantic." *Ga Rev,* 21 (1967), 491–502.

2036 WELSH, John R. "Washington Allston: Expatriate South Carolinian." *S C Hist Mag,* 57 (1966), 84–98.

5. Humorists

2037 ANDERSON, John Q., ed. and comp. *With the Bark On: Popular Humor of the Old South.* Nashville, Tenn., 1967.

2038 BETTERSWORTH, John K. "The Humor of the Old Southwest: Yesterday and Today." *Miss Q,* 17 (1964), 87–94.

2039 BLAIR, Walter. "Traditions in Southern Humor." *Am Q,* (1953), 132–142.

2040 BUDD, Louis J. "Gentlemanly Humorists of the Old South." *S Folklore Q,* 17 (1953), 232–240.

2041 CLARK, Thomas D. "Humor in the Stream of Southern History." *Miss Q*, 13 (1960), 176–188.

2042 COHEN, Hennig, and William B. DILLINGHAM, eds. *Humor of the Old Southwest*. Boston, 1964.

2043 CURRENT-GARCIA, Eugene. "Newspaper Humor in the Old South, 1835–1855." *Ala Rev*, 2 (1949), 102–121.

2044 CURRENT-GARCIA, Eugene. "Thomas Bangs Thorpe and the Literature of the Ante-Bellum Southwestern Frontier." *La Hist Q*, 39 (1956), 199–222.

2045 EATON, Clement. "Humor of the Southern Yeoman." *Sew Rev*, 49 (1941), 173–183.

2046 EATON, Clement. *The Mind of the Old South*. See **286**.

2047 ELLISON, George R. "William Tappan Thompson and the *Southern Miscellany*, 1842–1844." *Miss Q*, 23 (1970), 155–168.

2048 HARRIS, George W. *High Times and Hard Times: Sketches and Tales*. Ed. M. Thomas Inge. New York, 1976.

2049 HARRIS, George W. *Sut Lovingood's Yarns*. Ed. M. Thomas Inge. New Haven, Conn., 1966.†

2050 HOOLE, W. Stanley. *Alias Simon Suggs: The Life and Times of Johnson Jones Hooper*. Westport, Conn., 1970.

2051 HUDSON, Arthur P., ed. *Humor of the Old Deep South*. 2 vols. Port Washington, N. Y., 1970.

2052 JORDAN, Philip D. "Humor of the Backwoods, 1820–1840." *Miss Val Hist Rev*, 25 (1938), 25–38.

2053 MEINE, Franklin J., ed. *Tall Tales of the Southwest: An Anthology of Southern and Southwestern Humor, 1830–1860*. St. Clair Shores, Mich., 1971.

2054 MILLER, Henry P. "The Life and Works of William Tappan Thompson." Doctoral dissertation, University of Chicago, 1942.

2055 PARKS, Edd Winfield. "The Intent of the Ante-Bellum Southern Humorist." *Miss Q*, 13 (1960), 163–168.

2056 RICKELS, Milton. *George Washington Harris*. New York, 1965.†

2057 RICKELS, Milton. *Thomas Bangs Thorpe: Humorist of the Old Southwest*. Baton Rouge, 1962.

2058 STEWART, Samuel B. "Joseph Glover Baldwin." Doctoral dissertation, Vanderbilt University, 1942.

2059 WADE, John D. *Augustus Baldwin Longstreet: A Study of the Development of Culture in the South*. Athens, Ga., 1969.

2060 YATES, Norris. *William T. Porter and the "Spirit of the Times": A Study of Big Bear School of Humor*. New York, 1977.

6. *Historians*

2061 ANDERSON, Charles R. "Charles Gayarré and Paul Hayne: The Last Literary Cavaliers." *American Studies in Honor of William Kenneth Boyd*. Duke University. Americana Club. Freeport, N. Y., 1969.

2062 EATON, Clement. *The Waning of the Old South Civilization.* See **852**.

2063 HESSELTINE, William B. "Lyman Draper and the South." *J S Hist*, 19 (1953), 20–31.

2064 HESSELTINE, William B. "The Mississippi Career of Lyman C. Draper." *J Miss Hist*, 15 (1953), 165–180.

2065 KOCH, Adrienne. "The Versatile George Tucker." *J S Hist*, 29 (1963), 502–512. An essay review of Robert C. McLean's biography of Tucker.

2065a McLEAN, Robert C. *George Tucker: Moral Philosopher and Man of Letters.* See **2012**.

2066 OWSLEY, Frank L., Jr., "Albert J. Pickett: Planter-Historian of the Old South." *La Stud*, 8 (1969), 158–184.

2067 SOCOLA, Edward M. "Charles E. A. Gayarré: A Biography." Doctoral dissertation, University of Pennsylvania, 1954.

2068 YEARNS, Wilfred B., Jr. "Charles Gayarré, Louisiana's Literary Historian." *La Hist Q*, 33 (1950), 255–268.

7. Southern Speech Patterns; Southern Oratory

2069 CRUM, Mason. *Gullah: Negro Life in the Carolina Sea Islands.* Durham, N. C., 1940.

2070 DALE, Edward E. "The Speech of the Pioneers." *Ark Hist Q*, 6 (1947), 117–131.

2071 ELIASON, Norman E. *Tarheel Talk: An Historical Study of the English Language in North Carolina.* Chapel Hill, 1956.

2072 GREET, W. Cabell. "Southern Speech." *Culture in the South.* Ed. W. T. Couch. Westport, Conn., 1970.

2073 JOHNSON, Guy B. *Folk Culture on St. Helena Island, South Carolina.* Chapel Hill, 1930.

2074 KEPHART, Horace. *Our Southern Highlanders.* Ed. George Ellison. Knoxville, Tenn., 1976.

2075 MATHEWS, Mitford M. *Some Sources of Southernisms.* University, Ala., 1948.

2075a *Oratory in the Old South.* Ed. Waldo W. Braden. Baton Rouge, 1970.

2076 RANDOLPH, Vance, and George P. WILSON. *Down in the Holler: A Gallery of Ozark Folk Speech.* Norman, Okla., 1953.

2077 WOOD, Gordon R. "Dialect Contours in the Southern States." *Am Speech*, 38 (1963), 243–256.

XVII. Culture and the Arts

1. General

2078 BETTS, Edwin M. "Jefferson's Gardens at Monticello." *Ag Hist*, 19 (1945), 180–182.

2079 BOWES, Frederick P. *The Culture of Early Charleston.* Westport, Conn., 1978.

2080 BRIDWELL, Margaret M. "Kentucky Silversmiths before 1850." *Filson Club Hist Q*, 16 (1942), 111–126.

2081 BURTON, E. Milby. *Charleston Furniture, 1700–1825.* 2nd ed. Columbia, S. C., 1970.

2082 BURTON, E. Milby. *South Carolina Silversmiths, 1690–1860.* Rutland, Vt., 1968.

2083 CUTTEN, George B. *Silversmiths of North Carolina, 1696–1850.* Rev. ed., Mary R. Peacock. Raleigh, N. C., 1973.

2084 DAVIS, Richard Beale. *Intellectual Life in Jefferson's Virginia, 1790–1830.* Knoxville, Tenn., 1973.

2085 FLOURNOY, Mary H. "Art in the Early South." *S Atl Q*, 29 (1930), 402–418.

2086 GARRETT, Romeo B. "African Survivals in American Culture." *J Neg Hist*, 51 (1966), 239–245.

2087 HANCOCK, Harold B. "Furniture Craftsmen in Delaware Records." *Winterthur Port*, 9 (1974), 175–212.

2088 HINDES, Ruthanna. "Delaware Silversmiths, 1700–1850." *Del Hist*, 12 (1967), 247–308.

2089 LAGOUDAKIS, Charilaos. "Greece in Georgia." *Ga Hist Q*, 47 (1963), 189–192.

2090 MILES, Edwin A. "The Old South and the Classical World." *N C Hist Rev*, 48 (1971), 258–275.

2091 MILLER, Lillian B. *Patrons and Patriotism: The Encouragement of the Fine Arts in the United States, 1790–1860.* Chicago, 1974.†

2092 NEAL, Julia. "Shaker Industries in Kentucky." *Antiques*, 105 (1974), 603–611.

2093 SCAFIDI, Polly J. "Notes on Delaware Cabinetmakers." *Del Hist*, 14 (1971), 262–278.

2094 SHRYOCK, Richard H. "Cultural Factors in the History of the South." *J S Hist*, 5 (1930), 333–346.

2095 TAYLOR, Rosser H. *Ante-Bellum South Carolina.* See **803**.

2. *Architecture*

2096 ALLCOTT, John V. "Architectural Developments at 'Montrose' in the 1850's." *N C Hist Rev*, 42 (1965), 85–95.

2097 ANDREWS, Alfred J. "Gideon Shryock, Kentucky Architect and Greek Revival Architecture in Kentucky." *Filson Club Hist Q*, 18 (1944), 67–77.

2098 BEIRNE, Rosamond R. "William Buchland, Architect of Virginia and Maryland." *Md Hist Mag*, 41 (1946), 199–218.

2099 BONNER, James C. "Plantation Architecture of the Lower South on the Eve of the Civil War." *J S Hist*, 11 (1945), 370–388.

2100 COLEMAN, J. Winston, Jr. "Early Lexington Architects and Their Work." *Filson Club Hist Q*, 42 (1968), 222–234.

2101 COOPER, J. Wesley. *Ante-Bellum Houses of Natchez*. Natchez, Miss., 1970.

2102 FORMAN, Henry C. *The Architecture of the Old South: The Medieval Style, 1585–1850*. New York, 1957.

2103 GALLAGHER, Helen M. P. *Robert Mills*. New York, 1966.

2104 HAMLIN, Talbot F. *Benjamin Henry Latrobe*. New York, 1955.

2105 HAMLIN, Talbot F. "Benjamin Henry Latrobe: The Man and the Architect." *Md Hist Mag*, 37 (1942), 339–360.

2106 HAMLIN, Talbot F. *Greek Revival Architecture in America*. New York, 1944.†

2107 KIMBALL, Fiske. *American Architecture*. New York, 1970.

2108 KIMBALL, Fiske. *Domestic Architecture of the American Colonies and of the Early Republic*. Magnolia, Mass., [n. d.].

2109 LANCASTER, Clay. *Ante Bellum Houses of the Bluegrass*. Lexington, Ky., 1961.

2110 LANCASTER, Clay. *Back Streets and Pine Forests: The Work of John McMurtry*. Lexington, Ky., 1956.

2111 LINLEY, John. *Architecture of Middle Georgia: The Oconee Area*. Athens, Ga., 1972.

2112 MAHONEY, Nell S. "William Strickland and the Building of Tennessee's Capitol, 1945–1854." *Tenn Hist Q*, 4 (1945), 99–153.

2113 MASSEY, James C. "Robert Mills Documents, 1823: A House for Ainsley Hall in Columbia, South Carolina." *J Soc Arch Hist*, 22 (1963), 228–232.

2114 MUMFORD, Lewis. *The South in Architecture*. New York, 1967.

2115 NEWCOMB, Rexford. Architecture in Old Kentucky. Urbana, Ill., 1952.

2116 RUSK, William S. "Benjamin H. Latrobe and the Classical Influence in His Work." *Md Hist Mag*, 31 (1936), 126–154.

2117 SCULLY, Arthur, Jr. *James Dakin, Architect: His Career in New York and the South*. Baton Rouge, 1973.

2118 SIMONS, Albert, and Samuel LAPHAM, Jr., eds. *The Early Architecture of Charleston*, Columbia, S. C., 1970.

2119 SMITH, Joseph Frazer. *White Pillars: Early Life and Architecture of the Lower Mississippi Valley*. New York, 1941.

2120 WATERMAN, Thomas T., and John A. BARROWS. *Domestic Colonial Architecture of Tidewater Virginia*. New York, 1968.

3. *Painting and Sculpture*

2121 ADAMS, A. B. *John James Audubon, A Biography.* New York, 1966.

2122 ALLCOTT, John V. "Robert Donaldson, the First North Carolinian to Become Prominent in the Arts." *N C Hist Rev*, 52 (1975), 333–366.

2123 BLOCH, E. Maurice. *George Caleb Bingham: The Evolution of an Artist.* Berkeley, Cal., 1967.

2124 COLEMAN, J. Winston, Jr. "Edward Troye: Kentucky Animal Painter." *Filson Club Hist Q*, 33 (1959), 32–45.

2125 COLEMAN, J. Winston, Jr. "Samuel Woodson Price: Kentucky Portrait Painter." *Filson Club Hist Q*, 23 (1949), 5–24.

2126 COLEMAN, J. Winston, Jr. *Three Kentucky Artists: Hart, Price, and Troye.* Lexington, Ky., 1974.

2127 DEMOS, John. "George Caleb Bingham: The Artist as Social Historian." *Am Q*, 17 (1965), 218–228.

2128 FLEXNER, James T. *The Light of Distant Skies, 1700–1835.* New York, 1969.

2129 FORD, Alice. *John James Audubon.* Norman, Okla., 1964.

2130 FRASER, Charles. *Charleston Sketchbook.* 3rd ed. Charleston, S. C., 1972.

2131 HEITE, Edward F. "Painter of the Old Dominion [John Gadsby Chapman]." *Va Cav*, 17 (Winter, 1968), 11–19, and "Chapman Paints the Washington Legend—A Portfolio," 20–29.

2132 JOHNS, Elizabeth. "Washington Allston: Method, Imagination, and Reality." *Wintherthur Port*, (1977), 1–18.

2133 LONGAKER, Jon D. "Painting in the South—A Double Portrait." *Art and Music in the South.* Longwood College, Institute of Southern Culture. Farmville, Va., 1961.

2134 McDERMOTT, John F. *George Caleb Bingham, River Portraitist.* Norman, Okla., 1959.

2135 MIDDLETON, Margaret S. *Henrietta Johnson of Charles Town, South Carolina: America's First Pastellist.* Columbia, S. C., 1966.

2136 PINCKNEY, Pauline A. *Painting in Texas: The Nineteenth Century.* Austin, Tex., 1967.

2137 PLEASANTS, J. Hall. "Joshua Johnston, The First American Negro Portrait Painter." *Md Hist Mag*, 37 (1942), 121–149.

2138 PRICE, Prentiss. "Samuel Shaver: Portrait Painter." *E Tenn Hist Soc Pub*, 24 (1952), 92–105.

2139 RICHARDSON, Edgar P. *Washington Allston: A Study of the Romantic Artist in America.* See **2030**.

2140 RUDOLPH, Marilou A. "George Cooke and His Paintings." *Ga Hist Q*, 44 (1960), 117–153.

2141 RUTLEDGE, Anna Wells. *Artists in the Life of Charleston.* Philadelphia, Pa., 1949.

2142 SELLERS, Charles C. *Charles Willson Peale.* New York, 1969.

2143 SIMMS, L. Moody, Jr. "John Blennerhassett Martin, William Garl Brown and Flavius James Fisher: Three Nineteenth-Century Virginia Portraitists." *Va Cav*, 25 (Autumn, 1975), 72–79.

2144 SIMMS, L. Moody, Jr. "Talented Virginians: The Peticolas Family." *Va Mag Hist Biog*, 85 (1977), 55–64.

2145 WEEKS, Mangum. "On John James Audubon." *S Atl Q*, (1942), 76–87.

2146 WELSH, John R. "Washington Allston, Cosmopolite and Early Romantic." See **2035**.

2147 WELSH, John R. "Washington Allston: Expatriate South Carolinian." See **2036**.

2148 WRIGHT, Nathalia. "Francis Kinloch: A South Carolina Artist." *S C Hist Mag*, 61 (1960), 99–100.

4. Music

2149 CRIPE, Helen. *Thomas Jefferson and Music*. Charlottesville, Va., 1974.

2150 EADER, Thomas S. "Baltimore Organs and Organ Builders." *Md Hist Mag*, 65 (1970), 263–282.

2151 FISHER, Miles Mark. *Negro Slave Songs in the United States*. Ed. Ray A. Billington. Secaucus, N. J., 1969.†

2152 GOTTSCHALK, Louis Moreau. *Notes of a Pianist*. Ed. Jeanee Behrend. New York, 1964.

2153 HALL, Harry H. "The Moravian Wind Ensemble: Distinctive Chapter in America's Music." Doctoral dissertation, George Peabody College for Teachers, 1967.

2154 HINDMAN, John J. "Concert Life in Ante-Bellum Charleston." Doctoral dissertation, University of North Carolina, 1971.

2155 JACKSON, George P., ed. *White Spirituals in the Southern Uplands*. New York, 1965.†

2156 KMEN, Henry A. *Music in New Orleans: The Formative Years, 1791–1841*. Baton Rouge, 1966.

2157 LaFAR, Margaret F. "Lowell Mason's Varied Activities in Savannah." *Ga Hist Q*, 28 (1944), 113–137.

2158 LOGGINS, Vernon. *Where the Word Ends*. Baton Rouge, 1977.†

2159 McCORKLE, Donald M. "The 'Collegium Musicum' in Salem: Its Music, Musicans, and Importance." *N C Hist Rev*, 33 (1956), 483–498.

2160 MAURER, Maurer. "Music in Wachovia, 1753–1880." *Wm Mar Q*, 3rd ser., 8 (1951), 214–227.

2161 PROPHIT, Willie. "The Crescent City's Charismatic Celebrity: Louis Moreau Gottschalk's New Orleans Concerts, Spring 1853." *La Hist*, 12 (1971), 243–254.

2162 ROSE, Kenneth. "Jenny Lind, Diva." *Tenn Hist Q*, 8 (1949), 34–48.

2163 ROSE, Kenneth. "A Nashville Musical Decade, 1830–1840." *Tenn Hist Q*, 2 (1943), 216–231.

2164 SIMMS, David McD. "The Negro Spiritual: Origins and Themes." *J Neg Ed*, 35 (1966), 35–41.

2165 SIMMS, L. Moody, Jr. "Talented Virginians: The Peticolas Family." See **2144**.

5. *Theatre*

2166 ARMISTEAD, Margaret B. "The Savannah Theatre—Oldest in America." *Ga Rev*, 7 (1953), 50–56.

2167 BRISTOW, Eugene K. "Variety Theatre in Memphis, 1859–1862." *W Tenn Hist Soc Pap*, 13 (1959), 117–127.

2168 CURTIS, Mary Julia. "Charles-Town's Church Street Theatre." *S C Hist Mag*, 70 (1969), 149–154.

2169 DAVIS, Richard Beale. *Intellectual Life in Jefferson's Virginia, 1798–1830.* See **2084**.

2170 DODD, William G. "Theatrical Entertainment in Early Florida." *Fla Hist Q*, 25 (1946), 121–174.

2171 DORMON, James H., Jr. *Theatre in the Ante-Bellum South, 1815–1861.* Chapel Hill, 1967.

2172 EDWALL, Harry R. "The Golden Age of Minstrelsy in Memphis: A Reconstruction." *W Tenn Hist Soc Pap*, 9 (1955), 29–47.

2173 FREE, Joseph M. "The Ante-Bellum Theatre of the Old Natchez Region." *J Miss Hist*, 5 (1943), 14–27.

2174 GATES, William B. "Performances of Shakespeare in Ante-Bellum Mississippi." *J Miss Hist*, 5 (1943), 28–37.

2175 GATES, William B. "The Theatre in Natchez." *J Miss Hist*, 3 (1941), 71–129.

2176 HILL, Raymond S. "The Memphis Theatre—First Decades (1835–1846)." *W Tenn Hist Soc Pap*, 9 (1955), 48–58.

2177 HILL, West T., Jr. *The Theatre in Early Kentucky, 1790–1820.* Lexington, Ky., 1971.

2178 HOGAN, William R. "The Theatre in the Republic of Texas." *SW Rev*, 19 (1934), 374–401.

2179 HOOLE, William Stanley. *The Ante-Bellum Charleston Theatre.* University, Ala., 1946.

2180 HOOLE, William Stanley. "Charleston Theatres." *SW Rev*, 25 (1940), 193–204.

2181 HOOLE, William Stanley. "Two Famous Theatres of the Old South." *S Atl Q*, 36 (1937), 273–277.

2182 NELLIGAN, Murray H. "American Nationalism on the Stage: The Plays of George Washington Parke Custis (1781–1857)." *Va Mag Hist Biog*, 58 (1950), 299–324.

2183 RANKIN, Hugh F. *The Theatre in Colonial America.* Chapel Hill, 1965.

2184 RULFS, Donald J. "The Ante-Bellum Professional Theatre in Fayetteville." *N C Hist Rev*, 31 (1954), 125–133.

2185 RULFS, Donald J. "The Ante-Bellum Professional Theatre in Raleigh." *N C Hist Rev*, 29 (1952), 344–358.

2186 STOKES, D. Allen. "The First Theatrical Season in Arkansas: Little Rock, 1838–1839." *Ark Hist Q*, 23 (1964), 166–183.

2187 WATSON, Charles S. "Stephen Cullen Carpenter, First Drama Critic of the Charleston Courier." *S C Hist Mag*, 69 (1968), 243–252.

2188 WEISERT, John J. "Beginnings of German Theatricals in Louisville." *Filson Club Hist Q*, 26 (1952), 347–359.

XVIII. Religion

1. General

2189 BOLES, John B. *The Great Revival, 1787–1805*. Lexington, Ky., 1972.

2190 BOST, George H. "Samuel Davies, the South's Great Awakener." *J Presb Hist Soc*, 33 (1955), 135–155.

2191 BRUCE, Dickson D., Jr. *And They All Sang Hallelujah: Plain-Folk Camp-Meeting Religion, 1800–1845*. Knoxville, Tenn., 1974.

2192 BRUCE, Dickson D., Jr. "Religion, Society and Culture in the Old South: A Comparative View." *Am Q*, 26 (1974), 399–416.

2193 DesCHAMPS, Margaret Burr. "The Church as a Social Center." *J Presb Hist Soc*, 32 (1953), 157–165.

2194 EATON, Clement. "The Ebb of the Great Revival." *N C Hist Rev*, 23 (1946), 1–12.

2195 EATON, Clement. *The Mind of the Old South*. See **286**.

2196 GEWEHR, Wesley M. *The Great Awakening in Virginia, 1740–1790*. Magnolia, Mass., 1965.

2197 GILLESPIE, Neal C. *The Collapse of Orthodoxy: The Intellectual Ordeal of George Frederick Holmes*. Charlottesville, Va., 1972.

2198 GILLESPIE, Neal C. "The Spiritual Odyssey of George Frederick Holmes: A Study of Religious Conservatism in the Old South." *J S Hist*, 32 (1966), 291–307.

2199 HOLIFIELD, E. Brooks. *The Gentlemen Theologians: American Theology in Southern Culture, 1795–1860*. Durham, N. C., 1978.

2200 JOHNSON, Charles A. *The Frontier Camp Meeting*. Dallas, Tex, 1955.

2201 JOHNSON, Charles A. "The Frontier Camp Meeting: Contemporary and Historical Appraisals, 1805–1840." *Miss Val Hist Rev*, 37 (1950), 91–110.

2202 JOHNSON, Guion Griffis. "The Camp Meeting in Ante-Bellum North Carolina." *N C Hist Rev*, 10 (1933), 95–110.

2203 JOHNSON, Guion Griffis. "Revival Movements in Ante-Bellum North Carolina." *N C Hist Rev*, 10 (1933), 21–43.

2204 MATHEWS, Donald G. *Religion in the Old South*. Chicago, 1977.

2205 MATHEWS, Donald G. "Religion in the Old South: Speculation on Methodology." *S Atl Q*, 73 (1974), 34–52.

2206 MOORE, Margaret DesChamps. "Religion in Mississippi in 1860." *J Miss Hist*, 22 (1960), 223–238.

2207 MOUNGER, Dwyn. "History as Interpreted by Stephen Elliott." *Hist Mag Prot Epis Church*, 44 (1975), 285–317.

2208 NORTON, Wesley. "Religious Newspapers in Antebellum Texas." *SW Hist Q*, 79 (1975), 145–165.

2209 POSEY, Walter B. "The Earthquake of 1811 and Its Influence on Evangelistic Methods in the Churches of the Old South." *Tenn Hist Mag*, 2nd ser., 1 (1931), 107–114.

2210 POSEY, Walter B. *Frontier Mission: A History of Religion West of the Southern Appalachians to 1861.* Lexington, Ky., 1966.

2211 POSEY, Walter B. *Religious Strife on the Southern Frontier.* Baton Rouge, 1965.

2212 ROGERS, Tommy W. "Frederick A. Ross: Huntsville's Belligerent Clergyman." *Ala Rev*, 22 (1969), 53–67.

2213 SONNE, Niels H. *Liberal Kentucky, 1780–1828.* See **1631**.

2214 STOKES, Durward T. "North Carolina and the Great Revival of 1800." *N C Hist Rev*, 43 (1966), 401–412.

2215 STROUPE, Henry S. "The Beginnings of Religious Journalism in North Carolina, 1823–1865." *N C Hist Rev*, 30 (1953), 1–22.

2216 STROUPE, Henry S. *The Religious Press in the South Atlantic States, 1802–1865: An Annotated Bibliography with Historical Introduction and Notes.* Durham, N. C., 1956.

2217 SUAREZ, Raleigh A. "Religion in Rural Louisiana, 1850–1860." *La Hist Q*, 38 (1955), 55–63.

2218 SWEET, William W. *Religion in the Development of American Culture, 1765–1840.* Magnolia, Mass., 1963.

2219 SWEET, William W. *The Story of Religion in America.* Grand Rapids, Mich., 1973. Original edition bears the title *Story of Religions in America.*†

2220 WALHOUT, Clarence P. "John Pendleton Kennedy: Late Disciple of Enlightenment." *J S Hist*, 32 (1966), 358–367.

2221 WINDELL, Marie G. "The Camp Meeting in Missouri." *Mo Hist Rev*, 37 (1943), 253–270.

2. Baptist

2222 DALTON, Jack. "A History of Florida Baptists." Doctoral dissertation, University of Florida, 1952.

2223 EDWARDS, Lawrence. "History of the Baptists of Tennessee with Particular Attention to the Primitive Baptists of East Tennessee." Master's thesis, University of Tennessee, 1941.

2224 LINDSEY, Jonathan A. "Basil Manly: Nineteenth Century Protean Man." *Bapt Hist Heritage*, 8 (1973), 130–143.

2225 MORGAN, David T., Jr. "The Great Awakening in North Carolina, 1740–1775: The Baptist Phase." *N C Hist Rev*, 45 (1968), 264–283.

2226 PASCHAL, George W. *History of North Carolina Baptists.* 2 vols. Raleigh, N. C., 1930–1955.

2227 POSEY, Walter B. *The Baptist Church in the Lower Mississippi Valley, 1776–1845.* Lexington, Ky., 1957.

2228 POSEY, Walter B. "The Early Baptist Church in the Lower Southwest." *J S Hist*, 10 (1944), 161–173.

2229 POSEY, Walter B. "The Frontier Baptist Ministry." *E Tenn Hist Soc Pub*, 14 (1942), 3–10.

2230 SWEET, William W., ed. *The Baptists, 1783–1830, a Collection of Source Material*. New York, 1931.

2231 TOWNSEND, Leah. "Discipline in Early Baptist Churches." *S C Hist Mag*, 54 (1953), 129–134.

3. Christian, Church of Christ, Disciples of Christ

2232 GARRISON, Winfred E., and Alfred T. DeGROOT. *The Diciples of Christ: A History*. Rev. ed. Bethany, W. Va., 1958.

2233 HARRELL, David E., Jr. "The Sectional Origins of the Churches of Christ." *J S Hist*, 30 (1964), 261–277.

2234 HARRELL, David E., Jr. *Quest for a Christian America: The Disciples of Christ and American Society to 1866*. Nashville, Tenn., 1966.

2235 WAGNER, Harry C. "The Beginnings of the Christian Church in East Tennessee." *E Tenn Hist Soc Pub*, 20 (1948), 49–58.

4. Congregational

2236 EDWARDS, George N. *History of the Independent or Congregational Church of Charleston, South Carolina*. Boston, 1947.

2237 WINGFIELD, Marshall. "Tennessee's Oldest Congregational Church." *W Tenn Hist Soc Pap*, 8 (1954), 55–94.

5. Episcopal

2238 BROWN, Lawrence L. "Richard Channing Moore and the Revival of the Southern Church." *Hist Mag Prot Epis Church*, 35 (1966), 3–63.

2239 BURGER, Nash. "A Side-Light on an Ante-Bellum Plantation Chapel." *Hist Mag Prot Epis Church*, 12 (1943), 69–73.

2240 BURGER, Nash Kerr. "The Society for the Advancement of Christianity in Mississippi." *Hist Mag Prot Epis Church*, 14 (1945), 264–269.

2241 CHORLEY, E. Clowes. "The Reverend Devereux Jarratt, 1732–1801." *Hist Mag Prot Epis Church*, 5 (1936), 47–64.

2242 CUSHMAN, Joseph D., Jr. *A Goodly Heritage: The Episcopal Church in Florida, 1821–1892.* Gainesville, Fla., 1965.

2243 DUGAS, Vera L. "Episcopalian Expansion into the Lower Mississippi Valley." *La Hist Q*, 38 (July, 1955), 57–74.

2244 LEMMON, Sarah M. "The Genesis of the Protestant Episcopal Diocese of North Carolina, 1701–1823." *N C Hist Rev*, 28 (1951), 426–462.

2245 PENNINGTON, Edgar L. "The Episcopal Church in Florida, 1763–1892." *Hist Mag Prot Epis Church*, 7 (1938), 1–77.

2246 PENNINGTON, Edgar L. "The Episcopal Church in the Alabama Black Belt, 1822–1836." *Ala Rev*, 4 (1951), 117–126.

2247 PENNINGTON, Edgar L. "The Organization of the Episcopal Church in Tennessee." *Hist Mag Prot Epis Church*, 22 (1953), 13–44.

2248 PENNINGTON, Edgar L. "Stephen Elliott, First Bishop of Georgia." *Hist Mag Prot Epis Church*, 7 (1938), 203–263.

2249 POSEY, Walter B. "The Protestant Episcopal Church: An American Adaptation." *J S Hist*, 25 (1969), 3–30.

2250 SLACK, William S. "Bishop Polk and the Diocese of Louisiana." *Hist Mag Prot Epis Church*, 7 (1938), 360–377.

2251 THOMAS, Albert S. "Christopher Edwards Gadsden (1785–1852): Fourth Bishop of South Carolina, 1840–1852." *Hist Mag Prot Epis Church*, 20 (1951), 294–324.

2252 THOMAS, Albert S. "The Protestant Episcopal Society for the Advancement of Christianity in South Carolina." *Hist Mag Prot Epis Church*, 21 (1952), 447–460.

2253 THOMAS, Albert S. "A Sketch of the History of the Church in South Carolina." *Hist Mag Prot Epis Church*, 4 (1935), 1–12.

2254 WILLIAMS, George W. "Dr. Frederick Dalcho (1769–1836), First Diocesan Historian." *Hist Mag Prot Epis Church*, 26 (1957), 311–328.

2255 WILLIAMS, George W. *St. Michael's, Charleston, 1751–1951.* Columbia, S. C., 1951.

6. Jewish

2256 DINNERSTEIN, Leonard, and Mary Dale PALSSON, eds. *Jews in the South.* See **910**.

2257 ELZAS, Barnett Abraham. *The Reformed Society of Israelites of Charleston, S. C.* New York, 1916.

2258 MOISE, Lucius C. *Biography of Isaac Harby, with an Account of the Reformed Society of Israelites of Charleston, S. C., 1824–1833.* Columbia, S. C., 1931.

7. Lutheran

2259 BERNHEIM, Gotthardt D. *History of the German Settlements and of the Lutheran Church in North and South Carolina.* Baltimore, Md., 1975.

2260 BRANTLEY, Rabun Lee. "The Salzburgers in Georgia."*Ga Hist Q*, 14 (1930), 214–244.

2261 CASSELL, Charles W., W. J. FINCH, and Elon O. HENKEL, eds. *History of the Lutheran Church in Virginia and East Tennessee.* Strasburg, Va., 1930.

2262 EISENBERG, William Edward. *The Lutheran Church in Virginia, 1717–1962.* Roanoke, Va., 1967.

2263 HOFER, J. M. "The Georgia Salzburgers." *Ga Hist Q*, 18 (1934), 99–117.

2264 HORN, Edward T. "A Historic Sketch of St. John's Lutheran Church, Better Known . . . as 'Bachman's Chapel' . . . ." *Yearbook of Charleston, S. C.,* (1884), 262–279.

2265 RUBINCAM, Milton. "Historical Background of the Salzburger Emigration to Georgia." *Ga Hist Q*, 35 (1951), 99–115.

2266 STROBEL, Philip A. *The Salzburgers and Their Descendants.* Athens, Ga., 1953.

8. Methodist

2267 ASBURY, Francis. *The Journal and Letters of Francis Asbury.* Ed. Elmer T. Clark. 3 vols. Nashville, Tenn., 1958.

2268 BUCKE, Emory S., ed. *The History of American Methodism.* 3 vols. New York, 1964.

2269 MATHEWS, Donald G. "The Methodist Schism of 1844 and the Popularization of Antislavery Sentiment." *Mid-Am*, 51 (1969), 3–23.

2270 MATHEWS, Donald G. *Slavery and Methodism: A Chapter in American Morality, 1780–1845.* Princeton, 1965.

2271 NORWOOD, John N. *The Schism in the Methodist Episcopal Church, 1844.* Philadelphia, Pa., 1976.

2272 PILKINGTON, James Penn. *The Methodist Publishing House: A History—Beginnings to 1870.* Nashville, Tenn., 1968.

2273 POSEY, Walter B. "The Advance of Methodism into the Lower Southwest." *J S Hist*, 2 (1936), 439–452.

2274 POSEY, Walter B. *The Development of Methodism in the Old Southwest, 1783–1824.* Philadelphia, Pa., 1974.

2275 SWEET, William W. *Methodism in American History.* Rev. ed. Nashville, Tenn., 1954.

2276 SWEET, William W., ed. *The Methodists: A Collection of Source Material.* Chicago, 1946.

2277 SWEET, William W. "New Light on the Relations of Early American Methodism to the Anglican Clergy in Virginia and North Carolina." *Hist Mag Prot Epis Church*, 22 (1953), 69–90.

2278 SWEET, William W. *Virginia Methodism, a History.* Richmond, Va., [1955].

9. Mormon

2279 ROBERTSON, R. J., Jr. "The Mormon Experience in Missouri, 1830–1839." *Mo Hist Rev*, 68 (1974), 280–298, 393–415.

10. Moravian

2280 FRIES, Adelaide L., et al. *Records of the Moravians in North Carolina.* v. 1–. Raleigh, N. C., 1922–.

2281 REICHEL, Levin Theodore. *The Moravians in North Carolina.* Baltimore, Md., 1968.

11. Presbyterian

2282 BALDWIN, Alice M. "Sources of Sedition: The Political Theories of Some of the New Light Presbyterian Clergy of Virginia and North Carolina." *Wm Mar Q*, 3rd ser., 5 (1948), 52–76.

2283 BARRUS, Ben. "Factors Involved in the Origin of the Cumberland Presbyterian Church." *J Presb Hist*, 45 (1967), 273–289; 46 (1968), 58–73.

2284 BLANKS, W. D. "Corrective Church Discipline in the Presbyterian Churches of the Nineteenth Century South." *J Presb Hist*, 44 (1966), 89–105.

2285 BOZEMAN, Theodore Dwight. "Inductive and Deductive Politics: Science and Society in Antebellum Presbyterian Thought." *J Am Hist*, 64 (1977), 704–722.

2286 CAMPBELL, Thomas H. *Studies in Cumberland Presbyterian History.* Nashville, Tenn., 1944.

2287 DesCHAMPS, Margaret Burr. "The Presbyterian Church in the South Atlantic States, 1801–1861." Doctoral dissertation, Emory University, 1952.

2288 DesCHAMPS, Margaret Burr. "Presbyterians and Others in the South after 1800." *J Presb Hist Soc*, 31 (1953), 25–40.

2289 DesCHAMPS, Margaret Burr. "Union or Division? South Atlantic Presbyterians and Southern Nationalism, 1820–1861." *J S Hist*, 20 (1954), 484–498.

2290 GARDINER, John H., Jr. "The Beginnings of the Prebysterian Church in the Southern Colonies."*J Presb Hist Soc*, 34 (1956), 36–52.

2291 HUBBARD, Donald Peyton. "A Historical Study of the Cumberland Presbyterian Church in Tennessee, 1810–1860." Master's thesis, University of Tennessee, 1966.

2292 HUGHES, Richard B. "Old School Presbyterians: Eastern Invaders of Texas, 1830–1865." *SW Hist Q*, 74 (1971), 324–336.

2293 PALMER, Benjamin M. *The Life and Letters of James H. Thornwell*. New York, 1975.

2294 POSEY, Walter B. *The Presbyterian Church in the Old Southwest, 1778–1838*. Richmond, Va., 1952.

2295 POSEY, Walter B. "Presbyterian Church Influence in the Lower Mississippi Valley." *J Presb Hist Soc*, 33 (1955), 35–50.

2296 POSEY, Walter B. "The Presbyterian Ministry in the Early Southwest." *J Presb Hist Soc*, 26 (1949), 215–226.

2297 SMITH, Elwyn A. "The Role of the South in the Presbyterian Schism of 1837–1838." *Church Hist*, 29 (1960), 44–63.

2298 SWEET, William W., ed. *The Presbyterians, 1783–1840, a Collection of Source Material*. New York, 1936.

2299 THOMPSON, Ernest Trice. *Presbyterians in the South, 1607–1861*. Richmond, Va., 1963.

12. Quaker

2300 CARROLL, Kenneth. "Joseph Nichols and the Nicholites of Caroline County, Maryland." *Md Hist Mag*, 45 (1950), 47–61.

2301 CARROLL, Kenneth L. "More about the Nicholites." *Md Hist Mag*, 46 (1950), 278–289.

2302 CARROLL, Kenneth L. "The Nicholites of North Carolina." *N C Hist Rev*, 31 (1954), 453–462.

2303 GILBERT, Dorothy L. "Quaker Migration to the Western Waters." *E Tenn Hist Soc Pub*, 18 (1946), 47–58.

2304 ROBERTS, Lucien E. "Quarkers in Georgia: The Rise and Fall of the Wrightsborough Community." *Ga Rev*, 4 (1950), 297–303.

13. Roman Catholic

2305 BURNS, Thomas J. "The Catholic Church in West Florida, 1783–1850." Master's thesis, Florida State University, 1962.

2306 EDWARDS, Richard A. "Pioneer Catholics in Kentucky." *Reg Ky Hist Soc*, 68 (1970), 252–264.

2307 FLANIGEN, George J., ed. *Catholicity in Tennessee: Sketch of Catholic Activities in the State, 1541–1937*. Nashville, Tenn., 1937.

2308 GANNON, Michael V. *The Cross in the Sand: The Early Catholic Church in Florida, 1513–1870*. Gainesville, Fla., 1965.

2309 GRANT, Dorothy F. *John England, American Christopher*. Milwaukee, Wis., 1949.

2310 GUILDAY, Peter K. *The Life and Times of John England, First Bishop of Charleston, 1786–1842*. 2 vols. in 1. New York, 1969.

14. Unitarian

2311 CLAPP, Theodore. *Parson Clapp of the Strangers' Church of New Orleans*. Ed. John Duffy. Baton Rouge, 1957.

2312 EATON, Clement. "Winifred and Joseph Gales, Liberals in the Old South." *J S Hist*, 10 (1944), 460–474.

2313 GIBSON, George H. "Unitarian Congregations in Ante-Bellum Georgia." *Ga Hist Q*, 54 (1970), 147–168.

2314 GIBSON, George H. "The Unitarian-Universalist Church in Richmond." *Va Mag Hist Biog*, 74 (1966), 321–335.

2315 GOHDES, Clarence. "Some Notes on the Unitarian Church in the Ante-Bellum South: A Contribution to the History of Southern Liberalism." *American Studies in Honor of William Kenneth Boyd*. Duke University. Americana Club. Freeport, N. Y., 1968.

2316 REILLY, Timothy F. "Parson Clapp of New Orleans: Antebellum Social Critic, Religious Radical, and Member of the Establishment."*La Hist*, 16 (1975), 167–191.

15. The Church and Its Relationship with Blacks and Indians

2317 AFRICA, Philip. "Slaveholding in the Salem Community, 1771–1851." *N C Hist Rev*, 54 (1977), 271–307.

2318 ANDERSON, Charles A., ed. "Presbyterians Meet the Slavery Problem." *J Presb Hist Soc*, 29 (1951), 9–40.

2319 ANDREWS, Rena M. "Slavery Views of a Northern Prelate." *Church Hist*, 3 (1934), 60–78.

2320 APTHEKER, Herbert. "Quakers and Negro Slavery." *J Neg Hist*, 25 (1940), 331–362.

2321 BAILEY, Kenneth K. "Protestantism and Afro-Americans in the Old South: Another Look." *J S Hist*, 41 (1975), 451–72.

2322 BELLOTT, Leland J. "Evangelicals and the Defense of Slavery in Britain's Old Colonial Empire." *J S Hist*, 37 (1971), 19–40.

2323 BOLES, John B. "John Hersey: Dissenting Theologian of Abolitionism, Perfectionism, and Millenialism." *Meth Hist*, 14 (1976), 215–234.

2324 BOLLER, Paul F., Jr. "Washington, the Quakers, and Slavery." *J Neg Hist*, 46 (1961), 83–88.

2325 CARROLL, Kenneth L. "Maryland Quakers and Slavery." *Md Hist Mag*, 45 (1950), 215–225.

2326 CLARKE, T. Erskine. "An Experiment in Paternalism: Presbyterians and Slaves in Charleston, South Carolina." *J Presb Hist*, 53 (1975), 223–238.

2327 DANIEL, W. Harrison. "Southern Presbyterians and the Negro in the Early National Period." *J Neg Hist*, 58 (1973), 291–312.

2328 DRAKE, Thomas E. *Quakers and Slavery in America.* Magnolia, Mass., 1965.

2329 ENGLAND, John. *Letters to the Late Bishop England to the Hon. John Forsyth on the Subject of Domestic Slavery.* Westport, Conn., 1969.

2330 EPPS, Archie C., III. "The Christian Doctrine of Slavery: A Theological Analysis." *J Neg Hist*, 46 (1961), 243–249.

2331 FAUST, Drew Gilpin. "Evangelicalism and the Meaning of the Proslavery Argument: The Reverend Thornton Stringfellow of Virginia." *Va Mag Hist Biog*, 85 (1977), 3–17.

2332 FRANKLIN, John, Hope. "Negro Episcopalians in Ante-Bellum North Carolina." *Hist Mag Prot Epis Church*, 13 (1944), 216–234.

2333 GENOVESE, Eugene D. "Black Plantation Preachers in the Slave South." *La Stud*, 11 (1972), 188–214.

2334 GREEN, Fletcher M. "Northern Missionary Activities in the South, 1846–1861." *J S Hist*, 21 (1955), 147–172.

2335 HARWOOD, Thomas F. "British Evangelical Abolitionism and American Churches in the 1830's." *J S Hist*, 28 (1962), 287–306.

2336 HIEMSTRA, William L. "Early Presbyterian Missions among the Choctaw and Chickasaw Indians in Mississippi." *J Miss Hist*, 10 (1948), 8–16.

2337 HILTY, Hiram H. "North Carolina Quakers and Slavery." Doctoral dissertation, Duke University, 1969.

2338 HOWARD, Victor B. "The Kentucky Presbyterians in 1849: Slavery and the Kentucky Constitution." *Reg Ky Hist Soc*, 73 (1975), 217–240.

2339 JACKSON, James C. "The Religious Education of the Negro in South Carolina Prior to 1850." *Hist Mag Prot Epis Church*, 36 (1967), 35–61.

2340 JACKSON, Luther P. "Religious Development of the Negro in Virginia from 1760–1860." *J Neg Hist*, 16 (1931), 168–239.

2341 JACKSON, Luther P. "Religious Instruction of Negroes, 1830–1860, with Special Reference to South Carolina." *J Neg Hist*, 15 (1930), 72–114.

2342 JONES, Charles Colcock. *Religious Instruction of the Negro in the United States.* New York, 1969.

2343 KORN, Bertram W. *Jews and Negro Slavery in the Old South, 1789–1865.* Elkins Park, Pa., 1961.

2344 KULL, Irving S. "Presbyterian Attitudes toward Slavery." *Church Hist*, 7 (1938), 101–114.

2345 MATHEWS, Donald G. "Charles Colcock Jones and the Southern Evangelical Crusade to Form a Biracial Community." *J S Hist*, 41 (1975), 299–320.

2346 MATHEWS, Donald G. "The Methodist Mission to the Slaves, 1829–1844." *J Am Hist*, 51 (1965), 615–631.

2347 MATHEWS, Donald G. *Slavery and Methodism, a Chapter in American Morality.* See **2270**.

2348 MOFFITT, James W. "Early Baptist Missionary Work among the Cherokees." *E Tenn Hist Soc Pub*, 12 (1940), 16–27.

2349 MOORE, Edmund A. "Robert J. Breckridge and the Slavery Aspect of the Presbyterian Schism of 1837." *Church Hist*, 4 (1935), 282–294.

2350 MURRAY, Andrew E. *Presbyterians and the Negro—A History.* Philadelphia, Pa., 1966.

2351 NUERMBERGER, Ruth K. *The Free Produce Movement: A Quaker Protest against Slavery.* New York, 1970.

2352 OPPER, Peter K. "North Carolina Quakers: Reluctant Slaveholders." *N C Hist Rev*, 52 (1975), 37–58.

2353 PEACOCK, Mary Thomas. "Methodist Mission Work among the Cherokee Indians before the Removal." *Meth Hist*, 3 (April, 1965), 20–39.

2354 PENDLETON, Othniel A., Jr. "Slavery and the Evangelical Churches." *J Presb Hist Soc*, 25 (1947), 88–112, 153–174.

2355 PERKINS, Haven P. "Religion for Slaves: Difficulties and Methods." *Church Hist*, 10 (1941), 228–245.

2356 POSEY, Walter B. "The Baptists and Slavery in the Lower Mississippi Valley." *J Neg Hist*, 41 (1956), 117–130.

2357 POSEY, Walter B. "Influence of Slavery upon the Methodist Church in the Early South and Southwest." *Miss Val Hist Rev*, 17 (1931), 530–542.

2358 POSEY, Walter B. "The Slavery Question in the Presbyterian Church in the Old Southwest." *J S Hist*, 15 (1949), 311–324.

2359 PURIFOY, Lewis M. "The Methodist Anti-Slavery Tradition, 1784–1844." *Meth Hist*, 4 (1966), 3–16.

2360 PURIFOY, Lewis M. "The Methodist Episcopal Church South and Slavery, 1844–1865." Doctoral dissertation, University of North Carolina, 1965.

2361 PURIFOY, Lewis M. "The Southern Methodist Church and the Proslavery Argument." *J S Hist*, 32 (1966), 325–341.

2362 RABOTEAU, Albert J. *Slave Religion: The "Invisible Institution" in the Antebellum South.* New York, 1978.

2363 REINDERS, Robert C. "The Churches and the Negro in New Orleans, 1850–1860." *Phylon*, 22 (1961), 241–248.

2364 RICE, Madeline H. *American Catholic Opinion in the Slavery Controversy.* Magnolia, Mass., 1964.

2365 ROGERS, Tommy W. "Dr. F. A. Ross and the Presbyterian Defense of Slavery." See **507**.

2366 SCHWARZE, Edmund. *History of the Moravian Missions among Southern Indian Tribes of the United States.* Bethlehem, Pa., 1923.

2367 SMITH, H. Shelton. *In His Image But . . . : Racism in Southern Religion, 1780–1910.* Durham, N. C., 1972.

2368 STAIGER, C. Bruce. "Abolitionism and the Presbyterian Schism of 1837–1838." *Miss Val Hist Rev*, 36 (1949), 391–414.

2369 STEINER, Bruce E. "A Planter's Troubled Conscience." *J S Hist*, 28 (1962), 343–347.

2370 TODD, Willie Grier. "North Carolina Baptists and Slavery." *N C Hist Rev*, 24 (1947), 135–159.

2371 TODD, Willie Grier. "The Slavery Issue and the Organization of a Southern Baptist Convention." Doctoral dissertation, University of North Carolina, 1964.

2372 TYNER, Wayne C. "Charles Colcock Jones: Mission to Slaves." *J Presb Hist*, 55 (1977), 363–380.

2373 WEEKS, Stephen B. *Southern Quakers and Slavery*. New York, 1968.

2374 WINTER, Hauser. "The Division in Missouri Methodism in 1845." *Mo Hist Rev*, 37 (1942), 1–18.

2375 WOOLRIDGE, Nancy B. "The Slave Preacher—Portrait of a Leader." *J Neg Ed*, 14 (1945), 28–37.

XIX. Government and Politics

1. General

2376 ABERNETHY, Thomas P. "Democracy and the Southern Frontier." *J S Hist*, 4 (1938), 3–13.

2377 ABERNETHY, Thomas P. *The South in the New Nation, 1789–1819*. See **54**.

2378 ALEXANDER, Thomas B., et al. "The Basis of Alabama's Ante-Bellum Two Party System." *Ala Rev*, 19 (1966), 243–276.

2379 ALEXANDER, Thomas B. "The Presidential Campaign of 1840 in Tennessee." *Tenn Hist Q*, 1 (1942), 21–43.

2380 ALEXANDER, Thomas B. *Sectional Stress and Party Strength: A Study of Roll-Call Voting Patterns in the United States House of Representatives, 1836–1860*. Nashville, Tenn., 1967.

2381 BEAN, W. G. "Anti-Jeffersonianism in the Ante-Bellum South." *N C Hist Rev*, 12 (1935), 103–124.

2382 BRAVERMAN, Howard. "The Economic and Political Background of the Conservative Revolt in Virginia [1837]." *Va Mag Hist Biog*, 60 (1952), 266–287.

2383 CAPERS, Gerald M. "A Reconsideration of John C. Calhoun's Transition from Nationalism to Nullification." *J S Hist*, 14 (1948), 34–48.

2384 CARPENTER, Jesse T. *The South as a Conscious Minority, 1789–1861*. New York, 1930.

2385 COKER, Francis W. "Are There Distinctive Political Traditions for the South?" *J Pol*, 2 (1940), 3–22.

2386 CRAVEN, Avery O. "Democratic Theory and Practice." *Va Q Rev*, 19 (1943), 278–287.

2387 CRAVEN, Avery O. "The 1840's and the Democratic Process." *J S Hist*, 16 (1950), 161–176.

2388 CRAVEN, Avery O. *The Growth of Southern Nationalism, 1848–1861.* See **57**.

2389 CUNNINGHAM, Noble E., Jr. "Who Were the Quids?" *Miss Val Hist Rev*, 50 (1963), 252–263.

2390 CURRENT, Richard N. "John C. Calhoun, Philosopher of Reaction." *Antioch Rev*, 3 (1943), 223–234.

2391 DANGERFIELD, George. *The Awakening of American Nationalism 1815–1828.* New York, 1965.†

2392 DANGERFIELD, George. *The Era of Good Feelings.* New York, 1963.†

2393 EATON, Clement. "Everybody Liked Henry Clay." *Am Heritage*, 7 (October, 1956), 26–29, 108–109.

2394 EATON, Clement. "Southern Senators and the Right of Instruction, 1789–1860." *J S Hist*, 18 (1952), 303–319.

2395 FOLSOM, Burton W., II. "The Politics of the Elites: Prominence and Party in Davidson County, Tennessee, 1835–1861." *J S Hist*, 39 (1973), 359–378.

2396 FREEHLING, William W. "Spoilsmen and Interests in the Thought and Career of John C. Calhoun." *J Am Hist*, 52 (1965), 25–42.

2397 GOVAN, Thomas P. "John M. Berrien and the Administration of Andrew Jackson." *J S Hist*, 5 (1939), 447–468.

2398 GREEN, Fletcher M. "Democracy in the Old South." *J S Hist*, 12 (1946), 3–23.

2399 HOFSTADTER, Richard. *The American Political Tradition and the Men Who Made It.* New York, 1974.†

2400 JONES, Allen W. "Party Nominating Machinery in Ante-Bellum Alabama." *Ala Rev*, 20 (1967), 34–44.

2401 KATEB, George. "The Majority Principle: Calhoun and His Antecedents." *Pol Sci Q*, 84 (1969), 583–605.

2402 LEAVELLE, Arnaud B., and Thomas I. COOK. "George Hitzhugh and the Theory of American Conservatism." *J Pol*, 7 (1945), 145–168.

2403 LOWE, Richard G. "The Republican Party in Antebellum Virginia, 1856–1860." *Va Mag Hist Biog*, 81 (1973), 259–279.

2404 LOWE, Richard, and Randolph CAMPBELL. "Wealthholding and Political Power in Antebellum Texas." *SW Hist Q*, 79 (1975), 21–30.

2405 MALONE, Dumas. "The Great Generation." *Va Q Rev*, 23 (1947), 108–122.

2406 MATHIAS, Frank F. "The Turbulent Years of Kentucky Politics, 1820–1850." *Reg Ky Hist Soc*, 72 (1974), 309–318.

2407 MILES, Edwin A. "Andrew Jackson and Senator Poindexter." *J S Hist*, 24 (1958), 51–66.

2408 MONTGOMERY, Horace. *Cracker Parties.* Baton Rouge, 1951.

2409 MURRAY, Paul. "Party Organization in Georgia Politics, 1825–1853." *Ga Hist Q*, 29 (1945), 195–210.

2410 NAGEL, Paul C. "The Election of 1824: A Reconsideration Based on Newspaper Opinion." *J S Hist*, 26 (1960), 315–329.

2411 NUERMBERGER, Ruth K. *The Clays of Alabama: A Plantation-Lawyer-Politician Family.* Lexington, Ky., 1958.

2412 POLE, J. R. "Representation and Authority in Virginia from the Revolution to Reform."*J S Hist*, 24 (1958), 16–50.

2413 POTTER, David M. *The South and the Concurrent Majority.* Baton Rouge, 1972.

2414 RAYBACK, J. S. "The Presidential Ambitions of John C. Calhoun, 1844–1848." *J S Hist*, 14 (1948), 331–356.

2415 RILEY, Edward M. "Commentary on the Small Farmer in Politics." *Ag Hist*, 43 (1969), 103–106.

2416 ROBSON, C. B. "Francis Lieber's Theories of Society, Government, and Liberty." *J Pol*, 4 (1942), 227–249.

2417 ROGERS, A. A. "Constitutional Democracy in Ante-Bellum Virginia." *Wm Mar Q*, 2nd ser., 16 (1936), 399–407.

2418 SCHULTZ, Harold S. "A Century of Calhoun Biographies."*S Atl Q*, 50 (1951), 248–254.

2419 SELLERS, Charles G., Jr. "James K. Polk's Political Apprenticeship." *E Tenn Hist Soc Pub*, 25 (1953), 37–53.

2420 SHUGG, Roger W. "Suffrage and Representation in Ante-Bellum Louisiana." *La Hist Q*, 19 (1936), 390–406.

2421 STENBERG, Richard R. "The Jefferson Birthday Dinner, 1830." *J S Hist*, 4 (1938), 334–345.

2422 SYDNOR, Charles S. *The Development of Southern Sectionalism, 1819–1848.* See **63**.

2423 SYDNOR, Charles S. *Gentlemen Freeholders: Political Practices in Washington's Virginia.* Chapel Hill, 1952.

2424 TAYLOR, Joe Gray. "The Democratic Idea and the Deep South: An Historical Survey." *Miss Q*, 18 (1965), 201–215.

2425 THORNTON, J. Mills, III. *Politics and Power in a Slave Society: Alabama, 1800–1860.* Baton Rouge, 1978.

2426 VIERECK, Peter. "The Aristocratic Origin of American Freedom." *SW Rev*, 37 (1952), 331–334.

2427 VINSON, John C. "Electioneering in North Carolina, 1800–1835." *N C Hist Rev*, 29 (1952), 171–188.

2428 VINSON, John C. "Electioneering in the South, 1800–1840." *Ga Rev*, 10 (1956), 265–273.

2429 WALTON, Brian G. "Elections to the United States Senate in Alabama before the Civil War." *Ala Rev*, 27 (1974), 3–38.

2430 WILTSE, Charles M. "Calhoun's Democracy." *J Pol*, 3 (1941), 210–223.

2. State Constitutions and State Governments

2431 BACOT, D. Huger. "Constitutional Progress and the Struggle for Democracy in South Carolina after the Revolution." *S Atl Q*, 24 (1925), 61–72.

2432 BARNHART, John D. "The Tennessee Constitution of 1796: A Product of the Old West." *J S Hist*, 9 (1943), 532–547.

2433 CASSELL, Robert. "Newton Cannon and the Constitutional Convention of 1834." *Tenn Hist Q*, 15 (1956), 224–242.

2434 COUNIHAN, Harold J. "The North Carolina Constitutional Convention of 1835: A Study in Jacksonian Democracy." *N C Hist Rev*, 46 (1969), 335–364.

2435 DRAKE, W. Magruder. "The Framing of Mississippi's First Constitution." *J Miss Hist*, 29 (1967), 301–327.

2436 DRAKE, W. Magruder. "The Mississippi Constitutional Convention of 1832." *J S Hist*, 23 (1957), 354–370.

2437 GAINES, Francis P., Jr. "The Virginia Constitutional Convention of 1850–51: A Study in Sectionalism." Doctoral dissertation, University of Virginia, 1950.

2438 GREEN, Fletcher M. *Constitutional Development in the South Atlantic States, 1776–1860.* New York, 1971.

2439 IRELAND, Robert M. *The County Courts in Antebellum Kentucky.* Lexington, Ky., 1972.

2440 McCLURE, Wallace. "The Development of the Tennessee Constitution." *Tenn Hist Mag*, 1 (1915), 292–314.

2441 McMILLAN, Malcolm C. "The Alabama Constitution of 1819: A Study of Constitution-Making on the Frontier." *Ala Rev*, 3 (1950), 263–285.

2442 McMILLAN, Malcolm C. *Constitutional Development in Alabama, 1798–1901: A Study in Politics, the Negro, and Sectionalism.* Chapel Hill, 1955.

2443 MARTIN, Ida M. "Civil Liberties in Georgia Legislation, 1800–1830." *Ga Hist Q*, 45 (1961), 329–344.

2444 OLIVER, George B. "A Constitutional History of Virginia, 1776–1860." Doctoral dissertation, Duke University, 1959.

2445 PRUFER, Julius F. "The Franchise in Virginia from Jefferson through the Convention of 1829." *Wm Mar Q*, 2nd ser., 7 (1927), 255–270; 8 (1928), 17–32.

2446 STICKLES, A. M. *The Critical Court Struggle in Kentucky, 1819–1829.* Bloomington, Ind., 1929.

2447 WOOSTER, Ralph A. *The People in Power: Courthouse and Statehouse in the Lower South.* Knoxville, Tenn., 1969.

2448 WOOSTER, Ralph A. *Politicians, Planters, and Plain Folk: Courthouse and Statehouse in the Upper South, 1850–1860.* Knoxville, Tenn., 1975.

3. War of 1812

2449 COLES, Harry L. *The War of 1812*. Chicago, 1966.†

2450 GREEN, Philip J. "William H. Crawford and the War of 1812."*Ga Hist Q*, 26 (1942), 16–39.

2451 LATIMER, Margaret K. "South Carolina—A Protagonist of the War of 1812." *Am Hist Rev*, 61 (1956), 914–929.

2452 LEMMON, Sarah M. *Frustrated Patriots: North Carolina and the War of 1812*. Chapel Hill, 1974.

2453 PRATT, Julius. *Expansionists of 1812*. Magnolia, Mass., [n. d].

2454 RISJORD, Norman K. "1812: Conservatives, War Hawks, and the Nation's Honor." *Wm Mar Q*, 3rd ser., 18 (1961), 196–210.

2455 TALMADGE, John E. "Georgia's Federalist Press and the War of 1812." *J S Hist*, 19 (1953), 488–500.

2456 WALKER, William A. "Martial Sons: Tennessee Enthusiasm for the War of 1812." *Tenn Hist Q*, 20 (1961), 20–37.

2457 WARREN, Harris G. "Southern Filibusters in the War of 1812." *La Hist Q*, 25 (1942), 291–300.

2458 WEHTJE, Myron F. "Opposition in Virginia to the War of 1812." *Va Mag Hist Biog*, 78 (1970), 65–86.

4. State and Southern Sectionalism

2459 AMBLER, Charles H. *Sectionalism in Virginia from 1776–1861*. New York, 1964.

2460 AMMON, Harry. "The Richmond Junto, 1800–1824." *Va Mag Hist Biog*, 61 (1953), 395–418.

2461 BEACH, Rex. "Spencer Roane and the Richmond Junto." *Wm Mar Q*, 2nd ser., 22 (1942), 1–17.

2462 CARROLL, Mary S. "Tennessee Sectionalism, 1796–1861." Doctoral dissertation, Duke University, 1931.

2463 FERGUSON, E. James. "Public Finance and the Origins of Southern Sectionalism." *J S Hist*, 28 (1962), 450–461.

2464 JACK, T. H. *Sectionalism and Party Politics in Alabama, 1819–1824*. Menasha, Wis., 1919.

2465 MURRAY, Paul. "Economic Sectionalism in Georgia Politics, 1825–1855."*J S Hist*, 10 (1944), 293–307.

2466 ROBERTSON, James R. "Sectionalism in Kentucky from 1855 to 1865."*Miss Val Hist Rev*, 4 (1917), 49–63.

2467 RUSSEL, Robert R. *Critical Studies in Antebellum Sectionalism: Essays in American Political and Economic History*. Westport, Conn., 1972.

2468 RUSSEL, Robert R. *Economic Aspects of Southern Sectionalism, 1840–1861.* See **1303**.

2469 SCHAPER, William A. *Sectionalism and Representation in South Carolina.* Ed. with note, E. M. Lander, Jr. New York, 1968.

2470 SCHULTZ, Harold S. *Nationalism and Sectionalism in South Carolina, 1852–1860.* Durham, N.C., 1950.

2471 SMITH, James M. "The Grass Roots Origins of the Kentucky Resolutions." *Wm Mar Q,* 3rd ser., 27 (1970), 221–245.

2472 TURNER, Frederick J. "Geographic Sectionalism in American History." *Ann Assn Am Geog,* 16 (1926), 85–93.

2473 TURNER, Frederick J. *The United States, 1830–1850: The Nation and the Sections.* New York, 1935.

2474 VAN DEUSEN, John G. *Economic Bases of Disunion in South Carolina.* See **1312**.

5. *State Rights*

2475 BRUGGER, Robert J. *Beverley Tucker, Heart over Head in the Old South.* See **1590**.

2476 COIT, Margaret L. "Calhoun and the Downfall of States' Rights." *Va Q Rev,* 28 (1952), 191–208.

2477 CUNNINGHAM, Noble E., Jr. "Nathaniel Macon and the Southern Protest against National Consolidation." *N C Hist Rev,* 32 (1955), 376–384.

2478 CURRY, Roy W. "James A. Seddon, a Southern Prototype." *Va Mag Hist Biog,* 63 (1955), 123–150.

2479 DRELL, Bernard. "John Taylor of Caroline and the Preservation of an Old Social Order." *Va Mag Hist Biog,* 46 (1938), 285–298.

2480 FISHER, John E. "The Dilemma of a States' Rights Whig: The Congressional Career of R. M. T. Hunter, 1837–1841." *Va Mag Hist Biog,* 81 (1973), 387–404.

2481 FORTUNE, Porter L., Jr. "George M. Troup: Leading State Rights Advocate." Doctoral dissertation, University of North Carolina, 1949.

2482 GELBACK, Clyde C. "Spencer Roane of Virginia, 1762–1822, a Judicial Advocate of State Rights." Doctoral dissertation, University of Pittsburgh, 1955.

2483 HATCHER, William H. "John Marshall and States' Rights." *S Q,* 3 (1965), 207–216.

2484 HORSNELL, Margaret E. "Spencer Roane: Judicial Advocate of Jeffersonian Principles." Doctoral dissertation, University of Minnesota, 1962.

2485 MALONE, Dumas. *The Public Life of Thomas Cooper, 1783–1839.* See **1622**.

2486 MALONE, Dumas. "Thomas Cooper and the States Rights Movement in South Carolina, 1823–1830." *N C Hist Rev,* 3 (1926), 184–197.

2487 PHILLIPS, Ulrich B. *Georgia and State Rights.* Kent, Ohio, 1968.†

2488 SKELTON, Lynda W. "The States Rights Movement in Georgia, 1825–1850."
      Ga Hist Q, 50 (1966), 391–412.

2489 VENABLE, Austin L. "William L. Yancey's Transition from Unionism to State
      Rights." *J S Hist*, 10 (1944), 331–342.

6. Jeffersonian Democracy

2490 BEARD, Charles A. *Economic Origins of Jeffersonian Democracy*. New York,
      1952.

2491 CUNNINGHAM, Noble E., Jr. *The Jeffersonian Republicans in Power, Party
      Operations, 1801–1809*. Chapel Hill, 1963.

2492 GILPATRICK, Delbert H. *Jeffersonian Democracy in North Carolina*. New
      York, 1967.

2493 GRISWOLD, A. Whitney. "The Agrarian Democracy of Thomas Jefferson."
      Am Pol Sci Rev, 40 (1946), 657–681.

2494 KOCH, Adrienne. *Jefferson and Madison: The Great Collaboration*. New York,
      1964.

2495 KOCH, Adrienne. *The Philosophy of Thomas Jefferson*. New York, 1943.

2496 LEVY, Leonard W. *Jefferson and Civil Liberties: The Darker Side*. Rev. ed.
      New York, 1973.†

2497 MALONE, Dumas. "Presidential Leadership and National Unity: The
      Jeffersonian Example." *J S Hist*, 35 (1969), 3–17.

2498 MUDGE, Eugene T. *The Social Philosophy of John Taylor of Caroline*. New
      York, 1968.

2499 PETERSON, Merrill D. *The Jefferson Image in the American Mind*. New
      York, 1960.

2500 WHITE, Leonard D. *The Jeffersonians, a Study in Administrative History,
      1801–1829*. New York, 1951.

2501 WILTSE, Charles M. *The Jeffersonian Tradition in American Democracy*. New
      York, 1960.†

2502 WOLFE, John H. *Jeffersonian Democracy in South Carolina*. Chapel Hill,
      1940.

7. Jacksonian Democracy

2503 ABERNETHY, Thomas P. "Andrew Jackson and Southwestern
      Democracy."*Am Hist Rev*, 33 (1927), 64–77.

2504 ABERNETHY, Thomas P. "The Political Geography of Southern Jacksonism."
      E Tenn Hist Soc Pub, 3 (1931), 35–41.

2505 BROWN, Richard H. "The Missouri Crisis, Slavery, and the Politics of
      Jacksonianism." *S Atl Q*, 65 (1966), 55–72.

2506 FOLSOM, Burton W., II. "Party Formation and Development in Jacksonian America: The Old South." *J Am Stud*, 7 (1973), 217–229.

2507 HALLER, Mark H. "The Rise of the Jackson Party in Maryland, 1820–1829." *J S Hist*, 28 (1962), 307–326.

2508 HOFFMAN, William S. *Andrew Jackson and North Carolina Politics*. Chapel Hill, 1958.

2509 LATNER, Richard B. "A New Look at Jacksonian Politics." *J Am Hist*, 61 (1975), 943–969.

2510 LONGAKER, Richard P. "Was Jackson's Kitchen Cabinet a Cabinet?" *Miss Val Hist Rev*, 44 (1957), 94–108.

2511 McCORMICK, Richard P. "New Perspectives on Jacksonian Politics." *Am Hist Rev*, 65 (1960), 228–301.

2512 McCORMICK, Richard P. *The Second American Party System: Party Formation in the Jacksonian Era*. Chapel Hill, 1966.

2513 MARSHALL, Lynn L. "The Genesis of Grassroots Democracy in Kentucky." *Mid-Am*, 47 (1965), 269–282.

2514 MEYERS, Marvin. *The Jacksonian Persuasion: Politics and Belief*. Stanford, Cal., 1957.†

2515 MILES, Edwin A. *Jacksonian Democracy in Mississippi*. New York, 1970.

2516 NEWSOME, Albert Ray. *The Presidential Election of 1824 in North Carolina*. Chapel Hill, 1939.

2517 REMINI, Robert V. *The Election of Andrew Jackson*. Philadelphia, Pa., 1963.†

2518 SATTERFIELD, R. Beeler. "The Uncertain Trumpet of the Tennessee Jacksonians." *Tenn Hist Q*, 26 (1967), 79–96.

2519 SCHLESINGER, Arthur M., Jr. *The Age of Jackson*. Boston, [n.d.].†

2520 SELLERS, Charles G., Jr. "Andrew Jackson versus the Historians." *Miss Val Hist Rev*, 44 (1958), 615–634.

2521 SELLERS, Charles G., Jr. *"Jackson Men with Feet of Clay."* *Am Hist Rev*, 62 (1957), 537–551.

2522 SYDNOR, Charles S. *The Development of Southern Sectionalism, 1819–1848*. See **63**.

2523 VAN DEUSEN, Glyndon G. *The Jacksonian Era, 1828–1845*. New York, 1959.†

2524 WHITE, Leonard. *The Jacksonians: A Study in Administrative History, 1829–1861*. New York, 1954.

8. *Political Parties*

A. Federalist

2525 BROUSSARD, James H. "Regional Pride and Republican Politics: The Fatal Weakness of Southern Federalism, 1800–1815." *S Atl Q*, 73 (1974), 23–33.

2526 BROUSSARD, James H. *The Southern Federalists, 1800–1816.* Baton Rouge, 1978.

2527 COMETTI, Elizabeth. "John Rutledge, Jr., Federalist." *J S Hist,* 13 (1947), 186–219.

2528 COX, Joseph W. "Robert Goodloe Harper: The Evolution of a Southern Federalist Congressman." Doctoral dissertation, University of Maryland, 1967.

2530 RISJORD, Norman K. "The Virginia Federalists." *J S Hist,* 33 (1967), 486–517.

2531 ROSE, Lisle A. *Prologue to Democracy: The Federalists in the South, 1789–1800.* Lexington, Ky., 1968.

B. Democrat

2532 BONHAM, Milledge L. "A Carolina Democrat on Party Prospects in 1844." *Am Hist Rev,* 42 (1936), 79–80.

2533 HARRISON, Joseph H., Jr. "Martin Van Buren and His Southern Supporters." *J S Hist,* 22 (1956), 438–458.

2534 HARRISON, Joseph H., Jr. "Oligarchs and Democrats—The Richmond Junto." *Va Mag Hist Biog,* 78 (1970), 184–198.

2535 MOORE, Powell. "James K. Polk and Tennessee Politics, 1839–1841." *E Tenn Hist Soc Pub,* 9 (1937), 31–52.

2536 MOORE, Powell. "James K. Polk: Tennessee Politician." *J S Hist,* 17 (1951), 493–516.

2537 NORTON, Clarence C. "Democratic Newspapers and Campaign Literature in North Carolina, 1835–1861." *N C Hist Rev,* 6 (1929), 345–361.

2538 NORTON, Clarence C. *The Democratic Party in Ante-Bellum North Carolina, 1835–1861.* Chapel Hill, 1930.

2539 REMINI, Robert V. *Martin Van Buren and the Making of the Democratic Party.* New York, 1970.†

2540 SHUGG, Roger W. *Origins of Class Struggle in Louisiana, 1840–1875.* See **883**.

C. Whig

2541 ABERNETHY, Thomas P. "The Origins of the Whig Party in Tennessee." *Miss Val Hist Rev,* 12 (1926), 504–522.

2542 ALEXANDER, Thomas B., and Peggy J. DUCKWORTH. "Alabama Black Belt Whigs during Secession: A New Viewpoint." *Ala Rev,* 17 (1964), 181–197.

2543 ALEXANDER, Thomas B. "Thomas A. R. Nelson as an Example of Whig Conservatism in Tennessee." *Tenn Hist Q,* 15 (1956), 17–29.

2544 ALEXANDER, Thomas B. *Thomas A. R. Nelson of East Tennessee.* Knoxville, Tenn., 1956.

2545 ALEXANDER, Thomas B., et al. "Who Were the Alabama Whigs?" *Ala Rev,* 16 (1963), 5–19.

2546 BERGERON, Paul H. "The Election of 1843: A Whig Triumph in Tennessee." *Tenn Hist Q*, 22 (1963), 123–136.

2547 CAMPBELL, Randolph B. "The Whig Party of Texas in the Elections of 1848 and 1852." *SW Hist Q*, 73 (1969), 17–34.

2548 CARROLL, E. Malcolm. *Origins of the Whig Party*. Magnolia, Mass., [n.d.].

2549 COFFIN, John A. "A History of the Whig Party in Kentucky." Doctoral dissertation, Indiana University, 1933.

2550 COLE, Arthur C. *The Whig Party in the South*. Magnolia, Mass., [n.d.].

2551 DICKEY, Dallas C. *Seargent S. Prentiss, Whig Orator of the Old South*. Magnolia, Mass., 1970.

2552 DOHERTY, Herbert J., Jr. *The Whigs of Florida, 1845–1854*. Gainesville, Fla., 1959.

2553 GUNDERSON, Robert G. "The Great Baltimore Whig Convention of 1840." *Md Hist Mag*, 47 (1952), 11–18.

2554 GUNDERSON, Robert G. *The Log Cabin Campaign*. Lexington, Ky., 1957.

2555 HENRY, Milton. "What Became of the Tennessee Whigs?" *Tenn Hist Q*, 11 (1952), 57–62.

2556 HOFFMAN, William S. "John Branch and the Origins of the Whig Party in North Carolina." *N C Hist Rev*, 35 (1958), 299–315.

2557 HOFFMAN, William S. "Willie P. Mangum and the Whig Revival of the Doctrine of Instructions." *J S Hist*, 22 (1956), 338–354.

2558 JACKSON, Carlton L. "A History of the Whig Party in Alabama, 1828–1860." Doctoral dissertation, University of Georgia, 1963.

2559 LONDON, Lawrence F. "George Edmund Badger, Member of the Harrison-Tyler Cabinet, 1841." *S Atl Q*, 37 (1938), 307–327.

2560 McMILLAN, Malcolm C. "Joseph Glover Baldwin Reports on the Whig National Convention of 1848." *J S Hist*, 25 (1959), 366–382.

2561 McWHINEY, Grady. 'Were the Whigs a Class Party in Alabama?" *J S Hist*, 23 (1957), 510–522.

2562 MARSHALL, Lynn L. "The Strange Stillbirth of the Whig Party." *Am Hist Rev*, 72 (1967), 445–468.

2563 MERING, John V. *The Whig Party in Missouri*. Columbia, Mo., 1967.

2564 MOORE, Powell A. "The Establishment of the Whig Party in Tennessee." Doctoral dissertation, Indiana University, 1932.

2565 MOORE, Powell A. "The Revolt against Jackson in Tennessee, 1835–1836." *J S Hist*, 2 (1936), 334–359.

2566 MORRILL, James K. "The Presidential Election of 1852: Death Knell of the Whig Party of North Carolina." *N C Hist Rev*, 44 (1967), 342–359.

2567 MURRAY, Paul. *The Whig Party in Georgia, 1825–1853*. Chapel Hill, 1948.†

2568 NORTON, Leslie M. "A History of the Whig Party in Louisiana." Doctoral dissertation, Louisiana State University, 1940.

2569 PARKS, Edd Winfield. "Zollicoffer: Southern Whig." *Tenn Hist Q*, 11 (1958), 346–355.

2570 PARKS, Joseph H. "The Tennessee Whigs and the Kansas-Nebraska Bill." *J S Hist*, 10 (1944), 308–330.

2571 PEGG, Herbert D. *The Whig Party in North Carolina*. Chapel Hill, [1968?].

2572 POAGE, G. R. *Henry Clay and the Whig Party*. Magnolia, Mass., 1965.

2573 SELLERS, Charles G., Jr. "Who Were the Southern Whigs?" *Am Hist Rev*, 59 (1954), 335–346.

2574 SIMMS, Henry H. *Rise of the Whigs in Virginia, 1824–1840*. Richmond, Va., 1929.

2575 SMITH, W. Wayne. "The Whig Party in Maryland, 1826–1856." Doctoral dissertation, University of Maryland, 1967.

2576 STEEL, Edward M., Jr. *T. Butler King of Georgia*. Athens, Ga., 1964.

2577 STEPHENSON, Wendell H. *Alexander Porter, Whig Planter of Old Louisiana*. New York, 1969.

2578 TREGLE, Joseph G., Jr. "Through Friends and Foes with Alexander Porter." *La Hist*, 3 (1962), 173–191.

2579 VAN DEUSEN, Glyndon G. "Henry Clay, 1852–1857." *Filson Club Hist Q*, 26 (1952), 338–343.

2580 WILLIAMS, Max R. "The Foundations of the Whig Party in North Carolina: A Synthesis and a Modest Proposal." *N C Hist Rev*, 47 (1970), 115–129.

2581 WILLIAMS, Max R. "William A. Graham and the Election of 1844: A Study in North Carolina Politics." *N C Hist Rev*, 45 (1968), 23–46.

D. Know Nothing

2582 BEAN, William G. "An Aspect of Know Nothingism—The Immigrant and Slavery." *S Atl Q*, 23 (1924), 319–334.

2583 CARMAN, Harry J., and Reinhard H. LUTHIN. "Some Aspects of the Know-Nothing Movement Reconsidered." *S Atl Q*, 39 (1940), 213–234.

2584 COLLINS, Arthur L. "The Anti-Masonic Movement in Early Missouri." *Mo Hist Rev*, 39 (1944), 45–52.

2585 HOLT, Michael F. "The Politics of Impatience: The Origins of Know Nothingism." *J Am Hist*, 60 (1973), 309–331.

2586 McGANN, Sister Agnes Geraldine. *Nativism in Kentucky to 1860*. Washington, D.C., 1944.

2587 OVERDYKE, W. Darrell. "History of the American Party in Louisiana." *La Hist Q*, 15 (1932), 581–588; 16 (1933), 84–91, 256–278, 409–426, 608–627.

2588 OVERDYKE, W. Darrell. *The Know-Nothing Party in the South*. Magnolia, Mass., [n.d.].

2589 REINDERS, Robert C. "The Louisiana American Party and the Catholic Church." *Mid-Am*, 40 (1958), 218–228.

2590 RICE, Philip M. "The Know-Nothing Party in Virginia." *Va Mag Hist Biog*, 55 (1947), 61–75, 159–169.

2591 SMITH, Harold T. "The Know-Nothings in Arkansas." *Ark Hist Q*, 34 (1975), 291–303.

2592 SOULE, Leon C. *The Know-Nothing Party in New Orleans: A Reappraisal*. Baton Rouge, 1961.

2593 THOMPSON, Arthur W. "Political Nativism in Florida, 1848–1860: A Phase of Anti-Secessionism." *J S Hist*, 15 (1949), 39–65.

2594 WOOSTER, Ralph A. "An Analysis of the Texas Know-Nothings." *SW Hist Q*, 70 (1967), 414–423.

9. Tariff and Nullification

2595 BANCROFT, Frederic. *Calhoun and the South Carolina Nullification Movement*. Magnolia, Mass., 1966.

2596 BERGERON, Paul H. "Tennessee's Response to the Nullification Crisis." *J S Hist*, 39 (1973), 23–44.

2597 BOUCHER, Chauncey S. *Nullification Controversy in South Carolina*. Westport, Conn., 1969.

2598 FREEHLING, William W., ed. *Nullification Era: A Documentary Record*. Magnolia, Mass., [n.d.].

2599 FREEHLING, William W. *Prelude to Civil War: Nullification Controversy in South Carolina, 1816–1836*. New York, 1968.†

2600 GREENBERG, Irwin F. "Justice William Johnson: South Carolina Unionist, 1823–1830." *Pa Hist*, 36 (1969), 307–334.

2601 LESESNE, J. Mauldin. "The Nullification Controversy in an Up-Country District." *Proc S C Hist Assn*, 9 (1939), 13–24.

2602 PREYER, Norris W. "Southern Support of the Tariff of 1816: A Reappraisal." *J S Hist*, 25 (1959), 306–322.

2603 ROGERS, George C., Jr. "South Carolina Federalists and the Origins of the Nullification Movement." *S C Hist Mag*, 71 (1970), 17–35.

2604 ROLPH, Earl R. "The Economics of·the Nullification Movement." *W Ec J*, 11 (1973), 381–393.

2605 TREGLE, Joseph G., Jr. "Louisiana and the Tariff, 1816–1846." *La Hist Q*, 25 (1942), 24–148.

2606 WEHMANN, Howard H., ed. "Noise, Novelties and Nullifiers: A U.S. Navy Officer's Impression of the Nullification Controversy." *S C Hist Mag*, 76 (1975), 21–24.

2607 WILSON, Major L. " 'Liberty and Union': An Analysis of Three Concepts Involved in the Nullification Controversy." *J S Hist*, 33 (1967), 331–355.

10. Supreme Court and Its Decisions, Excepting the Dred Scott Case

2608 BEDFORD, Henry F. "William Johnson and the Marshall Court." *S C Hist Mag*, 62 (1961), 165–171.

2609 HAINES, Charles G. *The Role of the Supreme Court in American Government and Politics, 1789–1835*. Berkeley, Cal., 1934.

2610 HARRIS, Robert J. "Chief Justice Taney: Prophet of Reform and Reaction." *Van Law Rev*, 10 (1957), 227–257.

2611 LONGAKER, Richard P. "Andrew Jackson and the Judiciary." *Pol Sci Q*, 71 (1956), 341–364.

2612 MAGRATH, C. Peter. *Yazoo: Law and Politics in the New Republic: The case of Fletcher v. Peck*. Providence, R.I., 1966.

2613 MATHIS, Doyle. "*Chisholm v. Georgia*: Background and Settlement." *J Am Hist*, 54 (1967), 19–29.

2614 MILES, Edwin A. "After John Marshall's Decision: *Worcester v. Georgia* and the Nullification Crisis." *J S Hist*, 39 (1973), 519–544.

2615 MORGAN, Donald G. *Justice William Johnson, the First Dissenter: The Career and Constitutional Philosophy of a Jeffersonian Judge*. Columbia, S.C., 1944.

2616 NEWMYER, R. Kent. *The Supreme Court under Marshall and Taney*. Arlington Heights, Ill., 1969.

2617 PHILLIPS, Ulrich B. *Georgia and State Rights*. See **2487**.

2618 SMITH, Charles W. *Roger B. Taney: Jacksonian Jurist*. New York, 1973.

2619 SMITH, James M. "Sedition in the Old Dominion: James T. Callender and *The Prospect before Us*." *J S Hist*, 20 (1954), 157–182.

2620 SWISHER, Carl B. *Roger B. Taney*. New York, 1936.

2621 WARREN, Charles. *The Supreme Court in United States History*. 2 vols. Rev. ed. Boston, 1960.

11. *Indian Policy and Indian Removal*

2622 COTTERILL, Robert S. "Federal Indian Management in the South, 1789–1825." *Miss Val Hist Rev*, 20 (1933), 333–352.

2623 DeROSIER, Arthur H. "John C. Calhoun and the Removal of the Choctaw Indians." *Proc S C Hist Assn*, 27 (1957), 33–45.

2624 DeROSIER, Arthur H. *The Removal of the Choctaw Indians*. New York, 1972.†

2625 FAUST, Richard H. "Another Look at General Jackson and the Indians of the Mississippi Territory." *Ala Rev*, 28 (1975), 202–217.

2626 FOREMAN, Grant. *Indian Removal: Emigration of the Five Civilized Tribes*. Norman, Okla., 1976.

2627 HOFFMAN, William S. "Andrew Jackson, State Rightist: The Case of the Georgia Indians." *Tenn Hist Q*, 11 (1952), 329–345.

2628 MOULTON, Gary E. *John Ross, Cherokee Chief*. Athens, Ga., 1978.

2629 PRUCHA, Francis P. "Andrew Jackson's Indian Policy: A Reassessment." *J Am Hist*, 56 (1969), 527–539.

2630 STARKEY, M. L. *The Cherokee Nation*. New York, 1946.

2631 YOUNG, Mary E. "Indian Removal and Land Allotment: The Civilized Tribes and Jacksonian Justice." *Am Hist Rev*, 64 (1958), 31–45.

2632 YOUNG, Mary E. *Redskins, Ruffleshirts, and Rednecks: Indian Allotments in Alabama and Mississippi, 1830–1860*. Norman, Okla., 1961.

12. Biographies

AUSTIN, STEPHEN F.

2633 BARKER, Eugene C. *Life of Stephen F. Austin, Founder of Texas.* Austin, Tex., 1969.†

BELL, JOHN

2634 PARKS, Joseph H. *John Bell of Tennessee.* Baton Rouge, 1950.

BENTON, THOMAS HART

2635 BENTON, Thomas Hart. *Thirty Years' View.* 2 vols. St. Clair Shores, Mich., 1976.

2636 CHAMBERS, William N. *Old Bullion Benton, Senator from the New West: Thomas Hart Benton, 1782–1858.* New York, 1970.

2637 SMITH, Elbert B. *Magnificent Missourian: The Life of Thomas Hart Benton.* Westport, Conn., 1973.

BERRIEN, JOHN M.

2638 McCRARY, Royce C. "John MacPherson Berrien of Georgia (1781–1856): A Political Biography." Doctoral dissertation, University of Georgia, 1971.

BIRNEY, JAMES G.

2639 FLADELAND, Betty L. *James G. Birney: Slaveholder to Abolitionist.* Westport, Conn., 1969.

BLAIR, FRANCIS P.

2640 SMITH, William E. *The Francis Preston Blair Family in Politics.* 2 vols. New York, 1969.

BRECKINRIDGE, JOHN C.

2641 DAVIS, William C. *Breckinridge: Statesman, Soldier, Symbol.* Baton Rouge, 1974.

BROWN, ALBERT GALLATIN

2642 RANCK, James B. *Albert Gallatin Brown: Radical Southern Nationalist.* Philadelphia, Pa., 1974.

BROWN, JOHN

2643 OATES, Stephen B. *To Purge This Land with Blood: A Biography of John Brown*. See **743**.

BUCHANAN, JAMES

2644 KLEIN, Philip S. *President James Buchanan: A Biography*. University Park, Pa., 1962.

CALHOUN, JOHN C.

2645 CAPERS, Gerald M. *John C. Calhoun, Opportunist: A Reappraisal*. New York, 1969.†

2646 COIT, Margaret. *John C. Calhoun: American Portrait*. Boston, 1950.†

2647 SPAIN, August O. *The Political Theory of John C. Calhoun*. New York, 1968.

2648 WILTSE, Charles M. *John C. Calhoun*. 3 vols. New York, 1968.

CALL, RICHARD KEITH

2649 DOHERTY, Herbert J., Jr. *Richard Keith Call: Southern Unionist*. Gainesville, Fla., 1961.

CLAY, HENRY

2650 EATON, Clement. *Henry Clay and the Art of American Politics*. Boston, 1957.†

2651 VAN DEUSEN, Glyndon G. *Life of Henry Clay*. Boston, 1964.

COBB, HOWELL

2652 JOHNSON, Zachary T. *Political Policies of Howell Cobb*. Nashville, Tenn., 1929.

COOPER, THOMAS

2653 MALONE, Dumas. *The Public Life of Thomas Cooper, 1783–1839*. See **1622**.

CRAWFORD, WILLIAM H.

2654 MOONEY, Chase C. *William H. Crawford, 1772–1834*. Lexington, Ky., 1974.

CRITTENDEN, JOHN J.

2655 KIRWAN, Albert D. *John J. Crittenden*. Westport, Conn., 1974.

DAVIS, JEFFERSON

2656 McELROY, Robert M. *Jefferson Davis, the Unreal and the Real.* 2 vols. Millwood, N.Y., 1969.

DOUGLAS, STEPHEN A.

2657 CAPERS, Gerald M. *Stephen A. Douglas: Defender of the Union.* Boston, 1959.

2658 JOHANNSEN, Robert W. *Stephen A. Douglas.* New York, 1973.

FORSYTH, JOHN

2659 DUCKETT, Alvin L. *John Forsyth: Political Tactician.* Athens, Ga., 1962.

GAINES, EDMUND PENDLETON

2660 SILVER, James W. *Edmund Pendleton Gaines, Frontier General.* Baton Rouge, 1949.

GARRISON, WILLIAM LLOYD

2661 MERRILL, Walter M. *Against Wind and Tide: A Biography of William Lloyd Garrison.* See **741**.

2662 THOMAS, John L. *The Liberator, William Lloyd Garrison, a Biography.* See **762**.

GRUNDY, FELIX

2663 PARKS, Joseph H. *Felix Grundy, Champion of Democracy.* Baton Rouge, 1940.

HAMMOND, JAMES HENRY

2664 MERRITT, Elizabeth. *James Henry Hammond.* Baltimore, Md., 1923.

2665 TUCKER, Robert C. "James Henry Hammond, South Carolinian." Doctoral dissertation, University of North Carolina, 1958.

HAYNE, ROBERT Y.

2666 JERVEY, Theodore D. *Robert Y. Hayne and His Times.* New York, 1970.

HOUSTON, SAM

2667 JAMES, Marquis. *The Raven, a Biography of Sam Houston.* St. Simons Island, Ga., 1977.†

HUNTER, ROBERT M. T.

2668 SIMMS, Henry H. *Life of Robert M. T. Hunter: A Study in Sectionalism and Secession.* Richmond, Va., 1935.

JACKSON, ANDREW

2669 JAMES, Marquis. *Andrew Jackson.* 2 vols. in 1. New York, 1940.

2670 REMINI, Robert. *Andrew Jackson and the Course of American Empire.* New York, 1977.

2671 WARD, John W. *Andrew Jackson: Symbol for an Age.* New York, 1962.†

JEFFERSON, THOMAS

2672 KOCH, Adrienne. *Jefferson and Madison: The Great Collaboration.* See **2494**.

2673 MALONE, Dumas. *Jefferson and His Time.* v. 1–. Boston, 1951–.†

2674 MAYO, Bernard. *Myths and Men: Patrick Henry, George Washington, Thomas Jefferson.* New York, 1977.†

2675 PETERSON, Merrill D. *Thomas Jefferson and the New Nation.* New York, 1975.†

JOHNSON, HERSCHEL V.

2676 FLIPPIN, Percy S. *Herschel v. Johnson of Georgia, State Rights Unionist.* Richmond, Va., 1931.

JOHNSON, RICHARD M.

2677 MEYER, Leland W. *The Life and Times of Colonel Richard M. Johnson of Kentucky.* New York, 1967.

KING, THOMAS BUTLER

2678 STEEL, Edward M., Jr. *T. Butler King of Georgia.* See **2576**.

LAMAR, MIRABEAU BUONAPARTE

2679 GAMBRELL, Herbert P. *Mirabeau Buonaparte Lamar: Troubadour and Crusader.* Dallas, Tex., 1934.

LEGARÉ, HUGH SWINTON

2680 RHEA, Linda. *Hugh Swinton Legaré, a Charleston Intellectual.* See **1981**.

LIVINGSTON, EDWARD

2681 HATCHER, William B. *Edward Livingston: Jeffersonian Republican and Jacksonian Democrat.* See **960**.

LOVEJOY, ELIJAH P.

2682 DILLON, Merton L. *Elijah P. Lovejoy, Abolitionist Editor.* See **709**.

MADISON, JAMES

2683 BRANT, Irving. *James Madison.* 6 vols. Indianapolis, Ind., 1940–1961.

2684 KETCHAM, Ralph. *James Madison: A Biography.* New York, 1971.

MONROE, JAMES

2685 AMMON, Harry. *James Monroe: The Quest for National Identity.* New York, 1971.

2686 CRESSON, William P. *James Monroe.* Hamden, Conn., 1971.

NELSON, THOMAS A.R.

2687 ALEXANDER, Thomas B. *Thomas A. R. Nelson of East Tennessee.* See **2544**.

PERRY, BENJAMIN F.

2688 KIBLER, Lillian A. *Benjamin F. Perry, South Carolina Unionist.* Durham, N.C., 1946.

PETIGRU, JAMES LOUIS

2689 CARSON, James P. *Life, Letters, and Speeches of James Louis Petigru, the Union Man of South Carolina.* Washington, D.C., 1920.

PIERCE, FRANKLIN

2690 NICHOLS, Roy F. *Franklin Pierce, Young Hickory of the Granite Hills.* 2nd ed. Philadelphia, Pa., 1964.

PINCKNEY, CHARLES COTESWORTH

2691 ZAHNISER, Marvin R. *Charles Cotesworth Pinckney: Founding Father.* Chapel Hill, 1967.

POINSETT, JOEL R.

2692 RIPPY, J. Fred. *Joel R. Poinsett, Versatile American*. St. Clair Shores, Mich., 1970.

POLK, JAMES K.

2693 SELLERS, Charles G., Jr. *James K. Polk*. v. 1–. Princeton, 1957–.

PORTER, ALEXANDER

2694 STEPHENSON, Wendell H. *Alexander Porter, Whig Planter of Old Louisiana*. See **2577**.

PRENTISS, SEARGENT S.

2695 DICKEY, Dallas C. *Seargent S. Prentiss, Whig Orator of the Old South*. See **2551**.

RANDOLPH, JOHN

2696 BRUCE, William C. *John Randolph of Roanoke, 1773–1833*. 2 vols. New York, 1969.

2697 KIRK, Russell. *Randolph of Roanoke*. Indianapolis, Ind., 1978.

RHETT, ROBERT BARNWELL

2698 WHITE, Laura. *Robert Barnwell Rhett: Father of Secession*. Magnolia, Mass., 1965.

RITCHIE, THOMAS

2699 AMBLER, Charles H. *Thomas Ritchie: A Study in Virginia Politics*. New York, 1970.

RUFFIN, EDMUND

2700 CRAVEN, Avery O. *Edmund Ruffin, Southerner: A Study in Secession*. Baton Rouge, 1966.†

SCOTT, WINFIELD

2701 ELLIOTT, Charles W. *Winfield Scott: The Soldier and the Man*. New York, 1937.

SMITH, WILLIAM LOUGHTON

2702 ROGERS, George C., Jr. *Evolution of a Federalist: William Loughton Smith of Charleston, 1758–1812.* Columbia, S.C., 1962.

STEPHENS, ALEXANDER H.

2703 RABUN, James Z. "Alexander H. Stephens, 1812–61." Doctoral dissertation, University of Chicago, 1948.

2704 VON ABELE, Rudolph. *Alexander H. Stephens: A Biography.* New York, 1946.

SUMNER, CHARLES

2705 DONALD, David H. *Charles Sumner and the Coming of the Civil War.* New York, 1960.

TANEY, ROGER B.

2706 SMITH, Charles W. *Roger B. Taney: Jacksonian Jurist.* See **2618**.

2707 SWISHER, Carl B. *Roger B. Taney.* See **2620**.

TAYLOR, JOHN

2708 MUDGE, Eugene T. *The Social Philosophy of John Taylor of Caroline.* See **2498**.

2709 SIMMS, Henry H. *Life of John Taylor of Caroline.* Richmond, Va., 1932.

TAYLOR, ZACHARY

2710 DYER, Brainerd. *Zachary Taylor.* New York, 1946.

2711 HAMILTON, Holman. *Zachary Taylor.* 2 vols. Hamden, Conn., 1966.

TOOMBS, ROBERT

2712 THOMPSON, William Y. *Robert Toombs of Georgia.* Baton Rouge, 1966.

TUCKER, NATHANIEL BEVERLEY

2713 BRUGGER, Robert J. *Beverley Tucker: Heart over Head in the Old South.* See **1590**.

TYLER, JOHN

2714 CHITWOOD, Oliver P. *John Tyler, Champion of the Old South*. New York, 1964.

2715 SEAGER, Robert. *And Tyler Too: A Biography of John Tyler and Julia Gardiner Tyler*. New York, 1963.

UPSHUR, ABEL P.

2716 HALL, Claude H. *Abel Parker Upshur, Conservative Virginian, 1790–1844*. Madison, Wis., 1964.

VAN BUREN, MARTIN

2717 CURTIS, James C. *The Fox at Bay: Martin Van Buren and the Presidency, 1837–1841*. Lexington, Ky., 1970.

2718 REMINI, Robert V. *Martin Van Buren and the Making of the Democratic Party*. New York, 1970.†

WALKER, ROBERT J.

2719 SHENTON, James P. *Robert John Walker: A Politician from Jackson to Lincoln*. New York, 1961.

WALKER, WILLIAM

2720 GREENE, Laurence. *The Filibuster: The Career of William Walker*. Indianapolis, Ind., 1937.

2721 SCROGGS, William O. *Filibusters and Financiers: The Story of William Walker and His Associates*. New York, 1969.

WELD, THEODORE DWIGHT

2722 THOMAS, Benjamin P. *Theodore Weld, Crusader for Freedom*. See **761**.

WIGFALL, LOUIS T.

2723 KING, Alvy L. *Louis T. Wigfall: Southern Fire-Eater*. Baton Rouge, 1970.

WORTH, JONATHAN

2724 ZUBER, Richard L. *Jonathan Worth: A Biography of a Southern Unionist*. Chapel Hill, 1965.

YANCEY, WILLIAM L.

2725 DuBOSE, John W. *The Life and Times of William Lowndes Yancey*. 2 vols. Magnolia, Mass., 1942.

XX. Strain and Alienation
(see also Section XIX, part 12)

1. General Evidences of
Increasing Strain and Alienation

2726 BARNEY, William L. *The Road to Secession: A New Perspective on the Old South.* New York, 1972.†

2727 COLE, Arthur C. "The South and the Right of Secession in the Early Fifties." *Miss Val Hist Rev*, 1 (1914), 376–399.

2728 CRAVEN, Avery O. *Civil War in the Making, 1815–1860.* Baton Rouge, 1968.†

2729 CRAVEN, Avery O. *The Coming of the Civil War.* 2nd ed. Chicago, 1966.†

2730 CRAVEN, Avery O. *The Growth of Southern Nationalism, 1848–1861.* See **57**.

2731 CRENSHAW, Ollinger. *The Slave States in the Presidential Election of 1860.* Baltimore, Md., 1945.

2732 DUFFY, John. "A Note on Ante-Bellum Southern Nationalism and Medical Practice." See **1697**.

2733 EATON, Clement. "Censorship of the Southern Mails." *Am Hist Rev*, 48 (1943), 266–280.

2734 EATON, Clement. "Henry A. Wise and the Virginia Fire-Eaters of 1856." *Miss Val Hist Rev*, 21 (1935), 495–512.

2735 EATON, Clement. "The Resistance of the South to Northern Radicalism." *N Eng Q*, 8 (1935), 215–231.

2736 EZELL, John S. "A Southern Education for Southrons." See **1510**.

2737 FLOAN, Howard R. *The South in Northern Eyes, 1831–1861.* Austin, Tex., 1958.

2738 FREDRICKSON, George M. *The Inner Civil War: Northern Intellectuals and the Crisis of the Union.* New York, 1965.

2739 JOHANNSEN, Robert W. "Stephen A. Douglas and the South." *J S Hist*, 33 (1967), 26–50.

2740 McLENDON, James H. "John A. Quitman, Fire-Eating Governor." *J Miss Hist*, 15 (1933), 73–89.

2741 MERIWETHER, Robert L. "Preston S. Brooks on the Caning of Charles Sumner." *S C Hist Gen Mag*, 52 (1951), 1–4.

2742 MORISON, Elting. "Election of 1860." *History of American Presidential Elections, 1789–1968.* Eds. Arthur M. Schlesinger, Jr. and Fred L. Israel. 4 vols. New York, 1971.

2743 PHILLIPS, Ulrich B. *The Course of the South to Secession.* Ed. E. Merton Coulter. New York, 1964.†

2744 POTTER, David M. *The Impending Crisis, 1848–1861*. Ed. Don E. Fehrenbacher. New York, 1976.†

2744 POTTER, David M. *The South and the Sectional Conflict*. Baton Rouge, 1968.†

2746 SIMMS, Henry H. *A Decade of Sectional Controversy, 1851–1861*. Chapel Hill, 1942.

2747 STEPHENSON, Nathaniel W. "Southern Nationalism in South Carolina in 1851." *Am Hist Rev*, 36 (1931), 314–335.

2. Missouri Compromise

2748 BAILEY, Hugh C. "Alabama Political Leaders and the Missouri Compromise." *Ala Rev*, 9 (1956), 120–134.

2749 BROWN, Richard H. "The Missouri Crisis, Slavery, and the Politics of Jacksonianism." *S Atl Q*, 65 (1966), 55–72.

2750 ERNST, Robert. "Rufus King, Slavery, and the Missouri Crisis." *N-Y Hist Soc Q*, 46 (1962), 357–382.

2751 HODDER, Frank H. "Side Lights on the Missouri Compromise." *Ann Rept Am Hist Assn*, (1909), 151–161.

2752 JOHNSON, William R. "Prelude to the Missouri Compromise." *Ark Hist Q*, 24 (1965), 47–66.

2753 MOORE, Glover. *The Missouri Controversy, 1819–1821*. Lexington, Ky., 1966.†

2754 SIMPSON, Albert F. "The Political Significance of Slave Representation, 1787–1821." *J S Hist*, 7 (1941), 315–342.

3. Slavery in the Territories

2755 BERWANGER, Eugene H. *The Frontier against Slavery: Western Anti-Negro Prejudice and the Slavery Extension Controversy*. Urbana, Ill., 1967.

2756 BOUCHER, Chauncey S. "*In Re* That Aggressive Slavocracy." *Miss Val Hist Rev*, 8 (1921), 13–79.

2757 DAVIS, David Brion. *The Slave Power Conspiracy and the Paranoid Style*. Baton Rouge, 1969.

2758 FILLER, Louis. *The Crusade against Slavery, 1830–1860*. See **625**.

2759 GOVAN, Thomas P. "Slavery and the Civil War." *Sew Rev*, 48 (1940), 533–543.

2760 HUBBART, Henry Clyde. " 'Pro-Southern' Influences in the Far West, 1840–1865." *Miss Val Hist Rev*, 20 (1933), 45–62.

2761 MERK, Frederick. *Slavery and the Annexation of Texas*. New York, 1972.

2762 MERKEL, Benjamin C. "The Slavery Issue and the Political Decline of Thomas Hart Benton." *Mo Hist Rev*, 38 (1944), 388–407.

2763 NYE, Russel B. "The Slave Power Conspiracy, 1830–1860." *Sci and Soc*, 10 (1946), 262–274.

2764 RAMSDELL, Charles W. "The Natural Limits of Slavery Expansion." See **325.**

2765 RUSSEL, Robert R. "Constitutional Doctrines with Regard to Slavery in the Territories." *J S Hist*, 32 (1966), 466–486.

4. Texas and the Mexican War

2766 BARKER, Eugene C. "Annexation of Texas." *SW Hist Q*, 50 (1946), 49–74.

2767 BINKLEY, William C. *The Expansionist Movement in Texas, 1836–1859*. New York, 1970.

2768 BINKLEY, William C. *The Texas Revolution*. Baton Rouge, 1952.

2769 BOUCHER, Chauncey S. "The Annexation of Texas and the Bluffton Movement in South Carolina." *Miss Val Hist Rev*, 6 (1919), 3–33.

2770 BRAUER, Kinley J. *Cotton versus Conscience: Massachusetts Whig Politics and Southwestern Expansion, 1843–1848*. Lexington, Ky., 1967.

2771 FONER, Eric. "The Wilmot Proviso Revisited." *J Am Hist*, 56 (1969), 262–279.

2772 HENRY, Robert S. *The Story of the Mexican War*. Indianapolis, Ind., 1950.

2773 LATHROP, Barnes. *Migration into East Texas, 1835–1860*. Austin, Tex., 1949.

2774 MERK, Frederick. "A Safety Valve Thesis and Texas Annexation." *Miss Val Hist Rev*, 49 (1962), 413–436.

2775 MORRISON, Chaplain W. *Democratic Politics and Sectionalism: The Wilmot Proviso Controversy*. Chapel Hill, 1967.

2776 PHILLIPS, Ulrich B., ed. *Correspondence of Robert Toombs, Alexander H. Stephens, and Howell Cobb*. New York, 1970.

2777 POLK, James K. *Diary of James K. Polk during His Presidency, 1845–1849*. Ed. Milton M. Quaife. 4 vols. New York, 1970.

2778 RUIZ, Ramón Eduardo, ed. *Mexican War: Was It Manifest Destiny?* Magnolia, Mass., [n.d.].

2779 SANTA ANNA, Antonio López de. *The Mexican Side of the Texas Revolution*. Tr. Carlos E. Castañeda. 2nd ed. Austin, Tex., 1970.

2780 SEARS, L. M. "Nicholas P. Trist, a Diplomat with Ideals." *Miss Val Hist Rev*, 11 (1924), 85–98.

2781 SINGLETARY, Otis A. *The Mexican War*. Chicago, 1960.

2782 SMITH, Justin H. *Annexation of Texas*. New York, 1972.

2783 SMITH, Justin H. *The War with Mexico*. 2 vols. Magnolia, Mass., [n.d.].

2784 WINSTON, James E. "The Annexation of Texas and The Mississippi Democrats." *SW Hist Q*, 25 (1921), 1–25.

5. *Southern Imperialism*

2785 BRIDGES, C. A. "The Knights of the Golden Circle: A Filibustering Fantasy." *SW Hist Q*, 44 (1941), 287–302.

2786 BROUSSARD, Ray. "Governor John A. Quitman and the Lopez Expedition of 1851–1852." *J Miss Hist*, 28 (1966), 103–120.

2787 FORNELL, Earl W. "Texans and the Filibusters in the 1850's." *SW Hist Q*, 59 (1956), 411–428.

2788 FRANKLIN, John H. "The Southern Expansionists of 1846." *J S Hist*, 25 (1959), 323–338.

2789 FULLER, John D. P. "The Slavery Question and the Movement to Acquire Mexico, 1840–1848." *Miss Val Hist Rev*, 21 (1934), 31–48.

2790 GIBSON, George H. "Opinion in North Carolina Regarding the Acquisition of Texas and Cuba, 1835–1855." *N C Hist Rev*, 37 (1960), 1–21, 185–201.

2791 LANDER, Ernest M., Jr. "The Reluctant Imperialist: South Carolina, the Rio Grande, and the Mexican War." *SW Hist Q*, 78 (1975), 254–270.

2792 MAY, Robert E. *The Southern Dream of a Caribbean Empire, 1854–1861.* Baton Rouge, 1973.

2793 MERK, Frederick. *Manifest Destiny and Mission in American History.* New York, 1966.†

2794 MERK, Frederick. *The Monroe Doctrine and American Expansionism, 1843–1849.* New York, 1966.

2795 MOORE, J. Preston. "Pierre Soulé: Southern Expansionist and Promoter." *J S Hist*, 21 (1955), 203–223.

2796 PLETCHER, David M. *The Diplomacy of Annexation: Texas, Oregon, and the Mexican War.* Columbia, Mo., 1973.

2797 SCROGGS, William O. *Filibusters and Financiers: The Story of William Walker and His Associates.* See **2721**.

2798 SCROGGS, William O. "William Walker's Designs on Cuba." *Miss Val Hist Rev*, 1 (1914), 198–211.

2799 URBAN, C. Stanley. "The Ideology of Southern Imperialism: New Orleans and the Caribbean, 1845–1860." *La Hist Q*, 39 (1956), 48–73.

6. *Attempts to Achieve Southern Unity*

2800 BARNWELL, John Gibbes. "Robert W. Barnwell and South Carolina Politics, 1850–1852." Master's thesis, University of North Carolina, Chapel Hill, 1972.

2801 JENNINGS, Thelma N. "A Reappraisal of the Nashville Convention." Doctoral dissertation, University of Tennessee, 1968.

2802 McCARDELL, John M. "The Idea of a Southern Nation: Southern Nationalists and Southern Nationalism, 1830–1861." Doctoral dissertation, Harvard University, 1976.

2803 McCRARY, Royce C., ed. "Henry W. Hilliard and the Southern Caucus of 1848–49: A Letter to John MacPherson Berrien [May 1849]." *Ala Hist Q*, 37 (1975), 151–153.

2804 MONTGOMERY, Horace. "The Solid South Movement of 1855." *Ga Hist Q*, 26 (1942), 101–112.

2805 NEWBERRY, Farrar. "The Nashville Convention and Southern Sentiment of 1850." *S Atl Q*, 11 (1912), 259–273.

2806 PERKINS, Howard C. "A Neglected Phase of the Movement for Southern Unity, 1847–1852." *J S Hist*, 12 (1946), 153–203.

2807 STEPHENSON, Nathaniel W. "Southern Nationalism in South Carolina in 1851." See **2747**.

2808 TUCKER, Robert C. "James H. Hammond and the Southern Convention." *Proc S C Hist Assn*, 30 (1960), 4–14.

7. Compromise of 1850

2809 BROOKS, Robert P. "Howell Cobb and the Crisis of 1850." *Miss Val Hist Rev*, 4 (1917), 279–298.

2810 DOHERTY, Herbert J., Jr. "Florida and the Crisis of 1850." *J S Hist*, 19 (1953), 32–47.

2811 HAMILTON, Holman. " 'The Cave of the Winds' and the Compromise of 1850." *J S Hist*, 23 (1957), 331–353.

2812 HAMILTON, Holman. "Democratic Senate Leadership and the Compromise of 1850." *Miss Val Hist Rev*, 41 (1954), 403–418.

2813 HAMILTON, Holman. *Prologue to Conflict: The Crisis and the Compromise of 1850.* Lexington, Ky., 1964.

2814 HAMILTON, Holman. "Texas Bonds and Northern Profits: A Study in Compromise, Investment, and Lobby Influence." *Miss Val Hist Rev*, 43 (1957), 579–594.

2815 HODDER, Frank H. "The Authorship of the Compromise of 1850." *Miss Val Hist Rev*, 22 (1936), 525–536.

2816 HUBBELL, John T. "Three Georgia Unionists and the Compromise of 1850." *Ga Hist Q*, 51 (1967), 307–323.

2817 LONDON, Lawrence F. "George Edmund Badger and the Compromise of 1850." *N C Hist Rev*, 15 (1938), 99–118.

2818 McCARDELL, John. "John A. Quitman and the Compromise of 1850 in Mississippi." *J Miss Hist*, 37 (1975), 239–266.

2819 MARTIN, John M. "William R. King and the Compromise of 1850." *N C Hist Rev*, 39 (1962), 500–518.

2820 MEADOR, John. "Florida and the Compromise of 1850." *Fla Hist Q*, 39 (1960), 16–33.

2821 MONTGOMERY, Horace. "The Crisis of 1850 and Its Effect on Political Parties in Georgia." *Ga Hist Q*, 24 (1940), 293–322.

2822 NORTON, Wesley. "The Presbyterian Press and the Compromise of 1850." *J Presb Hist*, 40 (1962), 189–208.

2823 PARKS, Joseph H. "John Bell and the Compromise of 1850." *J S Hist*, 9 (1943), 328–356.

2824 RUSSEL, Robert R. "What Was the Compromise of 1850?" *J S Hist*, 22 (1956), 292–309.

2825 SHRYOCK, Richard H. *Georgia and the Union in 1850*. New York, [n.d.].

2826 SIOUSSAT, St. George L. "Tennessee, the Compromise of 1850, and the Nashville Convention." *Tenn Hist Mag*, 4 (1918), 215–247.

8. The Fugitive Slave Act and the Personal Liberty Laws

2827 CAMPBELL, Stanley W. *Slave Catchers: Enforcement of the Fugitive Slave Law, 1850–1860*. See **478**.

2828 GARA, Larry. "The Fugitive Slave Law: A Double Paradox." See **479**.

2829 JOHNSON, Allen. "Constitutionality of Fugitive Slave Acts." *Yale Law J*, 31 (1921), 161–182.

2830 LESLIE, William R. "The Constitutional Significance of Indiana's Statute of 1824 of Fugitives from Labor." *J S Hist*, 13 (1947), 338–353.

2831 LESLIE, William R. "The Pennsylvania Fugitive Slave Act of 1826." *J S Hist*, 18 (1952), 429–445.

2832 MORRIS, Thomas D. *Free Men All: The Personal Liberty Laws of the North, 1780–1861*. Baltimore, Md., 1974.

2833 NOGEE, Joseph L. "The Prigg Case and Fugitive Slavery, 1842–1850." *J Neg Hist*, 39 (1954), 185–194.

2834 NOGEE, Joseph L. "The Prigg Case and Its Consequences." *J Neg Hist*, 39 (1954), 195–205.

2835 ROSENBERG, Norman L. "Personal Liberty Laws and Sectional Crisis: 1850–1861." *Civ War Hist*, 17 (1971), 25–44.

2836 TALMADGE, John E. "Georgia Tests the Fugitive Slave Law." *Ga Hist Q*, 49 (1965), 57–64.

2837 THORNBROUGH, Emma Lou. "Indiana and Fugitive Slave Legislation." *Ind Mag Hist*, 50 (1954), 201–228.

9. The Kansas-Nebraska Act and "Bleeding Kansas"

2838 DAVIS, Granville D. "Arkansas and the Blood of Kansas." *J S Hist*, 16 (1950), 431–456.

2839 HARLOW, Ralph V. "Gerrit Smith and the John Brown Raid." *Am Hist Rev*, 38 (1932), 32–60.

2840 HARLOW, Ralph V. "The Rise and Fall of the Kansas Aid Movement." *Am Hist Rev*, 41 (1935), 1–25.

2841 HODDER, Frank H. "Genesis of the Kansas-Nebraska Act." *Proc Wis Hist Soc*, 16 (1912), 69–86.

2842 HODDER, Frank H. "The Railroad Background of the Kansas-Nebraska Act." *Miss Val Hist Rev*, 12 (1925), 3–22.

2843 ISELY, W. H. "The Sharps Rifle Episode in Kansas History." *Am Hist Rev*, 12 (1907), 546–566.

2844 MALIN, James C. "The Motives of Stephen A. Douglas in the Organization of Nebraska Territory: A Letter Dated December 17, 1853." *Kan Hist Q*, 19 (1951), 321–353.

2845 MALIN, James C. *The Nebraska Question, 1852–1854*. Lawrence, Kan., 1953.

2846 MALIN, James C. "The Proslavery Background of the Kansas Struggle." *Miss Val Hist Rev*, 10 (1923), 285–305.

2847 NICHOLS, Roy F. "The Kansas-Nebraska Act: A Century of Historiography." *Miss Val Hist Rev*, 43 (1956), 187–212.

2848 PARKS, Joseph H. "The Tennessee Whigs and the Kansas-Nebraska Bill." *J S Hist*, 10 (1944), 308–330.

2849 RAWLEY, James A. *Race and Politics: "Bleeding Kansas" and the Coming of the Civil War*. Philadelphia, Pa., 1969.†

2850 RAY, P. Orman. *Repeal of the Missouri Compromise, Its Origin and Authorship*. Boston, 1965.

2851 RUSSEL, Robert R. "The Issues in the Congressional Struggle over the Kansas-Nebraska Bill, 1854." *J S Hist*, 29 (1963), 187–210.

2852 RUSSEL, Robert R. "The Pacific Railway Issue in Politics Prior to the Civil War." *Miss Val Hist Rev*, 12 (1925), 187–201.

2853 SHOEMAKER, Floyd C. "Missouri's Proslavery Fight for Kansas (1854–55)." *Mo Hist Rev*, 48 (1954), 221–236, 325–340; 49 (1954), 41–54.

10. The Election of 1856

2854 COX, Monty W. "Freedom during the Fremont Campaign: The Fate of One North Carolina Republican in 1856." *N C Hist Rev*, 45 (1968), 357–383.

2855 NICHOLS, Roy F., and Philip S. KLEIN. "Election of 1856." *History of American Presidential Elections, 1789–1968*. Eds. Arthur M. Schlesinger, Jr., and Fred L. Israel. 4 vols. New York, 1971.

2856 RYLE, Walter H. "Slavery and Party Realignment in the State Elections of 1856." *Mo Hist Q*, 39 (1945), 320–322.

11. Dred Scott Decision

2857 ALEXANDER, Thomas B. "Historical Treatments of the Dred Scott Case." *Proc S C Hist Assn*, 23 (1953), 37–60.

2858 CATTERALL, Helen T. "Some Antecedents of the Dred Scott Case." *Am Hist Rev*, 30 (1924), 56–71.

2859 CORWIN, E. S. "The Dred Scott Decision in the Light of Contemporary Legal Doctrines." *Am Hist Rev*, 17 (1911), 52–69.

2860 EHRLICH, Walter. "Was the Dred Scott Case Valid?" *J Am Hist*, 55 (1968), 252–265.

2861 FEHRENBACHER, Don E. *The Dred Scott Case: Its Significance in American Law and Politics.* New York, 1978.

2862 HODDER, Frank H. "Some Phases of the Dred Scott Case." *Miss Val Hist Rev*, 16 (1929), 3–22.

2863 SCHWARTZ, Harold. "The Controversial Dred Scott Decision" *Mo Hist Rev*, 54 (1960), 262–272.

2864 STENBERG, Richard R. "Some Political Aspects of the Dred Scott Case." *Miss Val Hist Rev*, 19 (1933), 571–577.

2865 SWISHER, Carl B. "Dred Scott One Hundred Years After." *J Pol*, 19 (1957), 167–183.

12. The Lincoln-Douglas Debates

2866 ANGLE, Paul M., ed. *Created Equal? Lincoln-Douglas Debates.* Chicago, 1958.

2867 FEHRENBACHER, Don E. *Prelude to Greatness: Lincoln in the 1850's.* Stanford, Cal., 1962.†

2868 JOHANNSEN, Robert W., ed. *The Lincoln-Douglas Debates of 1858.* New York, 1965.†

2869 JOHANNSEN, Robert W. *Stephen A. Douglas.* See **2658**.

13. John Brown and Harper's Ferry

2870 HARLOW, Ralph V. "Gerrit Smith and the John Brown Raid." See **2839**.

2871 OATES, Stephen B. *To Purge This Land with Blood: A Biography of John Brown.* See **743**.

2872 QUARLES, Benjamin. *Allies for Freedom: Blacks and John Brown.* New York, 1974.

2873 WOODWARD, C. Vann. *The Burden of Southern History.* Baton Rouge, 1968.†

14. Southern Support for the Union

2874 BELOHLAVEK, John M. "John B. Floyd as Governor of Virginia, 1849–1852." *W Va Hist*, 33 (1971), 14–26.

2875 CARSON, James P. *Life, Letters, and Speeches of James Louis Petigru, the Union Man of South Carolina.* See **2689**.

2876 DOHERTY, Herbert J., Jr. *Richard Keith Call: Southern Unionist.* See **2649**.

2877 DOHERTY, Herbert J., Jr. "Union Nationalism in Florida." *Fla Hist Q*, 29 (1950), 83–95.

2878 EVITTS, William J. *A Matter of Allegiances: Maryland from 1850 to 1861.* Baltimore, Md., 1974.

2879 FLIPPIN, Percy S. *Herschel V. Johnson of Georgia, State Rights Unionist.* See **2676**.

2880 FOLK, Edgar E. "W. W. Holden and the Election of 1858." *N C Hist Rev*, 21 (1944), 294–318.

2881 GILLIAM, Will D., Jr. "Robert Jefferson Breckenridge, 1800–1871." *Reg Ky Hist Soc*, 72 (1974), 207–223, 319–336.

2882 GONZALES, John E. "Henry Stuart Foote: A Forgotten Unionist of the Fifties." *S Q*, 1 (1963), 129–139.

2883 GREENE, Helen I. "Politics in Georgia, 1853–1854: The Ordeal of Howell Cobb." *Ga Hist Q*, 30 (1946), 185–211.

2884 HITCHCOCK, William S. "Southern Moderates and Secession: Senator Robert M. T. Hunter's Call for Union." *J Am Hist*, 59 (1973), 871–884.

2885 JACKSON, Carlton. "Alabama's Hilliard: A Nationalistic Rebel of the Old South." *Ala Hist Q*, 31 (1969), 183–205.

2886 JAMES, Marquis. *The Raven: A Biography of Sam Houston.* See **2667**.

2887 KIBLER, Lillian A. *Benjamin F. Perry, South Carolina Unionist.* See **2688**.

2888 KIBLER, Lillian. "Unionist Sentiment in South Carolina in 1860." *J S Hist*, 4 (1938), 346–366.

2889 KIRWAN, Albert D. *John J. Crittenden.* See **2655**.

2890 KNOLES, George H., ed. *The Crisis of the Union, 1860–1861.* Baton Rouge, 1965.

2891 MAKER, Edward R., Jr. "Sam Houston and Secession." *SW Hist Q*, 55 (1952), 448–458.

2892 PARKS, Joseph H. *John Bell of Tennessee.* See **2634**.

2893 RABUN, James Z. "Alexander H. Stephens, 1812–61." See **2703**.

2894 SILBEY, Joel H. "The Southern National Democrats, 1845–1861." *Mid-Am*, 47 (1965), 176–190.

2895 SMYRL, Frank H. "Unionism in Texas, 1856–1861." *SW Hist Q*, 68 (1964), 172–195.

2896 VON ABELE, Rudolph. *Alexander H. Stephens: A Biography.* See **2704**.

2897 WHITE, Laura A. "The National Democrats in South Carolina, 1852 to 1860." *S Atl Q*, 28 (1929), 370–389.

2898 ZUBER, Richard L. *Jonathan Worth: A Biography of a Southern Unionist.* See **2724**.

15. The Election of 1860 and Secession

2899 BARNEY, William L. *The Secessionist Impulse: Alabama and Mississippi in 1860*. Princeton, 1974.

2900 BONNER, Thomas N. "Horace Greeley and the Secession Movement, 1860–1861." *Miss Val Hist Rev*, 38 (1951), 425–444.

2901 BRYAN, T. Conn. "The Secession of Georgia." *Ga Hist Q*, 31 (1947), 89–111.

2902 CAMPBELL, Mary R. "Tennessee's Congressional Delegation in the Sectional Crisis of 1859–1860." *Tenn Hist Q*, 19 (1960), 348–371.

2903 CAUTHEN, Charles E. "South Carolina's Decision to Lead the Secession Movement." *N C Hist Rev*, 18 (1941), 360–372.

2904 CHANNING, Steven. *Crisis of Fear: Secession in South Carolina*. New York, 1974.†

2905 COLE, Arthur C. "Lincoln's Election an Immediate Menace to Slavery in the States?" *Am Hist Rev*, 36 (1931), 740–767.

2906 CRENSHAW, Ollinger. "Christopher G. Memminger's Mission to Virginia, 1860." *J S Hist*, 8 (1942), 334–349.

2907 CURRENT, Richard N. *Lincoln and the First Shot*. Philadelphia, Pa., 1964.†

2908 DEW, Charles B. "Who Won the Secession Election in Louisiana." *J S Hist*, 36 (1970), 18–32.

2909 DONNELLY, William J. "Conspiracy or Popular Movement: The Historiography of Southern Support for Seccession." *N C Hist Rev*, 42 (1965), 70–84.

2910 DUMOND, Dwight L. *The Secession Movement, 1860–61*. New York, 1963.

2911 DUMOND, Dwight L., ed. *Southern Editorials on Secession*. Magnolia, Mass., 1964.

2912 GRAEBNER, Norman A., ed. *Politics and the Crisis of 1860*. Urbana, Ill., 1961.

2913 GUNDERSON, Robert G. *Old Gentlemen's Convention: The Washington Peace Conference of 1861*. Madison, Wis., 1961.

2914 HADD, Donald R. "The Irony of Secession." *Fla Hist Q*, 41 (1962), 22–28.

2915 HAMILTON, J. G. deRoulhac. "Lincoln's Election an Immediate Menace to Slavery in the States?" *Am Hist Rev*, 37 (1932), 700–711.

2916 HARRISON, Lowell H. "Governor Magoffin and the Secession Crisis." *Reg Ky Hist Soc*, 72 (1974), 91–110.

2917 HECK, Frank H. "John C. Breckinridge in the Crisis of 1860–1861." *J S Hist*, 21 (1955), 316–346.

2918 HESSELTINE, William B., and Hazel C WOLF. "Kentucky's Last Peace Effort." *Reg Ky Hist Soc*, 45 (1947), 335–339.

2919 IRONS, George V. "The Secession Movement in Georgia, 1850–1861." Doctoral dissertation, Duke University, 1936.

2920 LONG, Durward, "Unanimity and Disloyalty in Secessionist Alabama." *Civ War Hist*, 11 (1965), 257–273.

2921 MAYER, Henry. " 'A Leaven of Disunion': The Growth of the Secessionist Faction in Alabama, 1847–1851." *Ala Rev*, 22 (1969), 83–116.

2921a MORISON, Elting. "Election of 1860." See **2742**.

2922 PEARSON, Alden B., Jr. "The Tragic Dilemma of a Border-State Moderate: The Rev. George E. Eagleton's Views on Slavery and Secession." *Tenn Hist Q*, 32 (1973), 360–373.

2923 PERKINS, Howard C., ed. *Northern Editorials on Secession*. 2 vols. Magnolia, Mass., 1964.

2924 POTTER, David M. *Lincoln and His Party in the Secession Crisis*. New Haven, Conn., 1942.†

2925 POTTER, David M. "Why the Republicans Rejected Both Compromise and Secession." *The Crisis of the Union*. Ed. George H. Knoles. Baton Rouge, 1965.

2926 RAINWATER, Percy L. *Mississippi, Storm Center of Secession, 1856–1861*. New York, 1969.

2927 REYNOLDS, Donald E. *Editors Make War: Southern Newspapers in the Secession Crisis*. Nashville, Tenn., 1970.

2928 SCROGGS, Jack B. "Arkansas in the Secession Crisis." *Ark Hist Q*, 12 (1953), 179–224.

2929 SHANKS, Henry T. *The Secession Movement in Virginia, 1847–1861*. New York, 1971.

2930 SHORTRIDGE, Wilson P. "Kentucky Neutrality in 1861." *Miss Val Hist Rev*, 9 (1923), 283–301.

2931 SITTERSON, J. Carlyle. *The Secession Movement in North Carolina*. Chapel Hill, 1939.

2932 STAMPP, Kenneth M. *And the War Came: The North and the Secession Crisis, 1860–61*. Baton Rouge, 1950.†

2933 STAMPP, Kenneth M. "Lincoln and the Strategy of Defense in the Crisis of 1861." *J S Hist*, 11 (1945), 297–323.

2934 WOOSTER, Ralph A. "An Analysis of the Membership of Secession Conventions in the Lower South." *J S Hist*, 24 (1958), 360–368.

16. Historians and Causes of the War

2935 BEALE, Howard K. "What Historians Have Said about the Causes of the Civil War." *Soc Sci Res Coun Bul*, 54 (1946), 53–102.

2936 BESTOR, Arthur. "The American Civil War as a Constitutional Crisis." *Am Hist Rev*, 69 (1964), 327–352.

2937 DONALD, David. "American Historians and the Causes of the Civil War." *S Atl Q*, 59 (1960), 351–355.

2938 DRAY, William. "Some Causal Accounts of the American Civil War." *Daedalus*, 91 (1962), 578–598.

2939 FONER, Eric. "The Causes of the American Civil War: Recent Interpretations and New Directions." *Civ War Hist*, 20 (1974), 197–214.

2940 OWSLEY, Frank L. "The Fundamental Cause of the Civil War: Egocentric Sectionalism." *J S Hist*, 7 (1941), 3–18.

2941 OWSLEY, Frank L. "Origins of the American Civil War." *S Rev*, 5 (1940), 609–626.

2942 PRESSLY, Thomas J. *Americans Interpret Their Civil War*. New York, 1965.†

2943 RAMSDELL, Charles W. "The Changing Interpretation of the Civil War." *J S Hist*, 3 (1937), 3–27.

2944 SCHLESINGER, Arthur M., Jr. "The Causes of the Civil War: A Note on Historical Sentimentalism." *Part Rev*, 16 (1949), 969–981.

2945 STAMPP, Kenneth, ed. *The Causes of the Civil War*. Rev. ed. Englewood Cliffs, N.J., 1974.†

XXI. On Understanding the South

2946 BERTELSON, David. *The Lazy South*. New York, 1967.

2947 CASH, Wilbur J. *The Mind of the South*. New York, 1960.†

2948 DEGLER, Carl N. *The Other South: Southern Dissenters in the Nineteenth Century*. See **622**.

2949 DEGLER, Carl N. *Place over Time: The Continuity of Southern Distinctiveness*. Baton Rouge, 1977.

2950 GOVAN, Thomas P. "Was the Old South Different?" *J S Hist*, 21 (1955), 447–455.

2951 POTTER, David M. "On Understanding the South: A Review Article." *J S Hist*, 30 (1964), 451–462.

2952 RUBIN, Louis D., Jr., and James Jackson KILPATRICK, eds. *The Lasting South: Fourteen Southerners Look at Their Home*. Chicago, 1957.

2953 SELLERS, Charles G., Jr., ed. *The Southerner as American*. New York, 1966.†

2954 SIMKINS, Francis B. *The Everlasting South*. Baton Rouge, 1963.

2955 VANDIVER, Frank E., ed. *The Idea of the South: Pursuit of a Central Theme*. Chicago, 1964.

2956 WILLIAMS, T. Harry. *Romance and Realism in Southern Politics*. Baton Rouge, 1966.†

2957 WOODWARD, C. Vann *American Counterpoint: Slavery and Racism in the North-South Dialogue*. Boston, 1971.†

2958 WOODWARD, C. Vann. "The Irony of Southern History." *J S Hist*, 19 (1953), 3–19.

2959 WOODWARD, C. Vann. "The Search for Southern Identity." *Va Q Rev*, 34 (1958), 321–338.

INDEX

INDEX

INDEX

INDEX

INDEX

INDEX

INDEX

INDEX

INDEX

INDEX

INDEX

INDEX

INDEX

INDEX

INDEX

INDEX

INDEX

INDEX

NOTES